Ab Initio Language Teaching in British Higher Education

ADVANCES IN LANGUAGE EDUCATION

Series editor:
LI WEI (Director and Dean IOE, UCL's Faculty of Education and Society)

Applied Linguistics and Language Education are interdisciplinary fields at the forefront of policy and practice. Research in these areas is concerned with the cognitive and social benefits of language learning; equity and diversity of language learners and the language teaching profession; innovative pedagogy for language teaching and cross-curriculum connections; national language strategy; and language-in-education policies.

The unique aim of the *Advances in Language Education* series is to translate research-based knowledge of applied linguistics and language education into practical guidance for professionals. It turns the latest research findings into innovative pedagogies and guidance that will appeal to an international readership of language professionals, and language policy makers and practitioners. The research outlined in these books may be experimental, experiential, observational or action research, with impact on curriculum design and delivery, classroom management, pedagogy and school leadership all foregrounded. The books will be important reading for student educators and trainee teachers on PGCE, MEd and EdD programmes; and to language professionals, especially language teachers in universities, schools and other institutions. The books will also be of interest to language and education policymakers and stakeholders, early career researchers in applied linguistics and language education, including postgraduate students.

Series advisors:
Lourdes Ortega (Georgetown University); Norbert Pachler (UCL); Brian Paltridge (University of Sydney)

Ab Initio Language Teaching in British Higher Education

The case of German

Edited by
Ulrike Bavendiek, Silke Mentchen,
Christian Mossmann and Dagmar Paulus

First published in 2022 by
UCL Press
University College London
Gower Street
London WC1E 6BT

Available to download free: www.uclpress.co.uk

ISBN: 978-1-78735-928-4 (Hbk.)
ISBN: 978-1-78735-927-7 (Pbk.)
ISBN: 978-1-78735-926-0 (PDF)
ISBN: 978-1-78735-929-1 (epub)
DOI: https://doi.org/10.14324/111.9781787359260

Contents

List of figures and tables

Figures

Tables

List of contributors

Sabina Barczyk-Wozniak is a university teacher in the School of Modern Languages at Cardiff University where she has taught German on undergraduate programmes and across a range of levels for the Languages for All courses since 2016. As part of this role, Sabina has been responsible for designing the learning and assessment resources for the LfA German modules at B1–C1 language proficiency levels. Before coming to Cardiff, Sabina worked as a University Lecturer and Research Fellow in the Institute for German Studies and Applied Linguistics at Maria Curie-Skłodowska University in Lublin, Poland, where she carried out research into Glottodidactics and Psycholinguistics. Her research interests focus on the development of German learners' grammatical competence.

Ulrike Bavendiek is Senior Lecturer in the Department of Languages, Cultures and Film at the University of Liverpool. She has taught German language and linguistics in Goethe Institutes and at universities in Germany, Japan and the UK. At Liverpool she set up and has taught German *ab initio* for over 20 years. Her other teaching and research interests lie in the field of Applied Linguistics. She is the Director of the Centre for Teaching Excellence in Language Learning at the University of Liverpool.

Alexander Bleistein is DAAD-*Lektor* and Coordinator of German at the Centre for Languages and Inter-Communication (CLIC) of the Cambridge University Engineering Department. He has been teaching German in the UK at all levels with a focus on languages for specific purposes (LSP) since 2016 and has previously worked with the Goethe Institutes in London and Rotterdam. He is affiliated with Downing College, Cambridge, where he supervises students of German.

Daniela Dora is currently DAAD Teaching Fellow in German Studies at Gonville & Caius College/Trinity College (joint appointment) at the

University of Cambridge. Prior to coming to Cambridge, Daniela Dora taught at Ghent University and Université Saint-Louis Bruxelles in Belgium and King's College London. Her research deals with the interconnections between literary discourse and concepts of tourism in contemporary German-speaking literature. Further research interests include teaching literature and translation in the German as a Foreign Language (GFL) classroom.

Katharina Forster is DAAD-*Lektorin* and Teaching Fellow in German at University College London. Before joining UCL in 2019, she taught German at all levels at the Mongolian University of Science and Technology in Ulaanbaatar and the University of Regensburg. Her research interests include teaching literature and creative writing in the German language classroom.

Eva Gossner joined the German Department of Bristol University in 1993. She was the Language Co-ordinator from 2001 to 2011 and is now a Language Teaching Fellow. A graduate of the University of Munich, she has an MA in German from Arizona State University and a PGCE in Modern Languages from the University of Cambridge. She has also held teaching positions in Germany, Chile and Italy. Her main interests are *ab initio* teaching and teaching language through cultural topics.

Thomas Jochum-Critchley is a Lecturer in German at the University of York. He has over 20 years' experience of teaching German in a wide variety of UK and European higher education contexts. He co-organised and led professional development workshops and regularly shares his experience at national and international conferences. His scholarly interests lie in language learner autonomy, the role of grammar in language acquisition and in innovative pedagogies aiming to overcome institutional boundaries of language learning and teaching.

Annemarie Künzl-Snodgrass was DAAD-*Lektorin* for German at King's College London before moving to the University of Cambridge, where she subsequently was Senior Language Teaching Officer in the German Section at the Faculty of Modern and Medieval Languages and Linguistics until her retirement in 2018. She co-taught the *ab initio* German course from its inception. She is a Fellow and Tutor at Jesus College, Cambridge, and continues to teach German as a supervisor. She has co-authored an online German grammar programme and German language textbooks.

Kasia Łanucha gained her Master's degree in German as a Foreign Language at the University of Dresden before moving to the UK where she has been teaching German at various levels and for specific purposes (engineering students, medical school) for over 15 years at the University of Cambridge. She is particularly interested in developing cultural competence in the language classroom.

Theresa Lentfort is DAAD-*Lektorin* for German at St John's College, University of Cambridge. Before coming to Cambridge in 2018, she taught German at all levels at higher education institutes in Uzbekistan, Indonesia and Germany. At Cambridge, she supervises students of German throughout their undergraduate studies and delivers language courses at the Faculty of Modern and Medieval Languages and Linguistics. Her research interests lie in the field of linguistics, didactics and foreign language acquisition, with a particular focus on language criticism, the role of visualisations for grammar acquisition and computer-assisted language learning (CALL).

Silke Mentchen has been teaching German at the University of Cambridge since 1998. She is an Associate Professor at the Faculty of Modern and Medieval Languages and Linguistics with responsibilities for the curriculum and administration of various courses, including *ab initio* German. She is co-author of an online grammar programme, textbooks and articles on language pedagogy. She is also Fellow and Tutor at Magdalene College, Cambridge.

Christian Mossmann is Senior Lecturer in Modern Languages and Cultures at the University of Exeter and Language Coordinator for German in the university's Language Centre. He has been teaching German in the UK since 2007 and has been responsible for setting up the German *ab initio* pathway for degree students at Exeter. He is Senior Fellow of the Higher Education Academy and the Exeter Lead for the EU-funded European University Tandem (EuniTa) project.

Dagmar Paulus is Lecturer and Language Coordinator in German Studies at University College London where she is responsible for the German *ab initio* programme. Previously, she taught German at the University of Nottingham and at Tomsk State University, Russia. Her latest book, *Nationalism before the Nation State*, was published in 2020. Her current research project is a monograph on landscape and nationalism.

Mandy Poetzsch is Lecturer at the Department of German and the Language Director for German at the University of Bristol. She has been teaching German at all levels in the UK and abroad since 2007. Her research interests are language acquisition and CALL. She regularly presents her findings at conferences.

Birgit Smith was Director of Language Studies and Head of Department of Languages and Cultures at Lancaster University, where she taught German for 25 years from *ab initio* to advanced level, including Translation Studies at Master's level. Since taking early retirement, she continues her teaching of German with the Open University and through her role of External Examiner at a number of British universities.

Maren de Vincent-Humphreys has been a Language Teaching Officer for German at the University of Cambridge and a Fellow of Jesus College since 2019, where she teaches German at all levels. She had previously been appointed through the DAAD to teach at the University of Cambridge and the University of São Paulo. Furthermore, she worked on projects of multilingualism and second language acquisition at the universities of Hamburg and Bielefeld. Her research interests focus on students' agency of language learning, vocabulary learning and CALL, following a sociocultural approach.

Martina Wallner was Senior Lecturer in German at Keele University and Head of the Language Centre from 2010 until her retirement in 2021. She has extensive experience in designing, delivering and managing language learning and teaching at all levels. She remains associated to Keele as Honorary Fellow of the university.

Elisabeth Wielander is Senior Teaching Fellow at Aston University, Birmingham, and has been teaching German language, translation and content modules at undergraduate and postgraduate level at Aston University since 2007. In her role as departmental Director of Learning and Teaching, she was instrumental in introducing Aston's German *ab initio* stream in 2016. Her research interests include Content and Language Integrated Learning (CLIL) and second language acquisition. She is a member of the Centre for Language Research at Aston (ClaRA)'s Aston Language Education Research Group (ALE) and a Senior Fellow of the Higher Education Academy.

Ruth R. Winter is Lecturer and Deputy Language Director at the Department of German at the University of Bristol. She has been teaching German at Bristol for more than 20 years and is module leader for *ab initio* and German for Specific Purposes courses at the Department. Her main interests in language teaching research are effective feedback, learner autonomy and plurilingual learning.

Glossary and list of abbreviations

Ab initio	'From the beginning'. The term is used to refer to beginners' language teaching. In practice, this encompasses students with no or little prior knowledge.
A-levels	Advanced level subject-specific school-leaving qualifications taken in England, Wales and Northern Ireland that can lead to university study. Students are usually aged 16–18 and take A-levels in three or four subjects.
AR	Augmented reality.
CALL	Computer-assisted language learning.
CEFR	Common European Framework of Reference for Languages. An international standard developed by the Council for Europe for describing attainment levels in language learning. The framework describes abilities from beginners to near-native on a six-point scale (A1, A2, B1, B2, C1 and C2).
CLIL	Content and language integrated learning.
DAAD	*Deutscher Akademischer Austauschdienst* (German academic exchange service).
EBacc	English Baccalaureate. A set of school subjects studied at GCSE introduced in 2011 to measure student attainment that includes an ancient or modern foreign language.

ELQ	Equivalent or Lower Qualification. It describes a course at the same level or below an award already attained.
FHEQ	Framework of Higher Education Qualifications in England, Wales and Northern Ireland. All qualifications awarded by bodies with degree-awarding powers work within this framework.
GAIN	German *Ab Initio* Network. A network of teachers of German at UK universities founded in 2017 by Dagmar Paulus at UCL, currently with over 90 members.
GCSE	General Certificate of Secondary Education. An academic qualification in a specific subject taken in England, Wales and Northern Ireland. Students are usually aged 13–16 and take nine or ten GCSEs.
GFL	German as a Foreign Language.
HEFCE	Higher Education Funding Council for England. In 2017 it was replaced by the Office for Students (OfS).
HEI	Higher education institution.
HESA	Higher Education Statistics Agency in the UK.
IWLP	Institution-Wide Language Programme. They usually consist of elective, credit-bearing language modules at different levels to cater for the language learning needs of university students. Although IWLPs tend to have a more internal focus than LfA, there is considerable overlap in the use of both expressions. Both terms will be used interchangeably in this volume.
KS3	Key Stage 3. The UK's national curriculum is divided into Key Stages. At Key Stage 3, students are typically aged between 11 and 13.
L1, L2	L1 refers to a speaker's first language, L2 to the second language.
LfA	Languages for All. Language courses at different levels offered by universities to their students or members of the general public. These are not necessarily credit-bearing. Although LfA tend to have a more external

focus than IWLPs, there is considerable overlap in the use of both terms.

LMS	Learning Management System, see also VLE.
MFL	Modern foreign language.
Ofsted	Office for Standards in Education, Children's Services and Skills. A non-ministerial department of the UK government, the office inspects standards primarily in state schools in the UK and reports to Parliament.
POLAR	Young Participation of Local Areas. POLAR statistics measure how many young people in particular regions in the UK participate in higher education.
Russell Group	An association representing 24 public research-intensive universities in the UK.
SLA	Second language acquisition.
SRS	Student response system.
TBLT	Task-based language teaching.
UCAS	Universities and Colleges Admissions Service. An independent organisation that operates the student application process to UK higher education institutions.
VLE	Virtual learning environment. A web-based platform commonly used by schools and universities, such as Blackboard or Moodle.
VR	Virtual reality.
VUCA	Volatility, uncertainty, complexity and ambiguity. The term is used to characterise the world that the current generation of students find themselves in.

Foreword
Martin Durrell

As the editors point out in their Introduction, one of the most striking changes in British higher education over the last 25 years has been the increase in the opportunities to learn German *ab initio* as part of an honours degree. This had always been possible for those languages which were less widely taught in schools, such as Italian or Russian, but with the rapid decline in the numbers taking German at A-level after the surge in the early 1990s, institutions offering honours degree courses in German recognised the need to open these to potential students with no previous knowledge of the language. At the same time, the increased flexibility in student course choices brought about by the move away from the rigid structure of traditional honours degrees towards modular structures meant an increase in the number of students from all disciplines taking optional courses in a foreign language, typically within the framework of an Institution Wide Language Programme (IWLP) in a language centre.

One welcome consequence of these developments has been the increased professionalisation of language teaching in higher education as departments of individual languages and language centres have come to work more closely together. Previously the teaching of language within traditional degree programmes had typically tended to take the form principally of translation classes undertaken by members of the academic staff with little or no practical expertise in foreign language pedagogy, complemented by oral conversation classes with native speaker lectors who often lacked formal training. Such teaching was clearly going to be inadequate for *ab initio* students, who needed to acquire a high level of competence in a relatively short period of time, and it is now almost universally the case that language instruction in the context of both honours degree programmes and IWLP courses is undertaken by teachers with professional expertise in second language pedagogy. And it is absolutely clear that success in *ab initio* courses demands no less from the instructors.

In the present volume, the editors have collected an impressive set of chapters from colleagues who have been at the forefront of driving these changes in the teaching of German in British universities over the last two decades. Coming from ten different institutions – and in most cases with previous expertise in teaching German as a foreign language in Germany and several other countries – the contributors offer an insight into a wide range of approaches and techniques which will be of inestimable value to all those engaged in the task of guiding students on their first steps in acquiring a rounded competence in German.

Acknowledgements

First and foremost, we would like to thank all contributors to this handbook for their hard work and continued patience when teaching at universities went through challenging times due to the COVID-19 pandemic. Special thanks go to Pat Gordon-Smith, our editor at UCL Press, who guided us with steadfastness, helpful advice and good humour, and Li Wei as series editor for believing in our project, even when it was still in its early stages. We also wish to thank the wider community of practising language teachers at UK universities who contributed behind the scenes through conversations, answers to surveys and valuable tips. We owe gratitude to Alexander Steiner for kindly letting us use his photography for the front cover. Last but not least, we are delighted that Martin Durrell, author of the eminent *Hammer's German Grammar and Usage*, contributed the foreword to this volume.

Editors' introduction

Ulrike Bavendiek, Silke Mentchen,
Christian Mossmann and Dagmar Paulus

The teaching of modern languages at *ab initio* level in higher education has become a necessity for universities across the UK, given that the number of students studying for GCSEs and A-levels in Modern Foreign Languages (MFL) at school is in decline. Since 2003, the last year in which the taking of a modern foreign language in Year 10 was compulsory, entries for language GCSEs at schools in England have dropped by 41 per cent (Bawden, 2021; see also Durrell, 2017 for an overview and assessment of this development). A-level entries in French, German and 'other modern languages' have also dropped significantly since 2005, while Spanish entries have risen, though largely plateaued in recent years, as the British Council's *Language Trends 2021* report shows (British Council, 2021).

In England, studying a foreign language is one of the core subjects of the English Baccalaureate (EBacc), and some pin their hopes of an uptake of languages at secondary schools on this school performance indicator. The government has declared its intention to see 90 per cent of pupils studying the EBacc subject combination at GCSE by 2025 (Department for Education, 2019), but this goal seems rather ambitious at present. While it is too early to fully assess the long-term impact of either the COVID-19 pandemic or Brexit on language uptake at schools, large numbers of pupils at primary and secondary school did not receive any language education during national lockdowns (British Council, 2021), which has potential knock-on effects in subsequent years.

While the number of higher education institutions (HEIs) offering MFL degree programmes has decreased by 12 per cent between 2012 and 2018 (UCML and British Academy, 2021), the picture looks different for

IWLPs. A joint survey by the University Council of Modern Languages and the Association of University Language Communities in the UK and Ireland reports that 71 per cent of 49 responding institutions consider the future of their IWLP either very good or good (UCML and AULC, 2021: 28). French, Spanish and German remain the three dominant languages for MFL degree programmes. The outlook at IWLP provisions looks similar, with French in first and Spanish in second place, followed by Chinese and German on par (UCML and AULC, 2021: 28). The survey also detected a rise in the number of institutions offering *ab initio* languages and the fact that HEIs offer them almost universally. French and German, however, were the only languages that were not available *ab initio* in some HEIs, but have now been introduced or are planned to be introduced as a recent development (UCML and AULC, 2021: 18).

At a national level, the decline in language learning and the implications of foreign language proficiency in the UK have been recognised in a joint report of the British Academy, the Arts and Humanities Research Council, the Association of School and College Leaders, the British Council and Universities UK (2020). They declare languages to be strategically vital for the UK's future and its need to strengthen relationships globally, recognising overwhelming evidence of an insufficient and continuously decreasing supply of the language skills required to meet future needs. They call for a UK-wide national languages strategy: 'if we succeed in reversing the persistent decline in take up of languages throughout the education pipeline, the UK could become a linguistic powerhouse: more prosperous, productive, influential, innovative, knowledgeable, culturally richer, more socially cohesive and healthier' (British Academy et al., 2020: 3).

Given that German can be defined as an international language in the hierarchy of minority languages, official national languages, international languages and world languages based on numbers of speakers (Ammon, 2019: 7–8), it seems strategically sensible to fight against the decline of German in the UK education system. German is also the foreign language most sought after by employers, with an increasing number of job vacancies requiring German language skills in recent years (Woolcock, 2019).

In response to these developments, beginners' courses in higher education are on the rise, either as part of degree programmes or at language centres. Some institutions only started a few years ago, while for others, German *ab initio* already has a long tradition. According to McLelland, all universities still offering German as a degree course have now introduced German as an *ab initio* choice. At the same time, institutions with distinct German departments have declined in number; for 2017, McLelland cites 37 Heads of German, as opposed to 87 in 2002 (McLelland, 2019: 606).

As a result, the demand for teachers of *ab initio* has risen, along with the requirement for departments and schools to consider how to integrate their *ab initio* programme into existing programme diets in degree courses. We believe that it is vital for those involved in the subject to connect with colleagues and exchange experiences and expertise. One such example of a common question is when and how to integrate *ab initio* students into the main cohort of students with an A-level in the target language. Different institutions implement different solutions, with some universities uniting both cohorts as soon as the second year, while others wait until after the year abroad which is usually taken in the third year. It is useful for teachers and administrators to see how universities across the country fare with their respective methods.

This volume aims to support practitioners of *ab initio* language teaching by providing the expertise of contributors from a range of UK universities and at different stages in their careers. It is intended as a handbook for everyone involved with, or interested in, *ab initio* teaching. Inspiration for this book has come from a network for teachers of German *ab initio* courses at UK universities (GAIN), and we hope that we can extend, via this medium, the exchange and support that we have all found extremely helpful, not least during the pandemic.

Contributions focus on a variety of issues concerning *ab initio* teaching in higher education, both at modern language departments and at language centres. However, many challenges for beginners' language teaching, as opposed to the teaching at intermediate or higher levels, are comparable across different sectors and the volume is therefore relevant for language teachers at secondary level as well, for example when it comes to selecting a textbook, providing feedback, sustaining motivation, and using digital devices and resources. Readers will find introductory chapters reflecting on general trends or theoretical issues but also contributions with a focus on teaching methods and suggestions for lesson activities. While the main focus is on teaching German, most of the findings in the chapters can easily be applied to the teaching of other modern languages, too.

Primarily, this volume is aimed at teachers in the school and university classroom but also at decision makers such as heads of departments or schools who wish to gain insight into the landscape of German *ab initio* in the UK.

The volume is divided into four parts. In Part I's three chapters, the authors assess the role of *ab initio* provision within German Studies, and also within the wider context of modern languages and language centres. The five chapters in Part II reflect on *ab initio* teaching methods and pedagogy, while Part III's four chapters provide new approaches in the *ab initio* classroom. Part IV focuses on the learner in the *ab initio* context and its two chapters explore issues related to autonomy and working with learners' strengths.

Part I: Trends and developments

Martina Wallner and Elisabeth Wielander describe the current situation in their chapter, 'Beginners' German – *Ja bitte!* Development and status quo of German *ab initio* education in degree programmes and language centres at UK universities'. The chapter includes an overview of MFL teaching at UK secondary level in order to explain the recent rise in the number of students studying German as beginners in higher education. Using data collected through the German *Ab Initio* Network (GAIN), they describe how beginners' teaching has been integrated in traditional degree programmes which were originally designed for students starting with an A-level in the language. Different universities have developed different pathways. These are discussed taking into account factors like strategic decisions, progression, recruitment and widening participation. In the second section of the chapter, the authors discuss German *ab initio* teaching within IWLPs, highlighting the healthy and stable numbers of students. The overview is complemented by two case studies, exemplifying a degree pathway (Aston University) and IWLP delivery (Keele University). The conclusion considers the impact of national policy decisions like Brexit on German *ab initio* teaching in the UK.

In her chapter 'German *ab initio* in Languages for All programmes: student profiles and course design', **Sabina Barczyk-Wozniak** develops a profile of the *ab initio* German learner in Languages for All (LfA) programmes, based on data collected at Cardiff University. She investigates students' language learning biographies, their experiences, motivation, aspirations and needs in terms of language learning. The findings indicate that students from a wide range of degree programmes and linguistic backgrounds study German in the LfA programme. Their language learning tends to be intrinsically motivated, with learners enrolling in their courses to develop communication skills in the target language that they aim to apply in individual contexts. Based on her findings that speaking and listening skills are named frequently by students as particularly desirable, Barczyk-Wozniak provides practical examples of how to develop those in synchronous online teaching settings.

Kasia Łanucha and Alexander Bleistein consider the changing needs of *ab initio* language learners in UK universities. In their chapter 'Preparing Generation Z students for a VUCA world through language learning' they argue that teachers need to be aware of the implications of volatility, uncertainty, complexity and ambiguity (VUCA) for their students. As the first generation of digital natives now at university, these students' approach to learning is more focused on online materials, and teachers need to adapt in order to maintain the students' interest.

Part II: Pedagogy and teaching methods

Daniela Dora and Katharina Forster, in their chapter 'Reading literature in the *ab initio* classroom', start the discussion of teaching methods and pedagogy by highlighting the benefits of literary texts for language learning. They argue that the aesthetic value of literature can increase student motivation even in the beginners' classroom. Presenting guidelines for the evaluation of text difficulty for the *ab initio* classroom the authors consider not only the suitability of the texts in the wider curriculum but also language, narrative and thematic criteria. Some carefully chosen fictional texts are used to demonstrate how *ab initio* students in higher education can draw on their cognitive abilities and previous knowledge to access texts in spite of linguistic challenges.

Kirsten Mericka moves the focus to the role of music in her chapter 'Using music in *ab initio* courses'. She looks at various opportunities for integrating music into the *ab initio* curriculum. First, she outlines the benefits of music for language learners – for example, it offers an authentic piece of the target culture, its rhythm and melody can help with memorising vocabulary and the music itself can be relaxing and stimulating. Mericka then discusses several aspects of music as a teaching tool, including how music can help with pronunciation practice and how it tends to boost students' motivation. The chapter ends with a practice-oriented section, containing suggestions for songs and assignments, explaining in detail how teachers can use music in the *ab initio* classroom.

In her chapter 'Grammar teaching and learning in the German *ab initio* classroom', **Birgit Smith** explores the question of why grammar teaching and learning may be unpopular. She first gives a short historical overview on the role of grammar in language learning in the UK and then shows that there is now a focus on communication skills rather than linguistic knowledge in the language classroom, with less attention on grammar. Smith then argues that grammar is still relevant and necessary, and finally shows how grammar teaching can be integrated into *ab initio* teaching.

Finding the most suitable textbook for an *ab initio* course is crucial. In his chapter 'Selecting the right resources for beginners' level: a textbook evaluation', **Christian Mossmann** gathers a catalogue of criteria found in previous research to develop a practical and effective checklist. How a selection based on this list would work is exemplified by the author's scrutiny of two textbooks, one monolingual and one bilingual. In this way, evaluating one's own preferences as a teacher critically and continuously is made considerably easier.

In their chapter 'Intercultural awareness in the teaching and learning of German: the case of *ab initio*', **Eva Gossner and Dagmar Paulus** emphasise that engagement with intercultural awareness is vital for learners to become skilled intercultural communicators. Successful communication requires an awareness of behavioural and communicative codes, rules of social interaction and in-depth knowledge of a country's customs, traditions and history. A critical evaluation of current textbooks highlights their different approaches to cultural codes and reveals their various limitations. The authors present practical lesson activities, based on the themes of proxemics, cultural memory and gestures/facial expressions, which are aimed at encouraging students to develop their intercultural competence.

Part III: Innovative approaches

Mandy Poetzsch's chapter is titled 'The "flipped classroom" approach in the German beginners' context'. According to this approach, part of the traditional class content is delivered at home to free up class time for practice and further exploration. She argues that flipped learning techniques can increase student confidence in the classroom and allow teachers to use class time for active learning, student engagement and participation. The fact that most teachers have become more confident with the use of new technologies for language learning during the pandemic makes this a highly applicable approach that invites experimentation by *ab initio* teachers in different educational settings. The performance metrics available with many applications and software packages can provide crucial information for planning lessons according to the students' needs. Poetzsch illustrates new, blended delivery modes based on a range of selected digital tools.

Ruth R. Winter continues the discussion, exploring the use of student response systems (SRS) in her chapter 'New approaches to feedback in *ab initio* language classes: a case study'. During two academic years – one before the pandemic and one during – the author collected survey data to identify the benefits of an SRS called Socrative. These particular circumstances allow her to compare the use of feedback in face-to-face as opposed to online teaching. The author discusses the particular need for inclusive, constructive, and effective feedback for *ab initio* learners expected to achieve a high level of proficiency in a relatively short amount of time. Personalised and immediate feedback on students' progression is shown to be vital for student satisfaction, leading to a self-reflective and empowering learning experience.

Learning new words is the focus of **Silke Mentchen's** chapter 'Two for the price of one: using a cognitive theory of metaphors for vocabulary teaching and learning'. The author explores aspects of linguistic theories and their potential for application in *ab initio* teaching. The chapter includes examples for lesson planning showing how knowledge about conceptual metaphors can aid the learning process. The chapter also points out political dimensions of this approach by referring to research on ableist and racist use of metaphors, and explains how teaching methods based on cognitive theories can lead to intellectually stimulating learning and critically aware use of language(s).

Like Silke Mentchen, **Annemarie Künzl-Snodgrass, Theresa Lentfort and Maren de Vincent-Humphreys** recognise that effective vocabulary acquisition strategies are crucial to successful language learning. They evaluate vocabulary learning apps in their chapter 'Effective vocabulary learning apps: what should they look like?', exploring how CALL can support vocabulary acquisition, especially for *ab initio* learners. Drawing on recent research in second language acquisition and considering different learning styles, they offer a list of criteria that apps should fulfil in order to scaffold vocabulary learning effectively. Exploring the potential of virtual and augmented reality for vocabulary learning, they demonstrate how this cutting-edge technology allows learners to engage interactively and innovatively with their environment through their mobile devices.

Part IV: Learner focus

Thomas Jochum-Critchley, in his chapter 'Developing learner autonomy in German *ab initio* programmes', illuminates how encouraging students to take responsibility for and control over their learning can enhance learner autonomy. Based on the example of the German *ab initio* programme at the University of York, he outlines how the use of a portfolio can be harnessed to foster autonomy, creativity, reflexivity and engagement with authentic language input. An evaluation of student experiences at York reveals that such an approach can result in high student satisfaction and increased enjoyment of the language learning process. The chapter ends with a critical discussion of recent developments in online communication and mobile-assisted language learning tools, how they might enrich a portfolio approach and their potential to enhance the development of learner autonomy.

In her chapter, 'Individual differences in *ab initio* language learning: working with learners' strengths', **Ulrike Bavendiek** charts the constellation of factors that have an impact on language learners' progression and learning experiences. These include external and learner-specific variables. The author links new research in second language acquisition and Applied Linguistics with her experience as a teacher of German. If considered critically, acknowledgement of students' needs can be turned into the key for success in *ab initio* learning. The author analyses the concept of motivation as a cluster of individually differently expressed variables and discusses ways to sustain motivated learners in a potentially challenging *ab initio* context. How to let students take control of their learning process has become a crucial consideration in a context of anxiety and mental stress, and this chapter delivers helpful suggestions and strategies for teachers on the topic of feedback and task design. The chapter raises awareness for the use of English as a positive, contrastive interlanguaging tool in the German *ab initio* classroom.

The 14 chapters in this volume offer both general introductions to the theory and practice of beginners' language teaching and learning as well as more specific discussions of *ab initio* pedagogy and learner needs. We trust that readers will find this book useful and stimulating.

References

Ammon, U. (2019) 'Fördermöglichkeiten von Deutsch und Germanistik in der Welt im Überblick'. In *Förderung der deutschen Sprache weltweit: Vorschläge, Ansätze, Konzepte*, edited by U. Ammon and G. Schmidt , 3–24, Berlin and Boston, MA: De Gruyter.

Bawden, A. (2021) 'Millions of pupils in England had no language teaching in lockdowns – survey', 8 July. Online. www.theguardian.com/education/2021/jul/08/millions-of-pupils-in-england-had-no-language-teaching-in-lockdowns-survey (accessed 20 August 2021).

British Academy, the Arts and Humanities Research Council, the Association of School and College Leaders, the British Council and Universities UK (2020) *Towards a National Languages Strategy: Education and skills*. Online. www.thebritishacademy.ac.uk/documents/2597/Towards-a-national-languages-strategy-July-2020_R0FHmzB.pdf (accessed 18 August 2021).

British Council (2021) *Language Trends 2021. Language teaching in primary and secondary schools in England*. Online. www.britishcouncil.org/sites/default/files/language_trends_2021_report.pdf (accessed 18 August 2021).

Department for Education (2019) *Guidance. English Baccalaureate (EBacc)*. Online. www.gov.uk/government/publications/english-baccalaureate-ebacc/english-baccalaureate-ebacc (accessed 14 August 2021).

Durrell, M. (2017) 'Mündlichkeit und Schriftlichkeit im schulischen Deutschunterricht in England'. *Deutsch als Fremdsprache. Zeitschrift zur Theorie und Praxis des Faches Deutsch als Fremdsprache* 54:3, 131–41.

McLelland, N. (2019) 'Förderung von DaF in Großbritannien'. In *Förderung der deutschen Sprache weltweit: Vorschläge, Ansätze, Konzepte*, edited by U. Ammon and G. Schmidt, 599–613. Berlin and Boston, MA: De Gruyter.

UCML and AULC (2021) *Survey of Language Provision in UK Universities in 2021*. Online. https://university-council-modern-languages.org/wp-content/uploads/2021/07/UCML-AULC-Survey-2021-Report.pdf (accessed 19 August 2021).

UCML and British Academy (2021) *Report on Granular Trends in Modern Languages in UCAS Admissions Data 2012–18*. Online. https://university-council-modern-languages.org/wp-content/uploads/2021/07/UCML-BA-UCAS-Granularity-Report.pdf (accessed 12 January 2022).

Woolcock, N. (2019) 'German is more desirable than French for employers', 10 April. Online. www.thetimes.co.uk/article/german-is-more-desirable-than-french-for-employers-z7mbghm5t (accessed 14 September 2021).

Part I
Trends and developments

1

Beginners' German – *Ja, bitte!* Development and status quo of German *ab initio* education in degree programmes and language centres at UK universities

Martina Wallner and Elisabeth Wielander

Introduction

This book is an update and follow-up to Leder, Reimann and Walsh's (1996) volume that was among the first to shed light on the development of *ab initio* German teaching and learning at UK universities. In this chapter, we will first investigate twenty-first-century policy changes and developments in the Modern Foreign Language (MFL) landscape in the UK at secondary level and their impact on higher education, followed by an overview of the development of *ab initio* instruction of German in higher education, both at undergraduate degree level and through institution-wide language programmes for non-specialist language study. We will then outline one example for each model – undergraduate (UG) and IWLP – to demonstrate how *ab initio* German is delivered in practice.

25 years on: the MFL landscape in the UK today

It is widely known that student numbers in MFL degree programmes have been declining for a number of years. Nearly 20 years ago, Grix and Jaworska posited that '[a] lack of qualified teachers and low motivation among those teaching are ... contributing factors to the state of language learning in UK schools', along with 'limited contact with the language and culture' (2002: 4–5), and the situation has not changed significantly since then. Tinsley and Dolezal (2018: 8), for example, report that many schools have difficulty recruiting teachers for some languages or language combinations, and '60% of state schools and more than half of independent schools' struggle to recruit 'teachers of sufficient quality'.

Student motivation for learning foreign languages seems to have been at an alarming low for quite some time. At the turn of the millennium, the Nuffield Language Inquiry found that nine out of ten children stopped learning languages at 16. In its recommendations, the Inquiry called for a 'national strategy for developing capability in languages in the UK' (The Nuffield Languages Inquiry, 2000: 8), going so far as to propose that a language should be made a requirement for university entry. However, the opposite was the norm; in 2004, foreign languages became optional after the age of 14 in secondary state schools in England. These schools are highly dependent on their position in the annual league tables and on favourable assessments by Ofsted inspectors. Given that German is viewed as the most difficult language in the MFL curriculum, schools often encourage less able students to opt out of German post-KS3 (Reershemius, 2010: 1675), and other languages face their own preconceptions. As a result, between 2003 and 2007, during their steepest decline, GCSE entries in MFL overall fell by 27.6 per cent, with an even more marked decrease in German (-35.6 per cent) and French (-34.7 per cent). This ongoing development goes hand in hand with the fact that fewer state secondary schools offer German at KS3, falling from 48 per cent in 2015 to 41 per cent in 2018 (Tinsley and Dolezal, 2018: 10).

These conditions have meant that even fewer students have pursued MFL as a subject to A-level since 2004. As a result, A-level entries in German declined by 37 per cent between 2005 and 2017 (Tinsley and Dolezal, 2018: 4). Consequently, many university language departments struggle to draw a significant number of qualified students to their language degrees.

This development has only been exacerbated by the trebling of university fees in 2012. Until 2011, applications in European languages (and related subjects) had trended upwards, but in the first application cycle under the new fees regime (January 2012), the number of applications for European languages and related subjects decreased by 11.2 per cent. By 2018, applications for European languages and related studies had decreased by 33.1 per cent compared to 2012 (UCAS, 2018), and the latest UCAS figures show that 'the number of applicants accepted this year [2021] had fallen 36 per cent since 2011' (Baker, 2021: n.p.).

Those accepted are increasingly concentrated at a handful of institutions; around 60 per cent of students were accepted by only 13 institutions, whereas 36 universities accepted virtually no students or reduced acceptance numbers by more than half (Baker, 2021).

These recruitment trends have, of course, had a financial impact on MFL departments because of the comparatively high cost of delivery due to the nature of the discipline (the need for smaller groups, delivery of language-specific modules rather than cross-language provision of subject content and so on). By necessity or strategic consideration, a number of universities have discontinued their provision of degree programmes in MFL. Generally speaking, the younger universities and former polytechnics are more likely to phase out MFL programmes than older institutions, particularly the Russell Group, where MFL generally retain their traditional place in the Humanities (Reershemius, 2010: 1677). In October 2013, *The Guardian* reported that, since 2007, 11 universities had completely shut down all specialist language degrees, and a further 13 closed specialist language programmes but still offered languages in combination with other subjects (Bawden, 2013). In total, 'more than 50 universities in the UK have cut courses, or scrapped departments entirely since 2000' (Kelly, 2019). This development shows no sign of slowing down. Recent examples of universities that significantly reduced their language offer and/or staff numbers include Nottingham and Birmingham, and among the institutions that threatened or implemented the closure of their MFL programmes are Ulster, Salford, Hull and Aston.

The – mostly financial – pressures exerted on MFL departments in the current climate are only one side of the story. Since the late 1990s, experts have observed a national trend away from single honours degrees (Footitt, 2005: 9), and even dual language degrees are losing ground (Klapper, 2006: 2). Integrated degrees that combine a language and another non-linguistic discipline are still popular, but increasingly, universities 'are offering programmes in which a language is an optional rather than compulsory component' (Kelly and Jones, 2003: 24).

Among the reasons usually given for this general decline of MFL Studies are the fee-driven market's emphasis on direct routes to clearly defined careers and the assumption that languages are seen as most valuable in combination with other subjects, such as business, despite many voices from both academia and the private sector decrying the worrying lack of qualified linguists. The Confederation of British Industry, conducting its annual report in partnership with Pearson, found that the 'need for languages has been heightened by the UK's departure from the European Union. To achieve the government's ambition for a "Global

Britain", we have to get language teaching … right' (CBI/Pearson, 2018: 31). The latest report confirms that the major European languages most commonly listed by companies as being in demand are: German (37 per cent), Spanish (35 per cent) and French (32 per cent), with Mandarin catching up to or exceeding demand for European languages at 37 per cent for the first time (CBI/Pearson, 2019: 26–7).

To summarise, the high cost of delivering MFL programmes, combined with falling student numbers, means that many language departments, according to their institutions' resource models, are perceived as being in deficit and require cross-subsidy by other parts of the university, or face closure. In such cases, the decision to maintain MFL programmes often depends on high-level strategic considerations, for example the prioritising of MFL as part of an institution's international policy and its mission to train global citizens and enhance employability.

Ab initio German: a new delivery model at degree level

As we have seen, changes in provision and uptake at secondary level have had serious implications for recruitment into language degree programmes at many universities in the UK. Inevitably, German is no exception, in that the number of undergraduate students has fallen continuously – by 33 per cent between 1997 and 2006–7 (Reershemius, 2010: 1678), and even further since then. Ultimately, this trend has led to a wave of department closures: Where 126 universities in the UK offered German undergraduate programmes in 2000, by 2006, their number had fallen by 48 per cent to 65 (Reershemius, 2010: 1678), and in 2014–15, only 53 institutions offered German either as single honours or joint honours (Bawden, 2013).

One way in which universities have tried to make up for the steep decrease in A-level entries and the subsequent fall in university applications has been to open up alternative pathways into university language study. Where traditionally, it was necessary to have an A-level or equivalent qualification in a language to be able to enrol in a university language degree, fewer and fewer secondary schools, particularly in the state sector, offer their pupils the opportunity to attain such a qualification. Therefore, more and more universities have created so-called *ab initio* pathways that require no or very little prior knowledge of the language. These degree pathways usually focus very heavily on language acquisition and progression in the first year or two in order to enable students to achieve the same level of proficiency as their peers in the post-A-level pathway by the time they graduate.

Data collected during the inaugural meeting of the German *Ab Initio* Network (GAIN) at University College London in June 2017 show that the first *ab initio* programmes in German were introduced in the 1990s, but that the majority of such programmes have come online since the turn of the millennium. The GAIN findings indicate that there are a variety of different delivery models for *ab initio* degree programmes. They differ with regard to the number of weekly hours dedicated to language acquisition, the language level *ab initio* students are required to achieve in each academic year and the point at which these students are integrated with their post-A-level peers. An investigation of *ab initio* delivery at the institutions represented at the GAIN meeting in 2017 found that there were three main modules of integration with post-A-level pathway students: in some institutions, Year 2 *ab initio* students merge with Year 1 post-A-level students. In only a few universities, Year 2 *ab initio* students merge with Year 2 post-A-level students. Meanwhile, in half the institutions present, the two streams only merge in final year, usually after they have spent their third year abroad, studying at a German-speaking university or completing a work placement at a school or company in a German-speaking country.

At the 2017 GAIN meeting, *ab initio* programme leaders and tutors also discussed some of the challenges these programmes pose. Many reported that if their *ab initio* students are expected to join their post-A-level peers in Year 2, this often means that they have to put considerable efforts into developing their language independently during the summer holidays. In some places, they are expected or required to take part in intensive language courses during the summer months. Often, students feel that they do not get enough weekly hours dedicated to language development, and as a result ask for more contact time. At many institutions, tutors report discernible gaps, for example in vocabulary acquisition and self-confidence, between *ab initio* students and their post-A-level peers after integration of the two groups, requiring additional contact hours to be scheduled. And finally, many students underestimate the time, effort and dedication required to successfully complete an *ab initio* language degree, which can lead to significant differences in progression within the group and relatively high drop-out rates.

Some reports on *ab initio* provision have found that departments considering the introduction of *ab initio* pathways often feel that they may be a stop gap for falling recruitment from traditional student groups, but that they also have knock-on effects for the curriculum and for the workload of colleagues involved in their delivery (Footitt, 2005: 18).

On the other hand, these *ab initio* pathways provide an opportunity to study a language particularly to students from secondary schools who have limited or altogether eliminated language study. In that sense, they are an important instrument of widening participation. Modern foreign languages are increasingly offered predominantly at independent rather than state schools. As equality and diversity data from the Office for Students (OfS, n.d.) show, the student population on language degrees is made up of more than 80 per cent White students who come from mostly affluent homes, as is evidenced by the POLAR4 statistics. Due to the reduction of language teaching in state schools (Tinsley and Dolezal, 2018: 3; Collen, 2020: 3), language students are now typically from privileged backgrounds (Collen 2020), with easy access to language learning and international travel. In order to counter this development, *ab initio* pathways provide access to a discipline that would otherwise increasingly become the privilege of certain sectors of society.

The rise of IWLPs and German for non-specialists

Against the background of three decades of surveys, academic studies and newspaper reports analysing and lamenting the alarming decline in language learning in schools and in language degrees in UK higher education, a rather interesting phenomenon can be observed at tertiary level during the same period – namely the healthy recruitment to language learning in institution-wide non-specialist language programmes (IWLPs).

In their respective surveys of German Studies in the UK, Kolinsky and Tenberg concluded as early as 1993 that IWLP-type courses, and primarily *ab initio* IWLPs, 'constitute important dimensions of departments' contemporary teaching programmes' in the 'old' universities (Kolinsky, 1993: 122), and although a then 'relatively recent phenomenon' in the post-1992 universities, several institutions expected a threefold increase in IWLP German numbers over the following years (Tenberg, 1993: 155). This optimistic view was clearly borne out for languages in general, and for German in particular, in the years since. By 2001, Marshall (2001: 16) reported that 'the provision of less-specialist language learning in UK universities has grown exponentially in the last 10 years'. Coleman (2004: 150) also described a scenario where '[i]n a major power shift, language centres are increasingly supplying *all* the language classes for the institution – even where there are specialist degrees in Modern Languages.' Kelly and Jones highlighted that 'language centres are flourishing' (2003: 33), and towards the end of the decade, Worton (2009: 4) confirmed the 'considerable optimism across the Language Centre sector', reporting that 'most [respondents] felt that their language centre was strong and would remain so or grow' (Worton, 2009: 32). In the 2013–14 UCML-AULC survey of language centres, not a single respondent considered prospects for IWLP at their institution 'poor', whereas 65 per cent saw prospects as 'encouraging' (UCML-AULC, 2014: 11). This positive assessment was even improved upon in the following year when 80 per cent of respondents saw the future of their IWLP as 'encouraging' (UCML-AULC, 2015: 18).

The annual UCML-AULC/AULC-UCML surveys have provided a regular overview of the main trends and issues in IWLP since 2012. Due to the absence of UCAS or HESA statistics for the large number of students who study languages in non-credit-bearing modules, survey data relying on self-reporting by participating institutions can only give a general idea of the relative growth or decline of student numbers, and of the comparative position of individual languages within the whole IWLP student body. The fact that a similar number of institutions reported a rise from just under 50,000 to over 62,000 students in total between 2012–13 and 2016–17 (in 61 and 62 institutions respectively) can be seen as proof of the continued rapid rise of IWLPs and the consequent positive outlook of the sector. This trend only seemed to taper off in 2018–19 when the authors concluded that 'the overall numbers for IWLP appear to be stable' (UCML-AULC, 2019: 4).

The 2010s, of course, saw the entry of students into higher education who no longer had language education as a compulsory element at GCSE level. It can therefore be concluded that 'the success of IWLP perhaps reflects challenges elsewhere, including the reduction in take up of languages in schools and downward pressure on numbers being recruited to specialist degree programmes' (UCML-AULC, 2016: 19).

In the context of the overall positive trend of language study in non-degree higher education settings, it is interesting to observe the position of German. Throughout the AULC reporting period 2011–19, German remained the third most popular IWLP language after Spanish and French, thereby occupying the same position, if we exclude English Language, that it already held in 1998–9 (Marshall, 2001: 4). It therefore seems safe to assume that German benefitted from the general upward trend in IWPL student numbers during this period. In fact, the UCML-AULC data suggest that, unlike in degree settings where German was seen as 'the most vulnerable' of the languages (Worton, 2009: 29), it was a particularly popular choice in IWLP. German featured in the list of languages with increased demand by the greatest number of institutions in every single year of the UCML-AULC survey. It topped the list in 2013–14, 2014–15 and again (in joint first place) in 2015–16, when 'almost half of all participating institutions reported an increase in demand for German and Japanese' (UCML-AULC, 2016: 6).

This 'somewhat puzzling' popularity of German among IWLP learners was emphasised by the authors of the 2013–14 survey, in which respondents had cited 'the economic importance of Germany, employability reasons, and also the popularity of German with Engineering students and with some groups of international students' as potential reasons for the popularity of German (UCML-AULC, 2014: 7).

After several years, the continued growth of German has, however, now seemingly come to an end. By 2018–19, the number of institutions reporting a decline in German for the first time outnumbered those reporting increases. In fact, 'German was reported as showing a decrease in uptake by more respondents than for any other language' (AULC-UCML, 2019: 6). It is yet unclear to what extent this result heralds a new trend for IWLP German in the wake of the impact of Brexit. And unfortunately, it is not only German that saw a decline, but for the first time in a long period of growth, there appear to be signs that the seemingly unstoppable rise of IWLP has come, if not to an end, then at least to a stagnation in growth.

In the following section, we will examine two institutions' delivery of *ab initio* German to illustrate two different models – one at degree level and the other as part of an IWLP.

Case study 1: the *ab initio* degree pathway at Aston University[1]

Languages have made an important contribution to Aston's image and reputation from its beginnings as a university in 1966. Students choose Aston because they want to study languages applied to real-life settings and with a clear emphasis on the political, cultural and societal characteristics of target language regions. Target language instruction outside of the core language modules, also known as Content and Language Integrated Learning (CLIL), has been the USP of language study at Aston from the very outset, and Aston students complete a large proportion of their studies in the target language.

The German group at Aston is part of one of three academic departments that make up the School of Social Sciences and Humanities (SSH). Students can study a language in combination with either another language or with one of the subjects on offer in SSH. Depending on the subject combination, all language students acquire 40–80 of 120 required credits in each academic year through the medium of the target language. The basic 40 credits consist of a core language module and a core subject module such as Introduction to the French/Spanish(/etc.)-Speaking World or Politics & Society. The rest of the credits come from L2-taught optional modules, from English-taught modules in the combination subject or from another language studied as part of the IWLP (Languages for All). In addition, Aston offers an integrated degree in International Business and Modern Languages (IBML). All undergraduate language programmes feature a mandatory year abroad in one of the L2-speaking countries, where students undertake a work placement, work as language assistants through the British Council or study at an L2-speaking university after their second year of study.

As discussed previously, OfS equality and diversity data indicate that the vast majority of language students tend to be White and from affluent households. This is not a profile that matches the majority of Aston language students. Entry profiles show that most students are from the region, come largely from ethnic minority backgrounds, and often from low-income families. Aston's award as Guardian University of the Year 2020 was won in celebration of Aston's 'commitment to social mobility and diversity'. In MFL, this means giving students access to a subject they have previously had very limited opportunity to experience. Key to this strategy was the introduction of *ab initio* language routes in 2015 – first in German and French and a year later in Spanish, followed by Mandarin Chinese in 2018 – that allow students to study a language from beginners' level without A-level requirements.

The *ab initio* pathways at Aston follow a pattern similar to that of the post-A-level cohort: 40 of the 60 yearly credits for the half programme in the language are dedicated to an intensive language module, with five hours of contact time per week and an extensive array of learning tasks and formative assessment for another 10 hours of independent study per week. Usually, four of the five hours of contact time are delivered by the module convenor and structured around the chosen coursebook (*Motive A1-B1*), and an additional hour of language practice is delivered by language assistants. In March 2020 at the start of the COVID-19 pandemic, delivery was adapted to the new circumstances, particularly in the academic year 2020–1: students were asked to complete asynchronous tasks (mainly grammar explanations and exercises or vocabulary overviews) estimated to take one hour before joining the first of three hours of weekly synchronous webinars with the module convenor and an additional one-hour webinar with the language assistant.

This pattern of delivery applies to the first two years of the *ab initio* pathway. In addition to the language module, Year 1 *ab initio* students join their post-A-level counterparts in the module 'Introduction to Language and Communication', which is taught in English across the languages. In Year 2, the *ab initio* students face a much more challenging task: they join the Year 1 post-A-level cohort in a content module that introduces them to the history, society, geography and politics of German-speaking countries. This module is taught in the target language and assumes proficiency of at least B1 level. Since the *ab initio* students generally reach level A2 at the end of their first year of study, they have an additional seminar where the topics covered in the module are revised and where the students learn the specific language necessary to discuss them. All students spend their third year abroad.

Overall, the introduction of the *ab initio* pathway has seen mixed results. On the one hand, it has to some extent made up for the drop in post-A-level recruitment figures. In fact, in some years, more students enrol on the *ab initio* pathway than on the post-A-level stream. On the other hand, attrition is a more serious issue among *ab initio* students than for their post-A-level peers where few, if any, students leave the programme before graduation, whereas in *ab initio*, some years see up to half the cohort change programme or leave altogether before they go on their placement year. However, those who stick it out tend to catch up with, and at times even outperform, their post-A-level peers once they are integrated in the shared final year, a clear indication that *ab initio* provides an opportunity for very able students to excel.

Case study 2: the Keele 'with competency in German' degree designation

The national trends in recruitment to German were mirrored at Keele University: a period of strong recruitment to the German degree programme in the early 1990s was followed by a steady decline in applications in the early 2000s, when specialist language degrees that had hitherto been offered in a wide range of dual honours combinations were phased out. At the same time, the university committed to expanding the existing provision for students to study language electives as part of, or in addition to, non-language degrees via the creation of a new language centre in 2010.

Keele's founding ethos with its emphasis on interdisciplinarity had, since its post-war inception in 1949, ensured an element of breadth of education across all programmes. Undergraduate language subsidiary modules for students from all faculties had therefore already been a well-established and popular feature in students' foundation and first year programmes; and second- and third-year students were able to join on a non-credit-bearing basis, financed via separate lifelong learning funding which was available until HEFCE's ELQ policy change in 2008.

By 2001, it had become apparent that there was an increasing demand for a formal recognition of such extra-curricular language learning. Consequently, a 'Certificate of Language Competency in [Language]' was established that allowed students who successfully completed a series of language modules in each of their three years of study to graduate with a university-approved additional qualification.

A far-reaching curriculum reform at Keele in 2008–10 finally enabled the inclusion of language electives in each of the three years of study in many programmes. By this time, there was general recognition of the wider importance of language learning and the national skills gap in languages, but also general acknowledgement of the role that language learning could play in the enhancement of the university's internationalisation agenda, and in the development of graduate attributes as well as transferable and employability skills. This created a climate in which language electives could flourish.

The elevation of language modules to the status of credit-bearing modules – now counting towards degree classifications in students' second and final year presented additional challenges for the new language centre. A complete redesign of all modules with benchmarking against the Common European Framework of Reference for Languages (CEFR) set clear standards for learning outcomes and assessments at each level, thereby implementing a quality assurance mechanism that was to become the sector norm in the following years. By 2013–14 around 85 per cent of respondents to the UCML-AULC survey indicated reference to CEFR (2014: 9).

With languages firmly embedded within a large number of programmes, and student numbers for IWLP languages at Keele following the national upward trend, a further major development followed in 2015–16, when the separate 'Certificate of Language Competency' was withdrawn in favour of enhanced degree titles that include the designation 'with competency in [Language]' or 'with advanced competency in [Language]'. These formally recognise the sustained engagement with language learning during an undergraduate course and the wide-ranging benefits this can have on students' personal development, international outlook and transferable skills.

Over the course of a typical three-year undergraduate programme, students who start as *ab initio* German learners can normally reach the 'with competency in German' degree designation, equating to CEFR A2/B1 level, by completing six one-semester modules. Those who attend intensive summer residential courses at a partner university abroad can reach this level within two years. There is even a route from *ab initio* to 'advanced competency' level (CEFR B1/B2) for students who spend a year abroad or attend a minimum of eight weeks of intensive language courses over the period of three years. This accelerated pathway has in practice only been completed by one student in the past 20 years, whereas the basic 'with competency' is well within reach of any student who decides to persevere with their learning during their time at Keele. In summer 2020, 49 students graduated with degree enhancements across all languages, six of whom gained a formal recognition of studying German in awards such as 'LLB in Law with competency in German'.

Within the debate about *ab initio* language courses in an IWLP context, it has to be acknowledged that students who only receive two hours of contact time per week in their chosen language and who do not have a compulsory period abroad, will not reach the high level of linguistic proficiency and in-depth knowledge of culture and society that is expected of MFL graduates. Despite the extensive use of asynchronous self-study tasks delivered via the VLE, the relative lack of contact time is further exacerbated by the fact that students who study languages as a minor element in their degree at lower levels of proficiency are generally less likely to organise or take part in extra-curricular language activities. The term 'with competency in German' – rather than 'with proficiency in German' or simply 'with German' – is therefore deliberately used to acknowledge the student's considerable achievement of learning a language from beginners' to CEFR B1 level as a minor element within a non-MFL degree and, at the same time, to indicate that it is not providing the CEFR B2/C1 proficiency of MFL graduates. This should not be seen a deficit, however, as

> all linguistic skills, including those achieved at lower levels, can be of professional advantage, since employers do not only appreciate the instrumental value of linguistic skills, but also the additional

knowledge, cultural awareness and sensitivities that are brought about by language capability at all levels. (Skrandries, 2016: 17)

The 'Keele model' of allowing students to gain language skills and a qualification alongside their principal subjects is therefore well-placed to respond to the demand for linguistically and interculturally capable graduates in a climate where fewer and fewer applicants wish to commit to studying specialist language degrees. The success of the 'with-language competency' degree enhancements is, in fact, a key element in current discussions about adding additional (non-language) 'Global Challenges' enhancement pathways to the Keele portfolio in the near future.

Conclusion: Brexit and beyond

As the previous discussion has shown, a number of national policy decisions related to the British education system have had a direct or indirect impact on the fortunes of German provision at UK universities. The national discourse on the value of languages has been discouraging, despite recurring reports and commentaries in various news outlets bemoaning the negative impact on the skills gap in languages on society and the economy. At the time of writing, there are two major developments that will no doubt affect the long-term future for language learning in the UK – the combined impact of Brexit and of the COVID-19 pandemic.

Since the EU referendum in 2016, a shift in attitudes towards European languages has emerged. With Brexit now a reality, further detrimental developments are to be expected. To give but one example, many schools – both state and independent – have at least one teacher on staff who is from an EU country without UK citizenship, leaving many school managers worried about their ability to recruit and retain staff, so that 'finding language teachers of sufficient quality is a concern for 60 per cent of state schools and more than half of independent schools' (Tinsley and Dolezal, 2018: 8). And of the state schools that still offer German at and beyond KS3, more than half reported that pupils were 'less motivated' to study European languages after Brexit (Collen, 2020).

In the wake of the COVID-19 pandemic, the shift to fully online delivery of language modules was managed with admirable alacrity in MFL departments and language centres at many universities across the UK, aided by a subject community that has embraced technological innovations for many years. The new form of delivery has often meant a reduction of synchronous teaching and learning opportunities and often also a reduction in available spaces on IWLP courses that had to reduce student numbers to make online learning effective.

Finally, the recent call for a national languages strategy in a set of joint proposals from the British Academy, the Arts and Humanities Research Council, the Association of School and College Leaders, the British Council and Universities UK highlights the 'overwhelming evidence of an inadequate, longstanding, and worsening supply of the language skills needed by the UK to meet future needs' and emphasises the need for 'urgent, concerted and coordinated action at all levels from primary schools through to university and beyond' (British Academy et al., 2020: 2). In order to ensure that the ever-increasing skills gap in languages is reversed, the British government needs to make a strong commitment to language education at all levels.

Notes

1   Due to falling student numbers, Aston University management decided to discontinue recruitment to German degree programmes – both *ab initio* and post-A-level – from September 2020. The remaining language degree programmes in French, Spanish and Mandarin Chinese were closed down after a final admissions cycle in August 2021.

References

AULC-UCML (2018) AULC-UCML Survey of Institution-Wide Language Provision in Universities in the UK (2017–2018). Online. https://secureservercdn.net/160.153.138.219/sjc.1af. myftpupload.com/wp content/uploads/2021/03/AULC_UCML_2017-2018.pdf (accessed 20 April 2021).

AULC-UCML (2019) AULC-UCML Survey of Institution-Wide Language Provision in Universities in the UK (2018–2019). Online. https://secureservercdn.net/160.153.138.219/sjc.1af. myftpupload.com/wp-content/uploads/2021/03/AULC_UCML_2018-2019.pdf (accessed 20 April 2021).

Baker, S. (2021) 'Languages decline sees numbers drop to zero at UK universities'. *Times Higher Education*, 24 February. Online. www.timeshighereducation.com/news/languages-decline-sees-numbers-drop-zero-ukuniversities (accessed 26 April 2021).

Bawden, A. (2013) 'Modern languages: Degree courses in freefall'. *The Guardian*, 8 October. Online. www.theguardian.com/education/2013/oct/08/modern-foreign-language-degrees-axed (accessed 26 April 2021).

British Academy, the Arts and Humanities Research Council, the Association of School and College Leaders, the British Council and Universities UK (2020) *Towards a National Languages Strategy: Education and skills.* Online. www.thebritishacademy.ac.uk/documents/2597/Towards-a-national-languages-strategy-July-2020_R0FHmzB.pdf (accessed 4 May 2021).

CBI/Pearson (2018) Educating for the Modern World. CBI/Pearson education and skills annual report. Online. www.cbi.org.uk/media/1171/cbi-educating-for-the-modern-world.pdf (accessed 26 April 2021).

CBI/Pearson (2019) Education and Learning for the Modern World. CBI/Pearson education and skills annual report. Online. https://www.cbi.org.uk/media/3841/12546_tess_2019.pdf (accessed 16 June 2022).

Coleman, J.A. (2004) 'Modern languages in British universities: Past and present'. *Arts & Humanities in Higher Education* 3:2, 147–62.

Collen, I. (2020) *Language Trends 2020. Language teaching in primary and secondary schools in England*. London: British Council.

Footitt, H. (2005) The National Languages Strategy in Higher Education. Research Report No. 625. Southampton: LLAS. Online. https://dera.ioe.ac.uk/5561/1/RR625.pdf (accessed 26 April 2021).

Grix, J. and Jaworska, S. (2002) 'Responses to the Decline in Germanistik in the UK'. *German as a Foreign Language* 3, 1–24.

Kelly, M. (2019) 'Is the UK in a language crisis?'. *British Council*, 5 March. Online. www.britishcouncil.org/voices-magazine/uk-language-learning-crisis (accessed 26 April 2021).

Kelly, M. and Jones, D. (2003) *A New Landscape for Languages. A report commissioned by the Nuffield Foundation*. London: The Nuffield Foundation. Online. https://mk0nuffieldfounpg9ee.kinstacdn.com/wp-content/uploads/2019/11/new-landscape-for-languages.pdf (accessed 26 April 2021).

Klapper, J. (2006) *Understanding and Developing Good Practice. Language teaching in higher education*. London: CILT.

Kolinsky, E. (1993) 'Survey of German at the "old" Universities'. In *German Studies in the United Kingdom*, edited by R. Tenberg and R. Jones, 81–134. Cambridge: EBA.

Leder, G., Reimann, N. and Walsh, R. (1996) 'Introduction. The emergence and development of ab initio language courses'. In *Ab Initio Language Learning. A guide to good practice in universities and colleges. The example of German*, edited by G. Leder, N. Reimann and R. Walsh, 1–7. London: Centre for Information on Language Teaching and Research.

Marshall, K. (2001) *Report on Survey of Less Specialist Languages Learning in UK Universities (1998–99)*. Commissioned by University Council for Modern Languages. Published as Appendix 2 to: Marshall, K. (2002) *General Introduction to Modern Languages in Today's UK Universities*. Online. https://www.llas.ac.uk/resources/gpg/1392.html (accessed 29 April 2021).

The Nuffield Languages Inquiry (2000) *Languages: The next generation. The final report and recommendations of the Nuffield Languages Inquiry*. London: The Nuffield Foundation. Online. www.nuffieldfoundation.org/sites/default/files/languages_finalreport.pdf (accessed 26 April 2021).

OfS (n.d.) *Equality and diversity student data*. Online. www.officeforstudents.org.uk/data-and-analysis/equality-and-diversity-student-data/equality-and-diversity-data/ (accessed 7 May 2021).

Reershemius, G. (2010) 'Deutsch in Großbritannien'. In *Deutsch als Fremd- und Zweitsprache. Volume 2*, edited by H.-J. Krumm, C. Fandrych, B. Hufeisen and C. Riemer, 1674–80. Berlin: de Gruyter.

Skrandies, P. (2016) *Every Graduate a Linguist: Building strategic language capability through IWLP*. London: London School of Economics and Political Science, Language Centre. Online. http://eprints.lse.ac.uk/66055/?from_serp=1 (accessed 29 April 2021).

Tenberg, R. (1993) 'Survey of German at the "new" Universities'. In *German Studies in the United Kingdom*, edited by R. Tenberg and R. Jones, 135–67. Cambridge: EBA.

Tinsley, T. and Doležal, N. (2018) *Language Trends 2018. Language teaching in primary and secondary schools in England*. London: British Council.

UCAS (2018) *January Deadline Analysis*. Online. www.ucas.com/file/147861/download?token=v6pEGF8E (accessed 26 April 2021).

UCML-AULC (2013) *UMLC-AULC Survey of Institution-Wide Language Provision in Universities in the UK (2012–2013)*. Online. https://secureservercdn.net/160.153.138.219/sjc.1af.myftpupload.com/wp-content/uploads/2021/03/UCML_AULC_2012-2013.pdf (accessed 20 April 2021).

UCML-AULC (2014) *UMLC-AULC Survey of Institution-Wide Language Provision in Universities in the UK (2013–2014)*. Online. https://secureservercdn.net/160.153.138.219/sjc.1af.myftpupload.com/wp-content/uploads/2021/03/UCML_AULC_2013-2014.pdf (accessed 20 April 2021).

UCML-AULC (2015) *UMLC-AULC Survey of Institution-Wide Language Provision in Universities in the UK (2014–2015)*. Online. https://secureservercdn.net/160.153.138.219/sjc.1af.myftpupload.com/wp-content/uploads/2021/03/UCML_AULC_2014-2015.pdf (accessed 20 April 2021).

UCML-AULC (2016) *UMLC-AULC Survey of Institution-Wide Language Provision in Universities in the UK (2015–2016)*. Online. https://secureservercdn.net/160.153.138.219/sjc.1af.

myftpupload.com/wp-content/uploads/2021/03/UCML_AULC_2015-2016.pdf (accessed 20 April 2021).

UCML-AULC (2017) *UMLC-AULC Survey of Institution-Wide Language Provision in Universities in the UK (2016–2017)*. Online. https://secureservercdn.net/160.153.138.219/sjc.1af. myftpupload.com/wp-content/uploads/2021/03/UCML_AULC_2016-2017.pdf (accessed 20 April 2021).

Worton, M. (2009) *Review of Modern Foreign Languages Provision in Higher Education*. HEFCE. Online. https://discovery.ucl.ac.uk/id/eprint/329251/2/hereview-worton.pdf (accessed 29 April 2021).

2

German *ab initio* in Languages for All programmes: student profiles and course design

Sabina Barczyk-Wozniak

There is a growing trend within UK universities to offer institution-wide language programmes (IWLPs). This scheme is increasingly popular with students who can develop their foreign language skills alongside their degree programme (AULC and UCML, 2020). Students can learn a new language from scratch or continue to build on a language they started at school or college.

This chapter considers the German *ab initio* learners in the IWLP at Cardiff University, Languages for All (LfA), and discusses findings from an investigation into LfA German students of beginners' levels at Cardiff University. The discussion of the results gives an account of both students' linguistic characteristics, such as their language learning biographies, and their long- and short-term dispositions, for example, their experiences, interests, motivation, intentions, aspirations and needs in terms of German language learning.

The Languages for All programme at Cardiff University

LfA was founded in 2014 as part of Cardiff University's vision for the internationalisation and employability of its graduates and is part of the School of Modern Languages. It is a free, credit-bearing programme that the university offers to all its students from first-year undergraduate to final-year PhD students alongside their degree programmes. Recognition for student attainment in LfA courses is documented on degree transcripts as ten additional credits for each completed module. Students can study up to three modules per academic year. They may choose to focus on one language for the duration of their degree programme and attain a good level of language proficiency. Alternatively, students may choose to study a wider range of languages at *ab initio* level. LfA provides a range of levels, from *ab initio* (Common European Framework of Reference [CEFR] level A1) to proficiency (CEFR level C1).

The LfA programme offers two types of courses: (1) weekly classes with two contact hours per week and (2) intensive 'crash' courses delivered in 20 hours over one week, offered twice in the academic year. In addition, students can get further practice in the studied language(s) by using the autonomous learning option, which may include using a variety of physical and online resources to practice and improve their language skills outside the classroom, for example, in a language exchange scheme or in a language café where they can talk to native speakers in a relaxed, social environment. This wide range of flexible choice of study means that students can learn foreign languages in a way that suits their own preferences.

At Cardiff University, LfA courses divide the CEFR levels into smaller parts, with each course covering one part of the CEFR level. These parts accumulate and only on completion of the final part of the CEFR level are the CEFR competences met and, in some languages, externally certified through UniLang.[1] The decision to break down the CEFR levels into smaller components increases the flexibility of the language provision, enabling students to decide their language learning commitment semester by semester. The CEFR A1 and A2 courses are split into three parts, while the CEFR B1, B2 and C1 courses are split into four parts.

Students can enrol in LfA modules for a level that corresponds to their existing language proficiency. Student numbers indicate that A1 beginners levels are especially attractive. Until the academic year 2018/19, 71.2 per cent of LfA German students took a module at A1 level (1,905 out of a total of 2,676 students), while 44 per cent (1,177 out of 2,676 students) enrolled on the A1 part 1 module. The numbers during the COVID-19 pandemic remained high: in 2020/1, 238 students enrolled on A1 German beginners modules, with 153 students on the A1 part 1 module. This shows an increased demand for learning German *ab initio* with LfA, despite recent decreases in German student numbers reported in the AULC and UCML (2020) national survey of IWLP in universities in the UK.

Participants in the study

For better understanding of why students choose to learn German on the LfA programme, I conducted a survey among LfA German students in the summer semester of 2018/19. Students answered multiple choice and open questions in a questionnaire during the last class of the course. The research objective was to examine students' profiles, in particular their motivation and ambitions in terms of studying German *ab initio*.

The respondents were comprised of 54 students completing a LfA German module at beginners level or continuing learning German after starting German *ab initio*: 21 students in the A1 part 1 module, 10 students in the A1 part 2 module, 11 students in the A2 part 2 module, nine students in the A2 part 3 module and three students in the B1 part 3 module.

Instrument

The instrument used for gathering students' data was a questionnaire, which consisted of three parts. Part one asked about students' subjects and year of study, current module and any previous LfA German modules studied. The second part focused on students' language skills, that is, native language(s) and proficiency in other languages. The third part asked about students' motives for undertaking the German *ab initio* module, their motivation, goals and aspirations related to the application of German language in the future. Questions in this part consisted of a selection of randomly arranged statements (items) describing different reasons for undertaking the German module (12 items) and statements describing ways in which students plan to apply their German skills in the future (31 items), from which students were invited to choose all items they identified with.

Procedure

The questionnaire was administered to 54 LfA students at the end of their German course. The data gathered in the survey were firstly analysed using statistics to describe the results quantitatively. Secondly, they were analysed qualitatively to identify patterns that allowed a description of student profiles. The analysis focused on:
- the main subject of study, to identify preferences or links between studied courses and required language skills

- the number of languages spoken/learnt
- the intrinsic and extrinsic motivation to undertake the German *ab initio* course
- which key communicative language skills are at the centre of interest for LfA German *ab initio* students.

Findings and discussion

Students' backgrounds

The data showed that students come to study German *ab initio* in LfA courses from a variety of schools across the university. Among the 54 respondents, there were students from over 20 different subjects of study. However, it seemed that studying German as a beginner is especially popular among students of Medical Sciences, as they accounted for 18.5 per cent of the respondents (10 out of 54). This was followed by 13 per cent of students (7 out of 54) each coming from the School of Engineering and School of Business and another 11 per cent (6 out of 54) from different courses of study in the School of Modern Languages.[2]

The majority of respondents were first-year students (33 per cent; 18 out of 54) and postgraduate students (26 per cent; 14 out of 54), followed by second-year students (20 per cent; 11 out of 54). The remaining respondents were students in their third or final years (17 per cent; 9 out of 54) and Erasmus students (4 per cent; 2 out of 54). This showed that students at the beginning of their studies were particularly interested in starting learning German alongside their chosen course.[3]

Language learning biographies

Good language learning skills are often associated with being bi- or multilingual, or in general having experience of learning other languages. For the purposes of this study, I decided to look at students' language learning biographies, including native language(s) and other language skills to explore if students who already had some experience with learning languages are more inclined to learn a new language from scratch.

The group of questioned students shows a broad picture of native and previously studied languages. Some 18 native languages were spoken by the respondents, and the most common were English (57 per cent; 31 out of 54), varieties of Chinese (15 per cent; 8 out of 54) and Polish (9 per cent; 5 out of 54). The range of languages that students learned as a second/foreign language before they started their German module was even more noticeable, including 20 European and non-European languages (43 per cent English, 23 out of 54; 35 per cent French, 19 out of 54; 15 per cent Spanish, 8 out of 54; varieties of Chinese 13 per cent, 7 out of 54). The average number of languages previously studied by the respondents was three. However, some students listed more than five foreign languages and only three students had not learned a foreign language beforehand.

These data indicate a preference for language learning among students with prior language learning experience. Possible reasons might include that they understand the benefits of speaking foreign languages better, have already developed some language learning strategies and are not afraid to start learning a new language *ab initio*.

Motivational factors

Several studies in language learning pedagogy and foreign language acquisition clearly confirm that motives and motivations are essential for learning languages (for instance, Dörnyei, 2002; Kirchener, 2004; Riemer, 2006, 2011). The focus of this study was on answering the question to what extent students exhibit more intrinsic or extrinsic motivational factors, or in other words, whether they are driven rather by internal or external factors. It is worth noting here that motivation fluctuates and is made up of a number of both intrinsic and extrinsic factors, which can vary over time. As Dörnyei and Ryan (2015: 93) suggest, motivation is rather a complex, dynamic construct with temporal variations. Therefore, the explicit differentiation between intrinsic and extrinsic motivational factors is problematic (Edmondson, 2004; Dörnyei and Ushioda, 2011).

For intrinsic motivation the incentive to undertake an action comes from one's enjoyment and interest in a particular activity whereas controlled actions determined by an external force and not linked to personal enjoyment come as a result of extrinsic motivation. The distinction between the two types of motivation is crucial when discussing motivation, however, intrinsic and extrinsic motivation are not in conflict with each other but rather, should be understood as two components that work together toward motivated learning (Ryan and Deci, 2017).

Determining which motivational factors play an important role in the learning process of LfA German students aimed to better understand students' decision to undertake the German *ab initio* module and thus students' needs and goals in the course. Since the language learner is the subject in the language learning process and must be understood as the centre of any didactic practice in the language classroom (Grucza, 1993), more insights into students' motivational factors allow a better tailoring of the programme and the application of more successful strategies of delivery for this particular group of students.

Students could select all statements that applied out of 12 items describing reasons for choosing the German *ab initio* course. The statements such as 'I wanted to learn a new language', 'I have German-speaking friends' or 'I would like to work/do an internship at a German company in the UK/abroad', 'I would like to move abroad to a German-speaking country', correspond to two areas of motivation: learning German for interest, enjoyment or integrativeness,[4] which are related to intrinsic motivation, and learning German because of its value, usefulness or benefits, which relates more to extrinsic motivation.

Figure 2.1 presents the results with regards to motivation and demonstrates that LfA German students are more intrinsically than extrinsically oriented. The items 'I wanted to learn a new language/do something new' and 'I need German for my travel/holiday/leisure' were chosen more than 30 times (out of 125 responses for items in this category). There were 75 responses in the group of items corresponding to extrinsic motivation, with 'I would like to work/do an internship in a German company' chosen 33 times and 'I would like to move to Germany/Austria/Switzerland' chosen 18 times.[5] The results clearly indicate that

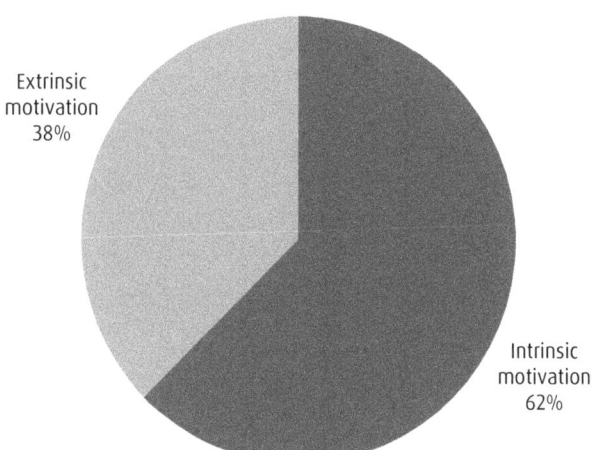

Figure 2.1 Proportion of intrinsic vs extrinsic motivation of LfA students in German *ab initio* courses. Source: Author.

students are self-driven to undertake an *ab initio* German course. They follow their interests, personal goals and understand the learning as an enrichment or an opportunity.

To investigate students' motives and goals in relation to using German skills in the future, respondents were asked to choose all statements that apply out of 33 items describing their aspired language skills in German. The randomly organised items were divided into three groups: (1) application of German skills in private areas of life; (2) application of German skills in professional areas of life; (3) tasks that require German skills in both professional and private areas of life.

Students' responses in relation to the aspirations and goals of using German in the future (presented in Table 2.1) show a clear predominance of responses related to the intended application of German skills in private areas of life. 'Asking for local information' and 'Socialising with local people/friends/neighbours' were chosen 37 times each. Highly rated statements also include: 'Listening to local radio/TV/online news' (28 responses) and 'Listening to public announcements' (24 responses).

From the items relating to professional areas of life students rated the highest: 'Socialising at the workplace' (22 responses) and 'Networking/ building professional relationships' (21 responses). It is interesting to note that the more frequent responses related to professional use of future German skills were recorded by students who continued learning German and achieved a higher level of proficiency (modules A2 part 2, B1 part 3). Those students aim at employment in German-speaking countries or companies and organisations that require German language skills and chose 'Participation in job interviews', 'Completing job applications', 'Reading scholarship articles/books/research reports' and 'Writing scholarship articles/research reports' more often than students from lower levels.

These results agree largely with the previous finding that students in LfA German *ab initio* courses are intrinsically determined to learn the new language and pursue enjoyment, confidence in the target country and opportunities to socialise while using their foreign language skills.

Table 2.1 Students' aspirations in applying German skills in relation to areas of life. Source: Author.

Area of application	Responses
Private application of German language skills	218
Professional application of German language skills	171
Application of German skills in private and professional areas	94
Total	483

Communicative language skills aspired to by LfA German *ab initio* learners

The main objective for the didactics of the foreign language is that learner develop communication competence in the target language (see for instance Grucza, 1993; Storch, 1999).[6] This can be mastered through the development and application of the key language skills of listening, speaking, reading and writing for actual communicative purposes. However, this didactic concept of four key language skills only partially corresponds with real communicative situations in which the communicative language skills tend to be used in connection with each other rather than applied separately. For instance, having a conversation with interlocuters is a sequence of listening and speaking where the roles change constantly between the communication partners.

The distribution of language skills in the mother tongue is highly debated. For example, Heyd (1991: 107–8) reports about studies that describe the ratio of listening–reading–speaking–writing as 8–7–4–2, while Rivers (1978) found that listening constitutes 45 per cent, speaking 30 per cent, reading 16 per cent and writing 9 per cent. In foreign language learning, to maintain and develop learners' motivation and sense of achievement, other factors than the weighting of the language skills in a native language communication need to be considered, for example, learners' aspirations and language learning psychology.

To determine which communicative language skills are of high importance for the LfA German *ab initio* students, I asked not directly about the skills but situations and tasks in which students intend to apply their German skills. After the first stage of analysis that focused on the motivation and area of application of German skills, all 31 items in this question were further broadly assigned to the four communicative language skills.

Figure 2.2 presents the results with regards to key language skills targeted by all participants. It shows clearly that LfA German beginners have a preference for speaking skills (35.7 per cent, 154 out of 459 responses) with frequently chosen items: 'Asking for local information' (36 responses), 'Socialising with local people and at the workplace' (35 and 20 responses respectively) and 'Telephoning' (13 responses). Reading comprehension with 24.4 per cent (122 out of 459 responses) followed in second place. The highest-rated purposes of using reading skills are: 'Reading emails' (20 responses), 'Reading local newspapers/online news' (17 responses) and 'Reading scholarship articles' (13 responses). Listening and writing follow almost equally with a weighting of 20 per cent (92 out of 459 responses) and 19.8 percent (91 out of459 responses)

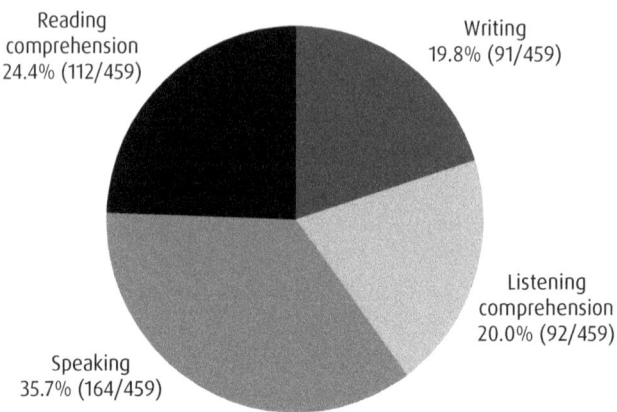

Figure 2.2 Communicative skills targeted by students of LfA German for Beginners modules. Source: Author.

respectively. The most frequently chosen items in those categories were: 'Writing emails' (23 responses), 'Sending text/WhatsApp messages, etc.' (21 responses), 'Listening to local radio/TV/online news' (27 responses) and 'Listening to announcements in public' (23 responses).

As already stated, these results need to be understood with reflection on the authentic communicative situation where the communicative language skills appear combined. Considering this, listening will gain importance, since it is an essential part of socialising or telephoning. Likewise, writing skills, such as sending text messages or emails, require good comprehension skills.

The discussion of the importance of individual communicative language skills for LfA students in German *ab initio* modules needs to take into consideration some differences in society before and after the COVID-19 pandemic. The pandemic forced the move from presence to distance in both private and professional areas of life. This was possible thanks to the availability of digital technologies but consequently caused a change in the channels of communication. Many of us experienced an increase in receiving and sending emails, text messages and posting on social media. In the professional areas of life, extensive email exchanges, preparing written presentations (sometimes pre-recorded with voice-overs), creating materials for autonomous use by the recipients (such as asynchronous learning resources for self-study in schools or universities) have become a new normality. Against this background written skills clearly gained in importance, and in our understanding, it is recommended to reflect on this by planning content and tasks for language courses accordingly.

Outcome of the study – Student profiles in LfA German *ab initio* modules

The analysis of the gathered data confirmed the significant academic heterogeneity of German *ab initio* groups in our LfA programme. Students come to study German at beginners level from many academic schools and students get to meet students from many different disciplines.

An average German student deciding to learn German *ab initio* speaks more than one language and during their educational pathway has some previous experience of learning other foreign languages. The existence of this cross-linguistic knowledge does not necessarily mean a simple transfer mechanism from the mother tongue or other languages. Several studies into foreign language acquisition demonstrated that the positive transfer or interference have a relatively small impact on the language learning process (Diehl et al., 2000; Barczyk, 2009). From already being multilingual, students can benefit in numerous other ways while learning German *ab initio*, for instance, to be knowledgeable about how to apply already developed (meta)linguistic knowledge during learning a new language by intra- and interlingual confrontative references might be one of the factors that motivates students to start learning another language.[7] This confirms the high number of responses that students wanted to 'learn a new language/do something different' (67 per cent, 36 out of 54). From a psycholinguistic point of view, having already gone through multiple language acquisition processes helps students develop language learning strategies and other communicative strategies, for instance, to focus on what is known and understood to decipher new/unknown information from context and to support comprehension in the foreign language, since they have already learned and applied those strategies while previously studying languages.

Taking students' motives and goals into consideration, the data allow the conclusion that LfA German *ab initio* students are mostly self-determined and their ambitions regarding the application of future German skills focus mostly on private areas of life. It becomes clear that in LfA modules the social aspect of learning plays an important part: students come to the course to socialise, want to communicate in the target language and intend to apply German skills pursuing personal rather than professional goals.

Didactical consequences for planning and delivery of LfA German *ab initio* modules

The LfA programme is tailored to the profiles of its students. Considering students' characteristics, motives and goals necessitates, among other things, a precise selection of topics, methods of presentation and practice, development of communicative language skills and forms of assessment. The following section briefly discusses the approach to developing oral and listening skills and the necessary adjustments made to mitigate changes caused by the COVID-19 pandemic in the academic year 2020/1.

The LfA programme mastered the transfer to online delivery quite early in the pandemic. Starting from semester two in the 2019/20 academic year, crash courses and then all modules in the academic year 2020/1 were delivered entirely online.

Development of free-speaking skills – an example from teaching practice

As already shown, free-speaking skills are of high importance for LfA German students. Speaking is a productive skill and its complexity for didactical purposes needs to be understood (Storch, 1999: 213). Free speaking can be developed best while performing the act of speaking. Spontaneity and fluency can be achieved better by promoting speaking fluently, even if mistakes occur, than by focusing on error-free but hesitant speech because of constant reflection on the rules (Neuf-Münkel and Roland, 1991: 109). In other words, factors such as adequacy, clarity, fluency and achieving communicative goals are more important during practising speaking than strict language correctness.[8]

LfA German students have multiple opportunities to practise free-speaking skills either in a traditional classroom or during synchronous delivery in breakout rooms. Students' feedback provided after completion of the modules in academic year 2020/1 shows clearly how much LfA students enjoy and value breakout room activities.

Practising speaking starts with standard beginners' topics, for example, personal information, family, daily routine, food and hobbies. After having the opportunity to speak about themselves, students practise different scenarios, pretending to be famous people, such as Angela Merkel, Manuel Neuer or Madonna. From the beginning, students are encouraged to use authentic short oral reactions, such as 'Echt!',

'Wirklich?' and 'Schade!'. The next step is to report back on celebrities from British or German societies (for example Boris Johnson or Angela Merkel) after reading fictive interviews with these people. The interviews are didactically prepared materials, easy to read for beginners, yet they accumulate vocabulary and grammar structures that need to be practised and acquired at this stage. An adequate level of redundancy allows students to focus on the content and the information they understood from the interview and try to give a free account of this. At the same time, they can practise a new structural pattern (third-person plural) and acquire (even if initially unreflective) the rule for subject–verb agreement.

Developing and assessing listening skills in synchronous delivery

While free speaking can still be practised effectively with the group in virtual classroom or in breakout rooms, there are certain limitations on developing and assessing listening skills with all students in a live virtual classroom. The experiences made during online synchronous teaching show that sharing audio or video files in sessions with students often results in technical problems, such as a delayed or robotic voice. Therefore, adjustments needed to be made in the form of delivery. After preparation for listening tasks in class (for example, activating or introducing key vocabulary, activating general knowledge or learners' expectations), learners often mute the call and complete the listening task individually on their devices offline. Afterwards, the results are discussed with the entire group online and feedback is provided. Similarly, listening comprehension is assessed in online digitised and self-marked tasks completed outside the classroom with feedback provided through an online mark and further feedback in class.

Changes to the assessment of LfA modules

In the academic year 2020/1, the assessment of LfA modules was changed. Firstly, to align with CEFR levels and to give students the possibility to gain UniLang certification, advising students on their language learning outcomes in case they would like to gain an international language certificate, such as Goethe Zertifikate.[9] Secondly, to better tailor the assessment types and feedback possibilities to online modes of delivery.

The different assessment forms aim to assess all four communicative language skills as well as grammar and vocabulary.[10] In each module, there are three summative assessments, preceded by formative exercises throughout the module in class, as follows:

1. Digitised auto-marked coursework (counting for 30 per cent of the module) submitted online through Cardiff University's virtual learning environment (VLE) with feedback provided through an online mark and by tutors in class.
2. Oral assessment (counting for 20 per cent of the module) in beginners' modules takes the form of a five-minute one-to-one speaking task with the tutor, with written feedback afterwards.
3. End-of-module class test (counting for 50 per cent of the module) – also an online assessment submitted through the VLE. It is timed and consists of an automated digitised part and a free-writing exercise marked by the tutor. Feedback is provided as an automated mark and further comments from the tutor.

All LfA German modules that complete a stage of the CEFR (that is, A1 part 3, A2 part 3 and B1 part 4) are accredited by UniLang. In the academic year 2020/1 there were 25 students enrolled on the A1 part 3 German module, of whom 23 achieved UniLang certification.

Conclusion

The results of the investigation indicate that students in the German *ab initio* modules are prompted to learn German by multiple motives and follow various aspirations. They have diverse linguistic knowledge gained through previous experiences with language learning. Although the profiles of students investigated in this study are to be interpreted as broad generalisations rather than definite descriptions, the awareness of those learner characteristics can be a decisive factor in the continued optimisation of the LfA programme. Moreover, teachers can systematically address learners' strengths, for example, by referring to and activating existing linguistic knowledge and language learning strategies, by choosing adequate content to enable students to fulfil their aspirational goals and developing a feeling of belonging to the speaker community. All those practices are highly recommendable to stimulate language learning in the *ab initio* modules.

Notes

1 UniLang is a UK-wide recognition scheme for language learning in higher education and runs alongside credits. It informs university students what their language learning outcomes mean in terms of the CEFR. Furthermore, it provides a recognised certificate that conveys the value of their language skills to careers services and employers. UniLang is administered through the Association of University Language Communities in the UK and Ireland (AULC) and is also part of the Network for University Language Testing in Europe, which offers mutual recognition of language learning between participating programmes in the UK, Czech Republic, France, Germany, Poland, Slovakia and Spain.

2 Other degree programmes include law, physics, mathematics, history and religion, journalism and architecture.

3 To explain this trend, further empirical data are needed. While it was not the subject of investigation in the discussed survey, it is likely that students in their first year have space available in their curriculum that could be filled by taking an LfA module.

4 This term refers here to a desire to communicate and participate in the target language community and culture.

5 As indicated earlier, the clear distinction between intrinsic and extrinsic motivational factors is sometimes challenging; the aspiration to secure a good job at a German company might be outcome-based but also be associated with enjoyment or personal volition.

6 Communication competence in Glottodidactics is a broad term used following Grucza (1993: 33) for the completion of the communicative competence *sensu stricto* which was not extensive enough to describe the full complexity of the objective of the foreign language teaching. It includes inter alia linguistics, communicative and (inter)cultural competence.

7 The term 'confrontative' is used in accordance with Zabrocki (1979: 33) who suggested this in opposite to 'contrastive' to emphasise language learners can benefit from analysing both differences and similarities between languages. 'Contrastive' analysis focuses more on differences.

8 It needs to be emphasised that linguistic corrections are still a fundamental condition for achieving communicative competence in the foreign language. A certain tolerance of language mistakes can only be accepted in learning phases while free speaking is practised. It does not mean ignorance of linguistic rules, in particular not in writing. Writing skills, because of their nature, allow application of declarative language knowledge and monitoring own written productions (Krashen, 1982).

9 Goethe Zertifikate seem to be a desirable target for LfA German students, with 31 out of 54 students responding that they would like to complete at least one Goethe examination.

10 Translation tasks are not included based on the fact that LfA students speak different native languages, and their English skills vary.

References

AULC and UCML (2020) *AULC-UCML Survey of Institution-Wide Language Provision in Universities in the UK (2019-2020)*. Online. https://aulc.org/wp-content/uploads/2021/07/AULC-UCML-survey-of-Institution-Wide-Language-Provision-in-universities-in-the-UK-2019-2020.pdf (accessed 18 August 2021).

Barczyk, S. (2009) *Der Erwerb syntaktisch-topologischer Regularitäten des Deutschen durch polnische Lerner und seine glottodidaktischen Implikationen*. Lublin: Wydawnictwo Uniwersytetu Marii Curie-Skłodowskiej.

Diehl, E., Christen, H., Leunenberger, S., Pelvat, I. and Studer, T. (2000) *Grammatikunterricht: alles für der Katz?: Untersuchungen zum Zweitsprachenerwerb Deutsch*. Tübingen: Niemeyer.

Dörnyei, Z. (2002) 'The motivational basis of language learning tasks'. In *Individual Differences in Second Language Acquisition*, edited by P. Robinson, 137–58. Amsterdam: John Benjamin.

Dörnyei, Z. and Ryan, S. (2015) *The Psychology of the Language Learner Revisited*. New York: Routledge.

Dörnyei, Z. and Ushioda, E. (2011) *Teaching and researching motivation*, second edition. Harlow: Longman.

Edmondson, W. (2004) 'Individual motivational profiles: The interaction between external and internal factors'. *Zeitschrift für Interkulturellen Fremdsprachenunterricht*, 9:2. Online. https://ojs.tujournals.ulb.tu-darmstadt.de/index.php/zif/article/view/487/463 (accessed 28 February 2022).

Grucza, F. (1993) 'Ansätze zu einer Theorie der Ausbildung von Fremdsprachenlernern'. In *Beiträge zur wissenschaftlichen Fundierung der Ausbildung von Fremdsprachenlernern*, edited by F. Grucza, H.-J. Krumm and B. Grucza, 7–96. Warsaw: Wydawnictow Uniwersytetu Warzawskiego.

Heyd, G. (1991) *Deutsch lernen. Grundwissen für den Unterricht in Deutsch als Fremdsprache*, second revised version. Frankfurt am Main: Diesterweg.

Kirchner, K. (2004) *Motivation beim Fremdsprachenerwerb. Eine qualitative Pilotstudie zur Motivation schwedischer Deutschlerner*. Online. https://ojs.tujournals.ulb.tu-darmstadt.de/index.php/zif/article/viewFile/486/462 (accessed 21 June 2021).

Krashen, S. (1982) *Principles and Practice in Second Language Acquisition*. Oxford: Pergamon.

Neuf-Münkel, G. and Roland, R. (1991) *Fertigkeit Sprechen*. (Erprobungsfassung 11/1991). Fernstudienprojekt zur Fort- und Weiterbildung im Bereich Germanistik und Deutsch als Fremdsprache. Berlin: Langenscheidt.

Riemer, C. (2006) 'Der Faktor Motivation in der empirischen Fremdsprachenforschung'. In *Motivation Revisited. Festschrift für Gert Solmecke*, edited by A. Küppers and J. Quetz, 35–48. Berlin: Lit. Verlag.

Riemer, C. (2011) 'Warum Deutsch (noch) gelernt wird – Motivationsforschung und Deutsch als Fremdsprache'. In *Deutsch bewegt. Entwicklungen in der Auslandsgermanistik und Deutsch als Fremd- und Zweitsprache*, edited by H. Barkowski, S. Demmig, H. Funk and U. Würz, 327–40. Baltmannsweiler: Schneider.

Rivers, W.M. (1978) *Der Französischunterricht: Ziele und Wege*, translated and revised for German by Heribert Walter. Frankfurt am Main: Diesterweg.

Ryan, R.M. and Deci, E.L. (2017) *Self-Determination Theory: Basic psychological needs in motivation, development, and wellness*. New York: Guilford Press.

Storch, G. (1999) *Deutsch als Fremdsprache – Eine Didaktik*. Munich: Wilhelm Fink Verlag.

Zabrocki, L. (1970) 'Grundfragen der Konfrontativen Grammatik'. In *Probleme der Kontrastiven Grammatik Jahrbuch 1969*, edited by H. Moser, 31–52. Düsseldorf: Schwann. Online. https://core.ac.uk/download/pdf/83651334.pdf (accessed 18 August 2021)

3

Preparing Generation Z students for a world of volatility, uncertainty, complexity and ambiguity (VUCA) through language learning

Kasia Łanucha and Alexander Bleistein

Introduction

With a new generation of learners being admitted to university courses, teachers are confronted with changing learning habits and preferences among students that tend to differ from the teachers' own experiences. Students find themselves in a world that is characterised by volatility, uncertainty, complexity, and ambiguity (VUCA) (Codreanu, 2016: 31), so this new generation of learners needs to be equipped with the appropriate skills. In this chapter, we argue that *ab initio* foreign language courses, with their high density of new content and steep learning curves to progress from no prior experience to a fluent discourse in the target language, can function as an ideal environment to acquire those skills. To best support learners towards their aim of fluency, it is crucial for teachers to understand their learners' profiles, and so this chapter opens with a brief characterisation of the Generation Z cohort. After presenting the challenges of the VUCA world that teachers should be aware of, we identify the transferable skills needed in such an environment and discuss how they relate to language learning. Finally, the chapter presents a list of questions and best practice to guide teachers in reflecting on their teaching so they can help students face the VUCA challenges both at present and in the future.

Who is Generation Z?

Born between 1995 and 2010 (Seemiller and Grace, 2017: 22), Generation Z is the population cohort that will be dominant in undergraduate courses until around 2030, while the preceding Generation Y (1981–94), often referred to as Millennials, will mostly have graduated and joined Generation X (1961–80) and the Baby Boomers (1945–60) in the labour market (Barclays, 2018). There will be at least three generations working alongside each other, which requires profound intergenerational understanding and sensitivity (Tual, 2021: 158). By no means do generational ascriptions apply to every individual of a cohort and they might vary depending on the cultural background. There is, however, a set of characteristics shared among many individuals due to similar experiences with regards to 'societal events, parental approaches experienced, changes in communication formats, and observations of the current global environment' (Carter, 2018: 3).

Generation Z can be seen as the first cohort of real digital natives who are comfortable handling technology from an early age. Using up to five screens on different devices at the same time (Kalkhurst, 2018), spending more than ten hours per day with internet content (Hebblethwaite, 2018) and engaging with many different social media platforms, the generation is plugged in and connected on many levels. While this development can be beneficial to an online learning environment, the amount of information at hand results in a reduced attention span and an expectation of instant gratification (Kalkhurst, 2018), as, due to streaming platforms, delivery services or search engines, most needs can be fulfilled in seconds through a single click or tap. At the same time, platforms for sharing short videos and images – such as TikTok, Instagram and Snapchat where contents are tailored to consumers with a short attention span – have become very popular exclusively among Generation Z. This is compared to Facebook and YouTube that are used across all age groups, as numbers in the US (Auxier and Anderson, 2021) suggest. In addition, data shows that, during the COVID-19 pandemic, the use of social media had a negative impact on young people's mental health, creating a vicious circle of social media fatigue through information overload on the one hand and FOMO (fear of missing out) on the other (Liu, 2021: 20).

The availability of numerous online content platforms and technical devices has effects on learning preferences. Compared to the preceding Millennials who value a collaborative approach highly (Schofield and

Honoré, 2009–10: 4), independent learning gains more importance for Generation Z (Seemiller and Grace, 2017: 23). While learner autonomy is far from being a new concept, it is apparent that technological progress and the accessibility of language learning tools and contents have significantly improved the conditions for individual progress at an appropriate pace and contributed towards the popularity of independent learning among Generation Z. Despite this development, considering the pandemic-related contact restrictions, more than half of UK students expressed a wish for a return to face-to-face teaching from September 2021 (UPP, 2021).

A Europe-wide project initiated by *The Guardian* (2021) on the post-COVID future of Generation Z revealed a growing frustration among the young, related to worries about the psychological and socio-economic effects of the pandemic and issues like climate change, as well as social and racial inequalities. High tuition fees and other costs related to higher education, often resulting in study loans and accumulating debts, are a worrying factor for many (Kalkhurst, 2018). Seemiller and Grace describe the will to change the world, to think globally and to work on societal issues as a 'we-centred mentality' (Seemiller and Grace, 2017: 22) focusing on the wider community rather than individual welfare. The characteristics of the Generation Z cohort, their learning preferences as well as their attitudes towards technology and society, impact the way these students approach language learning and the challenges arising, which we will discuss in the following sections.

VUCA as a framework to describe a challenging environment

The acronym VUCA found its place in leadership training in the early 2000s but was introduced much earlier in the late 1980s in an American war college to reflect 'a new emerging type of warfare' by referring to volatility, uncertainty, complexity and ambiguity of such an environment (Codreanu, 2016: 31). Codreanu argues that although the term VUCA has almost become a cliché, it is still useful (Codreanu, 2016: 31). Where there is a lack of a more suitable replacement umbrella term, the acronym seems very well suited to describe the modern global workplace where managers are facing all the VUCA key elements. VUCA reflected the reality of the pre-pandemic world well, for example the speed of change of an interconnected world, its disruptive technology, uncertainty of jobs linked to staff mobility and rotation, the complexity of international joint ventures and collaborations, not to mention the implications of working in foreign languages or using English as a lingua franca. Not all of these phenomena play a prominent role for Generation Z in a higher education context, but they are likely to become more important after graduation when entering the job market. In light of the pandemic, VUCA has gained a new meaning and has been applied to describe the current situation in different fields, including the higher education context, for example in a blog article by the Vice Chancellor of the University of Northampton related to COVID-19 challenges (Petford, 2020). In the bigger picture, VUCA is about the new reality the world has found itself in, and the smaller picture is contextual to each organisation or individual facing different challenges since 2020.

What is the VUCA of language teachers and learners? Other than all the factors mentioned above, there are new challenges caused by the COVID-19 pandemic that have added to the pre-pandemic situation and have accelerated certain developments. When it comes to volatility, speed of change applies for example to technological progress influencing teaching and learning methods. Additional volatility factors since March 2020 have been the different and ever-changing rules and restrictions, such as lockdowns or travel bans, which forced a swift switch to remote working and learning. This new situation also required teachers and students to familiarise themselves with new technology. Teachers have been faced with the challenge of adapting their methodology and materials to the needs of a virtual classroom at an unprecedented speed. All this contributes to a high level of uncertainty. A hybrid mode of delivery – partly in person and partly online – has become the norm at many institutions and it seems unlikely to disappear completely.

The complexity of online classrooms is obvious: new technology means that both students and teachers must navigate new tools (for instance, video conferencing platforms and collaboration tools), as well as the so-called 'Zoom fatigue' (Nadler, 2020: 1).

Ambiguity refers to the confusion associated with new ways of interacting online, like missing non-verbal cues or having to switch between an in-person and online environment. Although Generation Z students are potentially better prepared for this new way of interacting in the classroom because of their preferences for online communication in the social context, it is different from the way they used to learn before the pandemic, and therefore, one could argue that it requires much more of their conscious effort and focus.

A VUCA skill set through language learning

Fostering students' employability and preparing them to function in a multi-layered context by equipping them with appropriate transferable skills should be paramount for both the academy and praxis (Azionya and Oksiutycz, 2019: 6). Skills particularly useful in the VUCA environment described in the previous section are, among others, self-motivation and self-discipline, (learning) agility and autonomy, resilience and critical thinking as well as collaborative and communication skills.[1] A language course seems to be well placed to develop these skills, also due to the many benefits multilingualism has to offer in general. Researchers have stressed the positive implications of multilingualism in the past two decades, proving that speaking more than one language can, among other things, improve cognition (Kroll and Dussias, 2017: 248) and therefore, language learning is a relevant factor contributing to employability (Martinaj, 2020).

The language learning process offers an opportunity that goes well beyond pure linguistic skills by allowing students to foster the VUCA skill set referenced above. First and foremost, students need to be able to develop high self-motivation and sense of purpose to withstand the pressure of an ever-changing environment. Trying to learn a new language requires a tremendous amount of self-discipline and therefore is directly linked to learners' motivation to succeed.

Responding to the speed of change appropriately requires (learning) agility which means being able to come up with alternative solutions when faced with new problems. Research has shown that multilinguals are better equipped to find new directions in thinking, linked to the fact that 'mastering a foreign language in a classroom context dramatically increases the four components of divergent thinking ability, i.e., fluency, elaboration, originality, and flexibility' (Ghonsooly and Showqi, 2012: 161). A key element of learning agility is independent learning, that is being able to develop skills autonomously with guidance where needed.

Another crucial skill for future graduates is resilience – defined as 'the dynamic and negotiated process within individuals (internal) and between individuals and their environments (external) for the resources and supports to adapt and define themselves as healthy amid adversity, threat, trauma, and/or everyday stress' (Truebridge, 2014: 15). Language acquisition requires a high level of resilience because making mistakes and bouncing back when something goes wrong is part of the learning process. Therefore, teachers can champion and foster an approach of getting it wrong and getting over it quickly to encourage resilience in their learners.

When working in an environment in which individuals and organisations often encounter conflicting pieces of information, critical thinking is another necessary skill. A study by Keysar and colleagues revealed that, regardless of the foreign language they can speak, multilingual people are less likely to be biased in their decision making, linked to the fact that 'a foreign language provides greater cognitive and emotional distance than a native tongue does' (Keysar, Hayakawa and An, 2012: 661).

Finally, students need to develop both collaborative and communication skills to work successfully with others, to build relationships, to convey and receive messages and to foster understanding and enable exchange across generations, cultures and disciplines. It is self-explanatory that this should be a priority in language classrooms due to the nature of the subject matter – language is a natural enabler of any interaction including both collaboration and communication. Becoming a proficient communicator is challenging as such and even more so for *ab initio* students who must extend their vocabulary and sentence structures at a high pace. The next section exemplifies suitable teaching approaches and related considerations.

Implications for language teaching and learning

How can teachers implement these skills in the language classroom while considering the students' learning preferences? Of course adapting to the preferences should not be unidirectional – it can be beneficial for students to experience different learning approaches and teaching styles. In their role as facilitators, however, teachers must always try to tailor learning opportunities as adequately as possible to as many students as possible. Tual argues that '[u]niversities are the bridge between the Generation Z and the VUCA World, so they should take the time to define clear and concerted strategies to fulfil the mission' (Tual, 2021: 158).

For language professionals aiming to develop such a clear and concerted strategy, the following questions might be helpful when designing the syllabus and making decisions on the methods and materials used. The list is not exhaustive, but provides a springboard for reflection for, primarily but not exclusively, *ab initio* language teachers who want to support Generation Z students in developing the skill set needed in the post-pandemic VUCA world. All reflections are based on teaching experiences during German language classes at the Centre for Languages and Inter-Communication (CLIC) within the Engineering Department of the University of Cambridge.

1. Are the materials and course contents motivating and relevant to the students?

Considering the speed of societal and technological change, it is apparent that a lot of language material is outdated before it has even been published and therefore, it is not always useful for developing self-motivation, sense of purpose and ultimately self-discipline. Do Generation Z students in the 2020s still have to learn how to book a hotel room via phone? Is asking for directions an authentic scenario when navigation apps figure out the best route in seconds? To what extent are translation skills still necessary with the constantly improving accuracy of machine translation? For practical reasons, teachers must rely on existing material but should follow a learner-centred approach and amend exercises and scenarios to make them fit for the situation students currently find themselves in. Also, it is advisable to make resources available and easy to access online, not only to meet the learners' technological preferences but also to reduce costs for students and universities. Still, considering the saturation with technology, the widespread 'Zoom fatigue' (Nadler, 2020: 1) and social media overload, teachers should limit the platforms used and make sure that all of them bring a significant benefit to the classroom.

Involving students' interests in the course design is a factor that increases motivation in the classroom. Various online polling tools are a workable solution to find out about the learners' preferences during or before the first class. In order to develop a sense of purpose, the practical application of theoretical language and cultural knowledge is key for *ab initio* learners. For example, teachers are advised to facilitate situations allowing an authentic discourse with speakers of the target language. Online tandem projects with partner universities abroad have proven to be an effective way in language classes at CLIC to enable a meaningful exchange when restrictions make travel abroad unfeasible.

2. Can students develop learning agility?

Teachers play an important role in developing agility among the learners and moving them out of their comfort zones: they encourage students to take new directions and to approach problems from a different perspective. In language learning, there is no problem that cannot be solved, as long as learners have access to a wide range of techniques, exercises and explanations to tackle them. *Ab initio* classes offer the opportunity to implement various learning strategies from the very beginning, and the omnipresent technology focus of Generation Z enlarges the pool of resources and platforms. Learning agility also refers to being open to new types of tasks. For example, recording oneself can feel uncomfortable for the first few times, but students get used to it over time and acknowledge the potential of practising speaking and being able to listen back to the audio file. Equally important is the ability to work with and learn from different people, so mixing groups during classes should be a matter of course in *ab initio* groups.

During the pandemic, being able to switch between different modalities and platforms of communication has become another crucial skill, and one that is likely to gain importance and require agility in the future: students are expected to be confident to converse and collaborate online and in person, adapting to the conventions associated with each medium as well as to different communication styles.

3. Does the teaching foster learner autonomy and self-reflection?

From our experience, elements of autonomous learning, self-assessment and feedback seem to work particularity well when used with Generation Z students. To provide a comprehensive and personalised pathway, CLIC introduced a reflective portfolio as a new assessment element in language courses from 2020/1 onwards. This serves as a continuous log of the students' work and gives evidence of all relevant language skills. A viva at the end of the course requires students to defend the portfolio work submitted and allows teachers to check whether the skills meet the corresponding CEFR level (Council of Europe, 2020). Students are also asked to reflect in writing on their learning experiences and to answer questions like the following: 'Why did you choose this task?', 'How difficult was it to complete this task?', 'What would you like to work on in your next submissions?'. Answering questions of this sort not only activates a process of self-reflection within the students but also helps teachers develop a stronger connection with them and understand their learning styles and needs better.

While many students enjoy the high degree of flexibility and creativity allowed, a large proportion of learners, especially at beginners' level, require clear guidance and regular feedback from teachers to shape the personalised learning pathway. It is therefore necessary to establish a lively feedback culture in the classroom and to address the importance of giving and receiving feedback which is different to the act of instant gratification that Generation Z is used to in many scenarios (Kalkhurst, 2018). Altogether, students must learn to take responsibility for their own learning and can be held accountable for their progress, provided that the support and guidance from the teacher's side is sufficient and effective.

4. How can teachers help students in becoming more resilient?

Making mistakes is part of every language learning journey and should be considered normal. However, it is much easier to accept in children than in adult learners who are often more reluctant to embrace the fact that they will be wrong in the language course, and in fact, they will be wrong a lot – an inevitable by-product of language acquisition. If a message does not have the expected outcome or the interlocutor cannot understand it, teachers must encourage their students to try again, paraphrasing, or using other means of communication such as body language. Communicating the fact that trial and error is how we learn and that striving for perfection every time can be counterproductive is critical. This kind of stance from a teacher can boost creativity and encourage risk-taking (instead of always trying to play it safe) which should be reflected in the assessment and feedback where language accuracy is not the most important factor. In addition, non-native language teachers could also help learners by acknowledging their own vulnerability when they are not always sure of their language accuracy and yet constitute proficient language speakers which can be very empowering for the students.

Secondly, managing expectations of the learners is key, especially for those who enrol on a language class in hope for an easy gain of a credit. Language classes are often advertised as fun, and anecdotally, students at CLIC would sometimes drop off after a week or two once they realised that language learning is hard work too, especially when grammar is covered, which tends to be harder to make engaging (and therefore sometimes leads teachers to almost being apologetic for even talking about grammar in the class!).

5. What about critical thinking skills?

Critical thinking skills are particularly important when dealing with an overload of often conflicting and ambiguous information. Can teachers address this challenge in an *ab initio* language class? Shirkhani and Fahim argue that the best way of fostering critical thinking in the language teaching context is to include it in assignments by integrating language and critical thinking skills (Shirkhani and Fahim, 2011: 113). Although it might prove difficult to enhance critical thinking through engagement with sophisticated input at beginners' level, meta-reflection on language and cultural conventions (even if partly not in the target language), can form a part of language classes to critically shed a light on the learning contents: 'What is the benefit of having a system of cases in German?',

'Which function has the distinction between a formal and informal address (*du/Sie*)?', 'Do we need a gender-sensitive language?', 'Why are Germans considered as direct or even rude compared to the British?'. Cultural and linguistic questions like these could arise when dealing with language contents that touch on these topics explicitly or implicitly.

Another area to use critical skills is the choice of materials students engage with, such as online dictionaries, translation tools, YouTube videos or language programmes, perhaps by spending some time in the course on discussing the main features of reliable and credible (online) sources and by integrating traditional approaches like literature reviews or discourse analysis on a certain topic.

6. How can language teaching improve collaboration and communication skills?

Collaboration underpins every interactive language class and is present in different forms: work in pairs, smaller or bigger groups, in person or remotely or by using technology. Teachers can support their students, depending on the task and its length, by helping them establish the ground rules to make sure teamwork goes smoothly. When it comes to communication, it is unlikely that, at beginners' level, the target language will always be the language of instruction in the classroom. Instead, students have to use a lingua franca in their interactions, both synchronously and asynchronously, which the teacher can also model by setting the tone when interacting with the students as a group and individually.

Intercultural awareness is highly important when dealing with ambiguity and a key element of successful communication in the interconnected world Generation Z inhabit, and it goes beyond facts about a country and the dos and don'ts for visiting. It is also about understanding how national culture can affect the way we think, behave and therefore communicate. Certain cultural differences manifest themselves in German right from the start in a beginners' course, such as hierarchy and the use of both titles (for example, *Herr, Frau, Doktor*) and the formal and informal 'you'. Another one is communication style, especially requests such as *Buchstabieren Sie, bitte* (Please spell) or *Geben Sie mir bitte …* (Please give me …), which some students might consider inappropriate or simply rude. Teachers can also address other aspects randomly as the situation arises, for example when talking about how students from different national backgrounds feel about working times stated in teaching materials. Some might find that leaving the office at 5.00pm is late, some find it early. Discussions about what feels right in a given context go far beyond language learning and are closely linked to critical thinking skills (see Question 5). They raise awareness in the students of how their common sense is not at all that common when working across cultures which comes with many challenges in the VUCA world and in a language class, even at an *ab initio* level. This provides a fantastic opportunity for learning both about the target culture and other cultures (including one's own). The same applies to intergenerational learning and reflecting societal norms (for example, holding the door by a male for a female, which can be considered both polite and sexist in the same national culture).

Conclusion

Although generational differences are always at play in any educational setting, Generation Z with its particular characteristics is facing new challenges when it comes to *ab initio* language learning, especially in an online setting. In this chapter, we have examined how language acquisition can support students not only in the current COVID-19 pandemic, but also beyond their university course – two environments that can be described as VUCA. Language learning is suitable for fostering many transferable skills that can support today's students and future graduates. This is not to claim that the above questions regarding teaching practices have not been relevant for other generations in pre-pandemic times, but we are convinced that teachers must adapt teaching and assessment methods regularly to best address the needs of their current students. It is hard to predict how the situation is going to develop further, but the benefits of foreign language learning, especially at an *ab initio* level, should continue to be discussed in relation to transferable skills and employability.

Note

1 For a discussion of autonomy and learners' strengths see (respectively) Chapters 13 and 14 in Part IV.

References

Auxier, B. and Anderson, M. (2021) *Social Media Use in 2021*. Online. www.pewresearch.org/internet/2021/04/07/social-media-use-in-2021 (accessed 10 July 2021).
Azionya, C. and Oksiutycz, A. (2019) 'A teaching model to promote learning agility in a university course'. *The Independent Journal of Teaching and Learning* 14:1, 6–18.

Barclays (2018) *Gen Z: Step aside Millennials*. Online. www.investmentbank.barclays.com/our-insights/generation-z.html (accessed 5 July 2021).

Carter, T. (2018) 'Preparing Generation Z for the teaching profession'. *SRATE Journal* 27:1, 1–8.

Codreanu, A. (2016) 'A VUCA action framework for a VUCA environment. Leadership challenges and solutions'. *Journal of Defense Resources Management* 7:2, 31–8.

Council of Europe (2020) *Common European Framework of Reference for Languages: Learning, Teaching, Assessment. Companion volume*. Strasbourg: Council of Europe Publishing.

Ghonsooly, B. and Showqi, S. (2012) 'The effects of foreign language learning on creativity'. *English Language Teaching (Toronto)* 5:4, 161–7.

The Guardian (2021) '"So many revolutions to lead": Europe's Gen Z on their post-COVID future'. Online. www.theguardian.com/world/ng-interactive/2021/jun/02/so-many-revolutions-to-lead-europe-generation-z-on-their-post-covid-future (accessed 28 June 2021).

Hebblethwaite, C. (2018) 'Gen Z engaging with 10 hours of online content a day'. Online. https://marketingtechnews.net/news/2018/feb/09/gen-z-engaging-10-hours-online-content-day (accessed 15 July 2021).

Kalkhurst, D. (2018) 'Engaging Gen Z students and learners'. Online. www.pearson.com/ped-blogs/blogs/2018/03/engaging-gen-z-students.html (accessed 10 July 2021).

Keysar, B., Hayakawa, S. and An, S. (2012) 'The foreign-language effect: Thinking in a foreign tongue reduces decision biases'. *Psychological Science* 23:6, 661–8.

Kroll, J. and Dussias, P. (2017). 'The benefits of multilingualism to the personal and professional development of residents of the US'. *Foreign Language Annals* 50:2, 248–59.

Liu, H., Liu, W., Yoganathan, V. and Osburg, V. (2021) 'COVID-19 information overload and Generation Z's social media discontinuance intention during the pandemic lockdown'. *Technological Forecasting and Social Change* 166, 1–12.

Martinaj, F. (2020) 'Foreign languages: The key factor in employability'. *Management* 15:3, 161–78.

Nadler, R. (2020) 'Understanding "Zoom fatigue": Theorizing spatial dynamics as third skins in computer-mediated communication'. *Computers and Composition* 58:102613, 1–17.

Petford, N. (2020) 'Responding to COVID-19 challenges with VUCA action'. Online. https://www.ucea.ac.uk/news-releases/blog/19may20/ (accessed 24 August 2021).

Schofield, C.P. and Honoré, S. (2009–10) 'Generation Y and learning'. *360° – The Ashridge Journal* Winter 2009–10, 1–7.

Seemiller, C. and Grace, M. (2017) 'Generation Z: Educating and engaging the next generation of students'. *About Campus* 22:3, 21–6.

Shirkhani, S. and Fahim, M. (2011) 'Enhancing critical thinking in foreign language learners'. *Procedia, Social and Behavioral Sciences* 29, 111–15.

Truebridge, S. (2014) *Resilience Begins with Beliefs: Building on student strengths for success in school*. New York: Teachers College Press.

Tual, D. (2021) 'Gen Z in a VUCA world'. In *English Medium Instruction at European Universities*, edited by L. Szczuka Dorna and K. Matuszak, 153–8. Poznan: Publishing House of the Poznan University of Technology.

UPP Foundation (2021) 'Students prioritise a return to face to face teaching from September 2021'. Online. https://upp-foundation.org/student-futures-commission/news/students-prioritise-a-return-to-face-to-face-teaching-from-september-2021/ (accessed 20 July 2021).

Part II
Pedagogy and teaching methods

4

Reading literature in the *ab initio* classroom

Daniela Dora and Katharina Forster

Introduction

Leading voices in German as a foreign language research, such as Claus Altmayer (2014), have recently called for a reappraisal of the role of literature in language teaching. As rich sources of authentic linguistic material and useful starting points for explorations of German-speaking cultures, literary texts are seen as an antidote to the increasing standardisation and pragmatisation of language teaching with its emphasis on assessable skills. A contributing factor in the diminished role of literature in foreign language teaching was the rise of communicative approaches in the 1970s and '80s (Neidlinger and Pasewalck, 2014). Their preference for everyday communications seemed incompatible with the aesthetic qualities of literary texts, like ambiguity and deliberate subversions of linguistic norms. Despite these wider trends in foreign language teaching, however, reading literature remained standard practice in higher education. In this chapter, we set out to demonstrate the advantages of working with literary texts even at beginner level: it allows students to encounter target cultural contexts, provides abundant opportunities to reflect on language and offers meaningful incentives for the students' own language productions.

Drawing on recent research, the chapter outlines the benefits of integrating literature into foreign language teaching but also considers its challenges and addresses practical issues, like selection criteria to help identify suitable texts. To showcase the didactic potential of reading literature in the *ab initio* classroom, we present six text examples along with ideas for teaching.

Benefits of literature in foreign language teaching

Recent studies suggest three areas of teaching German as a foreign language where literary texts might be most productive: language, cultural studies and aesthetic education. Literature is seen as an opportunity to showcase the wealth of linguistic expression (and experimentation) inherent in the language system and as a way for students to engage with target cultural contexts. These potential applications, however, rely on a specific concept of literature. As Altmayer (2014) points out, literature is not conceived of as completely self-referential, but as a form of communication as well as a space of cultural meaning.

The range of new research published in the last few years illustrates the great variety of approaches integrating literary texts in foreign language teaching. Among those contributions that focus on the role literature can play in language acquisition, Dieter Neidlinger and Silke Pasewalck argue that the literary code is not defined by violations of linguistic norms but rather by their creative application. In engaging with literary texts, language learners are also prepared for the linguistic complexity of colloquial speech. Neidlinger and Pasewalck base their argument on a number of practical examples from Joseph von Eichendorff to Heinrich Heine and Ernst Jandl. By rejecting the conventional separation between literary discourse and everyday communication, they see literary texts as an opportunity for students to get used to the intricacy and flexibility of the linguistic system.

While Neidlinger and Pasewalck focus on the literary code, most studies concentrate on the interconnectedness of literature and culture, framing literature as a negotiation of meaning in social and cultural contexts. It is, however, important to note that the cultural subtext of literature should not be reduced to a narrow-minded essentialism. Engaging with the cultural aspects of a text, as Carlotta von Maltzan (2014) points out, is not about identifying 'objective' characteristics of German-speaking cultures (or, for that matter, differences and similarities between cultures), but about creating opportunities for students to reflect on the constructedness of cultures. The discursive processes that underlie the construction of cultural identities can also be explored in this context, for example, how cultural norms, values and practices are shaped by power relationships: '[Es] rückt u.a. die Frage ins Zentrum, wie und unter welchen Machtkonstellationen "Kulturen" oder Normen, Werte und Handlungsregeln konstruiert, bzw. geschaffen oder gemacht werden. Gerade in diesem Zusammenhang können literarische Texte eine entscheidende Rolle spielen' (Maltzan, 2014: 94).

Andrea Leskovec (2011), as well as Almut Hille (2014), assert that certain topics are particularly suitable as reading material for language students, both focusing on transnational aspects of literature and highlighting their pedagogical potential. Leskovec, for example, argues that literary texts dealing with alterity and sociocultural differences (in the context of migration or travel) can help readers develop 'intercultural skills' (Leskovec, 2011: 13). Like Maltzan, she describes these skills as an awareness of culture as a construct and a fuller perception of cultural heterogeneity. Leskovec also stresses that the estranging use of language in these texts, for example through linguistic experimentation, can trigger processes of reflection and deautomatisation: habitual ways of reading are disrupted, forcing readers to reflect on a text's formal aspects and explore alternative ways of understanding it. Similarly, Hille explains that literary texts are uniquely suited to engage with multi-faceted issues of global significance, like climate change, globalisation or inequity. Advocating the concept of 'global learning', which she adopts from English as a foreign language, Hille argues that language teaching should enable students to participate in current (ecological, global) discourses.

The issue of globalisation is also addressed by Claire Kramsch (2014). She notes that in a deterritorialised world literature 'offer[s] pathways for imagining other possible lives' (Kramsch, 2014: 308), engaging students' empathy and imagination. According to Kramsch, this is of particular importance to foreign language learners today as 'developing their own voice increasingly means developing an ear for the voices of others—no doubt a crucial, if lifelong, educational goal' (Kramsch, 2014: 309).

A plea for meaningful reading material also underpins Simone Schiedermair's argument that literature can counteract the 'dullness' of traditional language teaching. Referring to the concept of 'symbolic competence', first developed by Kramsch and Whiteside (2008), Schiedermair asserts that by reading literary texts students learn to engage with and appreciate the ambiguities and indeterminacy characteristic of literature (Schiedermair, 2014: 138). Yet, while all students may benefit from reading literary texts, reading literature with beginners requires some practical considerations and additional preparation.

Challenges and practical considerations

Having highlighted the advantages and unique benefits of incorporating literature into foreign language teaching, the following section will consider practical issues, such as selection criteria to help identify suitable texts, and discuss common ways of adapting literary texts for beginners.

Schmitz and colleagues describe reading comprehension as 'a complex interaction between readers' cognitive abilities, genre expectations, and text characteristics' (Schmitz, Gräsel and Rothstein, 2017: 1120). Besides topic and text length, the most salient text characteristic to consider when choosing reading material for *ab initio* students is text difficulty. An important fact to note at the very beginning is that the blanket assertion that non-fiction is generally easier to read than literature does not stand up to scrutiny. While readers do need longer to process literary texts (Zwaan, 1994), literature can be easier to understand than expository texts, especially if one considers prior knowledge. As Schmitz and colleagues explain, reviewing empirical studies by Alexander and Jetton (2000) as well as van Dijk (1995), reading expository texts comes with its own challenges: they 'often contain abstract terminology and their superstructure can change from subject to subject' (Schmitz, Gräsel and Rothstein, 2017: 1119), meaning that readers do not benefit from prior knowledge.

Reading modes also differ considerably between expository and literary texts. In what McDaniel and Einstein call 'relational processing' (McDaniel and Einstein, 1989: 118), readers look for 'sequential, conceptual, and/or causal relationships' (McDaniel and Einstein, 1989: 121) in literature, trying to construct larger themes from these connections. Expository texts, in contrast, 'invite processing that focuses on individual items or propositions' (McDaniel and Einstein, 1989: 125). Moreover, readers not only concentrate on different text aspects in relation to genre, but these processing modes are also characterised by different temporal structures: Readers delay interpretation when reading literary texts, which van Dijk and Kintsch describe as a 'wait-and-see strategy' (van Dijk and Kintsch, 1983: 208), but continually process 'specific components and distinctive information' (Schmitz, Gräsel and Rothstein, 2017: 1120) while reading expository texts.

What ultimately helps readers understand literary texts is their implicit knowledge of how literature works. As part of our socialisation as readers, we pick up on and internalise genre conventions, plot schemas and character types, as Schmitz and colleagues elaborate: 'As the familiarization with literary texts starts early, readers playfully acquire knowledge about superstructures, the story grammar, which relieves understanding considerably' (Schmitz, Gräsel and Rothstein, 2017: 1119). This 'expert' knowledge supports comprehension of literary texts despite the inherent complexity of literature. O'Reilly and McNamara (2007) present an example of how readers can use narrative schemata to construct a kind of mental 'scaffolding' which helps them anticipate plot developments and retain information: 'For instance, a war narrative usually involves at least two groups (characters) that compete for resources (motive) by attacking each other (means) to gain control over the other group (outcome)' (O'Reilly and McNamara, 2007: 143). Similarly, the verisimilitude of literary texts allows readers to tap into their life experiences and general world knowledge to facilitate comprehension.

What then are text characteristics that make some literary texts more difficult to read than others? Readability studies in the 1960s tried to establish seemingly objective parameters, like word and sentence length, connecting words and vocabulary level. Based on these factors specialised software like Lexile Analyze can compute a text's difficulty, though the process reveals its inherent limitations when confronted with literature. The software does not account for a text's intertextual potential or paratextual significance (such as sociohistorical contexts) while lacking sufficient complexity to deal with semantic ambiguity and indeterminacy (Frickel, 2007).

When it comes to literature, the accessibility of a text cannot be reduced to language difficulty – even though the latter is often the main obstacle to understanding at beginner level. As Frickel (2007) points out, how difficult a text is to read and understand plays out in the interaction between text and reader. Determining factors apart from text characteristics (for example, language, plot, intertextual references and sociohistorical context) are also the personal characteristics of the reader, like age, gender, prior knowledge, cognitive skills, emotional disposition and motivation. Frickel emphasises that an important part of assessing text difficulty is taking into account the specific student group as well as the institutional context.

The following informal guideline to assess text difficulty for *ab initio* readers in higher education is based on Sabine Pfäfflin's selection criteria for contemporary literature (2010) and Irene Pieper's LIFT-2 project (Literature Framework for Teachers in Secondary Education). A similar assessment tool – titled 'Fahrplan für die unterrichtsvorbereitende Textanalyse' – has been developed by Hermann Lösener (2010). The guidelines combine quantifiable criteria with subjective and interpretative text aspects:

Practical considerations:
- Text length/time requirements: how long will it take students to read the text? How long will it take to work with the text in class?
- Relevance for curriculum: Does the text fit into the curriculum thematically (for example, topic, themes)? Does the text highlight a relevant grammatical item? Can the text be used to practice a relevant skill (beyond reading)?

Language criteria:
- Structural complexity: how complex is the text in terms of sentence patterns and grammatical items?
- Verbal complexity: how challenging is the vocabulary (lexical fields, idiomaticity/level of abstraction, ambiguity)?
- Is the overall language use exemplary or experimental?

Narrative criteria:
- Level of indeterminacy: are there blanks in the story for readers to fill? To what degree is information implied? Is the meaning of the story confined to the text or does it transcend the text, for instance through intertextual references?
- Prior knowledge: does the text require prior (general or cultural) knowledge? Does the text require knowledge of specific literary genres, movements and periods?
- Time structure: is the story told chronologically? Does it feature temporal complications, such as flashbacks, foreshadowing?
- Plot: are there several plot lines and narrative levels (for example frame narrative, story-within-the-story)?
- Perspective: is the story told by multiple narrators? Are the narrators reliable? (Changes of perspective as well as narrative unreliability make stories more complex while omniscient narrators can act as mediators between text and reader. Although first- and third-person narrators offer only limited views of the fictional world, they also allow for more interesting creative writing tasks, such as retelling the story from the perspective of other characters.)
- Characters: how great is the distance between reader and characters (in terms of age, gender, morality)? Are the characters complex or literary types? How many characters has the reader to keep track of? (Ambiguous or contradictory relationships between characters can also make a story more complex.)

Thematic criteria:

- Interest: will young adults find the text interesting (youth-related topics, global or ecological issues, and so on)? Is the text funny, suspenseful or otherwise emotionally gripping?
- Relevance: Does the text deal with topics related to foreign language teaching (such as alterity, cultural differences, intercultural misunderstandings, migration, travel)? Does the text give insights into German-speaking cultures (for example, everyday life, social conventions, traditions)?

Literary texts that are assessed as too difficult to be read with beginners may be adapted to reduce difficulty. Thus, texts can be abbreviated, split into parts, read alongside English translations or even simplified, an example of which would be renarrations of fairy tales, which generally have multiple text versions. There are also annotated text editions specifically for German learners, such as the short story collection *Kurzgeschichten* (Radvan and Steiner, 2019).

Text examples

In this final section, we discuss six examples of literary texts for beginners, ranging from poems to essays and short stories. They can be used to encourage meaningful reflections on linguistic phenomena, but also allow for particularly active learning opportunities, such as role-play and creative (re)writing.

Ernst Jandl's *konkrete Poesie*, which frequently employs word play as well as visual and acoustic experiments, is a staple of literature lessons in German-speaking countries (e.g. *ottos mops*, *schtzngrmm*) but it is also often used in foreign language teaching. Rainer Wicke's textbook *Zwischendurch mal… Gedichte* (2012), for example, includes the poem 'fünfter sein'. Neidlinger and Pasewalck have argued that experimental poems like Jandl's 'lichtung' can prepare students (even at the beginner level) for the complexity of everyday language and inspire them to engage creatively with what they learn in class (Neidlinger and Pasewalck, 2014: 146). The poem 'lichtung' (Jandl, 1997: 171) is a clever play on the rule-based nature of language, confounding readers by presenting them with a made-up rule. Throughout the short text, the phoneme /r/ has been replaced by /l/ and vice versa. Ingeniously, this only becomes apparent halfway through the poem when the exchange first produces nonsensical words. In a puzzling case of left–right confusion, '*rechts*' (right) appears as '*lechts*' and '*links*' (left) as '*rinks*' (l. 2). Belatedly, the seemingly straightforward title acquires an ambiguous quality: it can be read as both '*Lichtung*' (clearing) and '*Richtung*' (direction), adding unexpected layers of meaning to the text.

An engaging and productive way to work with the poem is to present it as a riddle, prompting readers to make sense of it by spotting meaningful patterns (r = l). As a follow-up activity, students can come up with their own language rules and apply them to a short text. Finally, Jandl's poem also presents a great opportunity to make learners aware of phonemic differences between words (e.g. *Lichtung* vs. *Richtung*) and may be a starting point for pronunciation exercises with minimal pairs.

A poem that explicitly links poetry and everyday language by pointing to the poetic qualities of mundane conversations is Jandl's dialogic poem 'im park' (Jandl, 1992: 57). The poem records a promenader's quest to find a place to sit in a busy park, consisting of variations of just one question: 'ist hier frei' [Is this seat taken] (l. 1). Except for the very end of the poem, the request is always met with refusal – though some replies are more polite ('nein hier ist leider besetzt,' l. 26) than others ('besetzt', l. 23). While repetition is a common feature of the literary code, it is taken to extremes in Jandl's poem, highlighting the fact that everyday speech, like literature, is often highly structured. The poem can be used as exercise material for conversational patterns, that is, learners can act out the conversation in the poem, trying out different emotions and emphases. Presenting the poem without a title gives students the added opportunity to speculate about appropriate speech situations. As an easy creative writing task, students may write their own poems based on other formulaic everyday conversations.

Yoko Tawada's poem 'Vor einem hellen Vokal' (2010) is not overtly subverting linguistic rules like Jandl's 'lichtung', but rather a literary illustration of a specific rule – the allophonic variation of the digraph <ch>, which depends on the quality of the preceding vowel. The complexity of the poem lies in its double structure. On the level of form, the text is dominated by an accumulation of words containing <ch>, serving as a vivid demonstration of the digraph's complex pronunciation: <ch> represents the palatal fricative [ç] after /i/, /e/ or /ei/, but the velar fricative [x] after dark vowels like /a/, /o/, /u/ or /au/. Yet the poem also has a pronounced narrative quality. It presents a fantastical chain of events that involves German oak trees, blasphemous writings and flying carpets. There are no overt connections between the poem's content and form until the last two lines when the speaker explicitly addresses the formal principle of the text by conceding that the 'sacred characters / *c* and *h*' remain elusive.

Vor einem hellen Vokal

Gleich werde ich meinen
Bauch zeigen und tanzen an einem
Teich wo eine deutsche
Eiche steht. Ein gottloses
Buch werde ich
euch schreiben und steige
hoch auf den Galgen. Ich bin ein fliegender
Teppich mit einem
Kopftuch. So ein
Pech! Kann ich fliehen? Kennst du das Land
CH?
Die Lesart der heiligen Schriftzeichen
c und h bleibt weiter offen.
(Tawada, 2019: 5–6)
© Konkursbuch Verlag Claudia Gehrke, Yoko Tawada, from the book
Abenteuer der deutschen Grammatik, first edition, 2010; sixth edition, 2019

Listening to a recording or reading of the poem, students can first infer, then practise the correct pronunciation of <ch>. The text may also serve as a starting point for engaging with other pronunciation rules, such as the vocalisation of <r>. Once students have understood when <r> is vocalised and when it is not, they may collect suitable words for both categories before using these examples in their own nonsensical poems (e.g. 'Nach einem langen Vokal'). Like the original poem, these texts can also be based on free association.

Joachim Ringelnatz's poetry is characterised by a similar playfulness as Ernst Jandl's and Yoko Tawada's. The poem 'Ein männlicher Briefmark' (1912), however, features a simple plot with well-known fairy tale tropes, which considerably facilitates comprehension. It tells a tragicomic love story whose central stylistic device is personification: A postage stamp falls hopelessly in love after being 'kissed' by a princess.

Ein männlicher Briefmark

Ein männlicher Briefmark erlebte
was Schönes, bevor er klebte.
Er war von einer Prinzessin beleckt.
Da war die Liebe in ihm erweckt.
Er wollte sie wieder küssen,

da hat er verreisen müssen.
So liebte er sie vergebens.
Das ist die Tragik des Lebens!
(Ringelnatz, 2013: 15)

By anthropomorphising a mundane object like the stamp and framing it as the ill-fated admirer of a princess, the poem acquires a mock-heroic quality that accounts for its quirky humour. In 2008, the German postal service published a special issue stamp with the poem (Figure 4.1). The tiny spiral design not only highlights the text's laconic style and brevity, it also requires the reader to turn the stamp while reading, drawing out the reading process and enhancing the sense of surprise created by the unusual love story. With beginner readers, the poem can be read as a miniature love story, serving as an inspiration for creative writing activities. Students may be asked to write their own tiny love stories, conveying the entire plot in a few short sentences – to possibly humorous effects. Similar to Ringelnatz's poem, which relies on fairy tale elements, students can draw from their own prior knowledge of story patterns, which facilitates the writing process.

Figure 4.1 Special issue stamp by the German postal service (2008). Source: Author

The anthropomorphising of everyday objects is also a central feature of Yoko Tawada's literary essay 'Von der Muttersprache zur Sprachmutter' (2011). The narrator, a Japanese native, overhears her German colleague scolding a pencil for breaking every time she tries to write with it. Mystified by the casual personification of writing utensils, the narrator attributes it to the German grammatical gender.

> In meinem ersten Jahr in Deutschland schlief ich täglich über neun Stunden, um mich von den vielen Eindrücken zu erholen. Jeder normale Büroalltag war für mich eine Kette rätselhafter Szenen. [...] Eines Tages hörte ich, wie eine Mitarbeiterin über ihren Bleistift schimpfte: 'Der blöde Bleistift! Der spinnt! Der will heute nicht schreiben!' Jedesmal, wenn sie ihn anspitzte und versuchte, mit ihm zu schreiben, brach die Bleistiftmine ab. In der japanischen Sprache kann man einen Bleistift nicht auf diese Weise personifizieren: Ein Bleistift kann weder blöd sein noch spinnen. In Japan habe ich noch nie gehört, dass ein Mensch über seinen Bleistift schimpfte, als wäre er eine Person. (Tawada, 2011: 9–10)

Tawada's story of the recalcitrant pencil is an example of how linguistic differences can serve as a source of inspiration and how reflexions on language may produce literary texts. When the narrator gives insights into her own native language, the text also highlights the fascinating weirdness of languages. Since Japanese lacks grammatical gender, when it comes to grammar even men are not considered 'masculine' in Japan:

> In der japanischen Sprache sind alle Wörter geschlechtslos. Die Substantive lassen sich zwar – wie das bei den Zahlwörtern sichtbar wird – in verschiedene Gruppen aufteilen, aber diese Gruppen haben nie das Kriterium des Männlichen oder des Weiblichen: Es gibt zum Beispiel eine Gruppe der flachen Gegenstände oder der länglichen oder der runden. Häuser, Schiffe und Bücher bilden jeweils eigene Gruppen. Es gibt natürlich auch die Gruppe der Menschen: Männer und Frauen gehören zusammen dahin. Grammatikalisch gesehen ist im Japanischen nicht einmal ein Mann männlich. (Tawada, 2011: 11)

Tawada's essay and Ringelnatz's poem are examples of texts that support processes of deautomatisation and promote more attentive modes of reading. Both lend themselves to comparative activities, e.g. students can be asked to research a feature of their native language that is different from German (or simply particularly striking).

In foregrounding linguistic experimentation and creativity, all five examples discussed so far not only make for interesting reading material, but also provide students with important insights about language: experimental forms of expression, i.e. the breaking and subverting of linguistic rules, are a common feature of (literary) language and an outside perspective on any specific language can be a source of creativity.

The final example to be discussed here is Peter Stamm's short story 'Alles, was fehlt' (2003), about the first days of a Swiss expat in London's Canary Wharf district. It explores themes like loneliness, anonymity and modern love in Stamm's typical concise style that has been likened to Ernest Hemingway and Jean-Paul Sartre. The humdrum plot tracks the protagonist's arrival in his exclusive yet utterly unwelcoming flat, an aborted day trip to Greenwich and awkward attempts to connect with his Japanese neighbour. The story's linguistic simplicity – characterised by short sentences and a dearth of adjectives and other descriptive features – belies its semantic complexity. Stamm's prose is rich in allusions and provides blanks for readers to fill with their own interpretations. Part of the indeterminacy of the story is the open ending, in which the protagonist finally musters up the courage to introduce himself to his neighbour.

> Es war sehr still in der Wohnung. Erst jetzt bemerkte David die leisen Geräusche aus den Nachbarwohnungen. Er hörte Wasser rauschen, Schritte, ein Radio. Er stand auf und trat auf den Balkon. Nebenan stand die Japanerin und goss die Pflanzen, die dort in großen Tontöpfen wuchsen. Er grüßte sie, und sie grüßte zurück.
>
> 'Ich bin der neue Nachbar', sagte er.
>
> '*Nice to meet you*', sagte die Japanerin und lächelte.
>
> '*Nice to meet you, too*', sagte David. Er wollte noch etwas sagen, aber dann ging er zurück in die Wohnung. Ich habe Zeit, dachte er, es wird schon irgendwie gehen. (Stamm, 2003: 93–4)

The hopeful ambiguity that marks the ending of the story again lends itself to creative writing exercises. Students can, for example, continue the story or write a postcard David sends to a friend some weeks after his arrival in London, addressing questions such as: Will David's life have changed? Has the tenuous contact to his neighbour developed into a personal relationship? Richard Bamberger and Richard Vanecek (1984) note that formal simplicity in combination with semantic indeterminacy or ambiguity is not an unusual feature of literary texts. They explicitly mention the works of Franz Kafka, which are a staple of introductory literature classes in higher education. The example of Kafka illustrates that a high level of indeterminacy is not an insurmountable obstacle when it comes to reading a text with beginning learners, particularly in higher education. While their active and passive language skills might still be limited, the students' cognitive abilities and extensive prior knowledge as 'expert' readers can facilitate understanding. Polyvalency and indeterminacy may in fact have an empowering effect on readers and make for particularly engaging reading experiences.

Conclusion

Against the backdrop of the increasingly standardised nature of foreign language teaching, where literature and the study of literary texts often take a back seat to non-fiction, this chapter sought to highlight the benefits of reading literary texts right at the beginner level. While it might require additional preparation and particularly careful planning, the advantages in terms of student motivation and authenticity of learning material cannot be denied. Although we have focused mainly on short literary forms like poems and essays to give students the opportunity to read and explore a range of different texts, reading longer stories or even full-length novels (for example, those by Erich Kästner, Rafik Schami or Franz Kafka) may also be a viable option in some language modules.

References

Alexander, P. and Jetton, T. (2000) 'Learning from text: A multidimensional and developmental perspective'. In *Handbook of Reading Research*, edited by M.L. Kamil, P.B. Mosenthal, P.D. Pearson and R. Barr, vol. 3, 285–310. Mahwah, NJ: Lawrence Erlbaum.

Altmayer, C. (2014) 'Zur Rolle der Literatur im Rahmen der Kulturstudien Deutsch als Fremdsprache'. In *Literatur in Deutsch als Fremdsprache und internationaler Germanistik. Konzepte, Themen, Forschungsperspektiven*, edited by C. Altmayer, M. Dobstadt, R. Riedner and C. Schier, 25–39. Tübingen: Stauffenburg.

Bamberger, R. and Vanecek, E. (1984) *Lesen – Verstehen – Lernen – Schreiben. Die Schwierigkeitsstufen von Texten in deutscher Sprache*. Vienna: Sauerlaender.

Frickel, D. (2014) 'Literarische Textschwierigkeit interpretieren. Didaktische Analyse(kompetenzen) von Lehrkräften und ihre Voraussetzungen'. *GFL Journal* 2, 4–24.

Hille, A. (2014) 'Literarische Texte im Kontext eines globalen Lernens im Unterricht Deutsch als Fremdsprache und in der internationalen Germanistik'. In *Literatur in Deutsch als Fremdsprache und internationaler Germanistik. Konzepte, Themen, Forschungsperspektiven*, edited by C. Altmayer, M. Dobstadt, R. Riedner and C. Schier, 13–24. Tübingen: Stauffenburg.

Jandl, E. (1992) 'im park'. In *idyllen. Gedichte*. Hamburg: Luchterhand, 57.

Jandl, E. (1997) 'lichtung'. In *poetische werke 2. Laut und luise. Verstreute gedichte 2*. Munich: Luchterhand, 171.

Kramsch, C. (2014) 'Teaching foreign language in an era of globalization. Introduction'. *Modern Language Journal* 98:1, 296–311.

Kramsch, C. and Whiteside, A. (2008) 'Language ecology in multilingual settings. Towards a theory of symbolic competence'. *Applied Linguistics* 29, 645–72.

Leskovec, A. (2011) *Einführung in die interkulturelle Literaturwissenschaft*. Darmstadt: WBG.

Lösener, H. (2010) 'Poetisches Verstehen bei der Unterrichtsvorbereitung. Überlegungen zur literaturunterrichtlichen Sachanalyse'. In *Poetisches Verstehen. Literaturdidaktische Positionen – empirische Forschung – Projekte aus dem Deutschunterricht*, edited by C. Altmayer, M. Dobstadt, R. Riedner and C. Schier, 82–97. Baltmannsweiler: Schneider.

McDaniel, G.O. and Einstein, M.A. (1989) 'Material-appropriate processing: A contextualist approach to reading and studying strategies'. *Educational Psychology Review* 1:2, 113–45.

Neidlinger, D. and Pasewalck, S. (2014) 'Das Potenzial literarischer Sprache und Form im Bereich Deutsch als Fremdsprache. Ein Plädoyer für Komplexität im Fremdsprachenunterricht'. In *Literatur in Deutsch als Fremdsprache und internationaler Germanistik. Konzepte, Themen, Forschungsperspektiven*, edited by C. Altmayer, M. Dobstadt, R. Riedner and C. Schier, 141–52. Tübingen: Stauffenburg.

O'Reilly, T. and McNamara, D. (2007) 'Reversing the reverse cohesion effect: Good texts can be better for strategic, high-knowledge readers'. *Discourse Processes* 43:2, 121–52.

Pfäfflin, S. (2010) *Auswahlkriterien für Gegenwartsliteratur im Deutschunterricht*. Baltmannsweiler: Schneider.

Pieper, I. (2014) 'Den Schüler vor Augen, den Anspruch im Sinn: Der internationale Referenzrahmen LIFT-2 zu Progression und Textauswahl für den Literaturunterricht der Sekundarstufen'. In *Aktuelle Fragen der Deutschdidaktik*, edited by V. Frederking and A. Krommer, 586–609. Baltmannsweiler: Schneider.

Radvan, F. and Steiner, A. (2019) *Kurzgeschichten: Textausgabe – Text – Erläuterungen – Materialien*. Berlin: Cornelsen.

Ringelnatz, J. (2013) 'Ein männlicher Briefmark'. In *Gedichte, Prosa, Bilder*, 15. Ditzingen: Reclam.

Schiedermair, S. (2014) 'Deutsch als (ver)fremde(te) Sprache. Literarische Verfremdung als Kategorie im Fach Deutsch als Fremdsprache'. In *Literatur in Deutsch als Fremdsprache und internationaler Germanistik. Konzepte, Themen, Forschungsperspektiven*, edited by C. Altmayer, M. Dobstadt, R. Riedner and C. Schier, 131–40. Tübingen: Stauffenburg.

Schmitz, A., Gräsel, C. and Rothstein, B. (2017) 'Students' genre expectations and the effects of text cohesion on reading comprehension'. *Reading and Writing* 30:5, 1115–35.

Stamm, P. (2003) 'Alles, was fehlt'. In *In fremden Gärten. Erzählungen*, 78–94. Frankfurt am Main: Fischer.

Tawada, Y. (2011) 'Von der Muttersprache zur Sprachmutter'. In *Talisman. Literarische Essays*, 9–15. Tübingen: Konkursbuch.

Tawada, Y. (2019) 'Vor einem hellen Vokal'. In *Abenteuer der deutschen Grammatik*, 5–6. Tübingen: Konkursbuch.

van Dijk, T.A. (1995) 'On macrostructures, mental models and other inventions. A brief personal history of the Kintsch-van Dijk theory'. In *Discourse comprehension. Essays in Honor of Walter Kintsch*, edited by C. Weaver III, S. Mannes and C.R. Fletcher, 383–410. Hillsdale, NJ: Lawrence Erlbaum.

van Dijk, T.A. and Kintsch, W. (1983) *Strategies of discourse comprehension*. New York: Academic Press.

von Maltzan, C. (2014) 'Zum Wert von Kultur und Literatur im Fremdsprachenunterricht: Beispiel Südafrika'. In *Literatur in Deutsch als Fremdsprache und internationaler Germanistik. Konzepte, Themen, Forschungsperspektiven*, edited by C. Altmayer, M. Dobstadt, R. Riedner and C. Schier, 87–96. Tübingen: Stauffenburg.

Wicke, R. (2012) *Zwischendurch mal … Gedichte. Niveau A1-C1. Deutsch als Fremdsprache*. Munich: Hueber.

Zwaan, R.A. (1994) 'Effect of genre expectations on text comprehension'. *Journal of Experimental Psychology: Learning, Memory, and Cognition* 20:4, 920–33.

5
Using music in *ab initio* courses
Kirsten Mericka

Introduction

There is a long tradition of using music in the foreign language classroom. Teachers of foreign languages know the importance of listening comprehension and train this skill regularly in class; music can be used for that. In this chapter, music and songs refer to any authentic musical piece with German lyrics in any kind of format, including both audio and video. I chose to focus on authentic songs (rather than didactic songs that are made especially for the foreign language classroom) as native speakers of German enjoy them, too. Especially since the beginning of the twenty-first century, German-speaking music including singing in dialect has become mainstream in German-speaking countries.

The chapter is divided into two parts – one theoretical and one practical. First, I present reasons for using music in the foreign language classroom, followed by specific conditions for using it in the *ab initio* classroom. I then provide an overview of how music is included in textbooks as well as explaining its role as motivation to learn a foreign language. Subsequently, I write about singing and pronunciation as another aspect of music in the classroom. In the second part of the chapter, I propose concrete suggestions for embedding music in a course, that is, how to choose a song, the assignments and activities connected with it. I will not, however, present pre-made didactisations or show how a specific song can be used in particular ways, as that can be easily found on the internet. I list resources at the end of the chapter. Rather, I would like to encourage teachers to come up with their own didactisations, for which I offer ideas. In this chapter, there is a greater emphasis on using music for listening than participating in, for example, singing along to learn specific grammar structures, which is not to say that what is presented here cannot be used for that purpose, too.

Music is part of the lives of teachers and students alike. People often remember their first record, tape, CD or MP3 file download, or the first live concert they went to. Melodies get stuck in people's heads. There are (young) people with headphones everywhere. To apply their habits and interests in class is motivating for the students.[1] Popular music (rock, pop, hip hop, RnB, jazz, blues, reggae and so on), is perhaps more connected to young people's everyday lives, providing a base for authentic communication in the target language (Oebel, 2002: 2). This is one of the most compelling reasons for using music in the classroom but there are more, which I will discuss in the next section.

Reasons for using music in the classroom

Language and music are connected. Both have pitch, melody, timbre, rhythm, tempo and volume (Wild, 2014: 336). Even if a direct and beneficial connection between learning a language and music is not immediately evident, cognitive scientists and neuropsychologists are increasingly finding that the processing of music and language is similar, and a positive reciprocity between the two can therefore be assumed (Blell, 2010: 227). Measurable linguistic advantages have been verified for word recognition, text comprehension, pronunciation, grammar, vocabulary, cultural knowledge, listening and reading comprehension and authentic intonation (Perner, 2014: 323). Furthermore, babies learn to imitate sounds before they are able to speak words (Stansell, 2005: 6). However, only a few empirical studies with adults in the foreign language classroom have been conducted (Morgret, 2015: 71).

Oebel lists various reasons for using music in the German foreign language classroom. Popular songs in particular often use simple and easily accessible language, as well as short, yet demanding texts regarding content. Songs relate to a lot of different topics linked to young adults' lives. Music is relaxing, yet stimulating. It can be emotionally touching, and therefore motivating, and additionally offers positive connotations with foreign language learning (Oebel, 2002: 2–3).

Music may also awaken and engage the learners' interest in the target language and culture. Teachers are then able to maintain this interest by using the learners' favourite music, helping them understand its message, and engage in creative activities with the linguistic material. With music initiating genuine interest, students can practise their skills in speaking (wanting to talk about what they hear), listening (wanting to know more about what the music is about), reading (wanting to read the lyrics), as well as writing (responding to writing prompts).

Rodríguez Cemillán also writes that music and singing are simply fun. Using songs creates a learning atmosphere free from fear, which is also better for the learners' motivation (which will be discussed later in this chapter). Music is authentic advertising for a language, especially considering the presence of colloquial language and dialects (typical for music), which can lead to an appreciation of register. Even at the most basic level, songs can be used to consolidate and expand vocabulary. Their repetitive elements can be utilised for practising and revising grammatical structures (Rodríguez Cemillán, 2014: 53). Additionally, it helps break up the routine and monotony of lessons (Rodríguez Cemillán, 2000).

Other foreign language teachers even state that grammar and vocabulary should be taught with the aid of songs whenever possible because they are one of the most effective teaching methods as a person remembers a song more easily once they have learned it (Buttner, 2012: 66). Humans are better at recalling information when the words are linked to rhythm, which can be the reason for successful learning of new linguistic phrases (Stansell, 2005: 13). Applying mnemonic principles, teachers may use rhythm, rhyme and categories to organise complex information in an easy way (Stansell, 2005: 26).[2]

Apart from these reasons related to language learning, music offers a great way to motivate students to engage with a topic or to become interested in the (musical) culture of a country. Badstübner-Kizik argues that songs support language activities in the classroom, which can further provide an authentic glimpse into the foreign culture as they are a product of the German-speaking culture (Badstübner-Kizik, 2004: 11). By looking at what kind of music German speakers listen to, and what images are conveyed by music videos, for example, learners gain an insight into the culture and could therefore also be motivated to listen to songs because they are authentic elements of that culture. Furthermore, words may introduce a cultural association, for example, the German word *Heimat* refers to different concepts and translations depending on the culture.

Finally, teachers should not underestimate music as a source of aesthetic pleasure and students can be very creative if they are stimulated by the tasks. All of these reasons apply to *ab initio* classrooms but there are other aspects to consider too, which I address in the following.

Using music in the *ab initio* classroom

Using music in class presents numerous benefits for *ab initio* students. Ultimately, teachers decide how to use a song and why they want to include it in their lesson, for example, for grammar, cultural studies or creative work. Depending on the class, teachers may use the music without lyrics, only the lyrics or just the music video. Beginners might not be able to understand the lyrics completely, but they can develop a feeling for the target language speech melody. Music videos may help with comprehension as listening comprehension becomes easier with visual cues, that is, seeing a person's face while they are speaking rather than just hearing the person's voice.

Choosing contemporary songs with few words, repetition and clearly intonated lyrics is important. The catchy rhythm of a pop song can spur a desire to learn the language and to find out more about a culture. Songs used for beginners could cover topics and vocabulary that the learners already know, such as hobbies, family and relationships, daily life and so on. This allows them to understand and express their thoughts effectively, which in turn makes the song interesting to them.

However, teachers could also choose songs with more complex content, but should then avoid working with the lyrics in too much detail. One of the advantages of using music is that teachers can, for example, choose to focus only on the chorus, even though the class might listen to the whole song. The chorus is often short and repeated multiple times. It also usually contains the main message of the song and has a catchy melody. Either way, it seems reasonable to start with slower songs so that the learners may feel a sense of achievement after listening.

Music is authentic teaching material, which means its vocabulary is not necessarily introduced in *ab initio* textbooks and it might be difficult to understand for learners without corresponding tasks. Overwhelming the learners will likely result in the teacher having to take over, which would move the pedagogic focus away from the learner (Waychert, 2015: 48). This would then negate the purpose of using music as a learner-centric approach. However, it is quite easy to choose an appropriate song for beginners as discussed later in this chapter. But first, I want to look at how textbooks have included music.

Music in textbooks

The importance of music is not necessarily represented in textbooks. Looking at German foreign-language textbooks from the later second half of the twentieth century and the beginning of the twenty-first century, Badstübner-Kizik noticed that if activities for music were included, they would rarely focus on speech production but rather on comprehension (Badstübner-Kizik, 2004: 9). She found songs are used for listening exercises, rarely singing, and as a stimulus for communicative language teaching and cultural studies (Badstübner-Kizik, 2010a: 114).

Since the 1970s, more rock and pop music has been included in textbooks, with classical music limited to a few musical works and composers (especially Joseph Haydn, Wolfgang Amadeus Mozart and Ludwig van Beethoven). Beginning in the 1990s, textbooks started to include music more often, for example, in supplementary pages for a chapter (Badstübner-Kizik, 2010b: 1599).

Since the 2000s, considerably more textbooks have included didactic songs.[3] Karyn found that textbooks for adolescents had a lot more didactic songs with less varied song lyrics and activities than textbooks for adults, and that textbook authors frequently focused on the lyrics, disregarding the musical aspect of the melody or rhythm (Karyn, 2006: 549–52).

Waychert suggests that in textbooks for beginners, the topic of music is usually introduced with relevant vocabulary as part of a chapter about hobbies (for example, *Musik hören, ein Instrument spielen, ins Konzert gehen*). Consequently, teachers have to decide if they want to introduce music more generally before ever listening to a song. This can be done with questions about the learners' musical tastes, the circumstances of listening to music, whether they make music themselves, music genres and knowledge of German-speaking artists. Here, teachers may also introduce or revise expressions for personal taste and its reasoning (Waychert, 2017).

Singing and pronunciation

Music in the classroom can also play a role in pronunciation training of foreign languages. There is a link between singing and speaking as these acts are activated in similar areas of the brain. They both use the vocal motor system, so there is a strong similarity between the production of speech and song (Christiner and Reiterer, 2015: 5–6). Musical people are better at imitating the pronunciation of a foreign language than people who do not sing (Stansell, 2005: 10). With singing, the song and lyrics help to improve pronunciation memory (Stansell, 2005: 31).

Sposet looked at 23 studies and agreed that music has a positive effect on pronunciation, with regard to rhythm, intonation, improved fluency and produced fewer pronunciation mistakes (Sposet, 2008: 91). However, Wild criticises that most research designs of these studies were not transparent enough (Wild, 2014: 339). Her study of word stress acquisition with new rhythmic exercises at a UK university showed that these exercises did not help to raise awareness for word stress problems. Students who play an instrument or sing made fewer word stress mistakes, but Wild found that the new exercises with music were not necessarily better than traditional exercises without music (Wild, 2014: 342–4).

Morgret found that there are almost no music didactisations focusing on the pronunciation of adult learners (Morgret, 2015: 88), but she provides a variety of exercises in her doctoral thesis. She concludes that teachers should take more advantage of music, which offers automation through repetition, but without boredom.

I undertook a project with post-A-level first-year university students of German at the University of St Andrews (approximately corresponding to level A2/B1 according to the Common European Framework of Reference for Languages – CEFR), in which students created a LipDub video (a music video that combines lip-synching and audio dubbing and can be filmed on any recording device with a camera). For motivational reasons, the learners used German songs of their choice, which made them think about the song's message and its cultural meaning, ideally also sparking a general interest in music from German-speaking countries. In creating their own music videos outside the classroom, they learned to work collaboratively and autonomously. The students used their listening skills because they had to listen very carefully to imitate the sounds of the song. Looking up the lyrics, they also used their reading skills and sometimes translated parts of the song (or the whole thing). As this project combined various motivating elements, not least because it was seen as an enjoyable activity, I recommend trying it with beginners.[4]

By using music as an authentic part of the learners' lives, teachers engage with their students' motivation. In the following, I look at the role of motivation in this context.

The role of motivation

A statement often quoted suggests that there are hardly any learners who are not motivated to learn a language by some form of music (Blell and Hellwig, 1996: 7). Therefore, I presuppose that music is a source of motivation for language learning, which is especially relevant for *ab initio* students as their teachers want them to be successful learners and continue with their study of German.

Motivation is multidimensional, dynamic and constantly able to change or be influenced by teaching. Therefore, it is difficult for teachers to assess the motivation of individual leaners and purposefully initiate or foster it; it is impossible to empirically observe motivation (Riemer, 2017: 4). But motivation as well as its encouragement and maintenance are essential to achieve the desired learning outcome of the lesson (De Florio-Hansen, 2014: 59–60).

Correspondingly, foreign language teachers should strive to increase their students' motivation, to avoid demotivation, and to reduce fear in order to help their learners. They need to support the development of the students' motivation by identifying existing incentives and fostering those. This can happen when teachers let the learners engage with the language in a way that is of real meaning for their present and future selves, such as in activity-orientated work and project work. An example in the context of music could be a WebQuest about the Eurovision Song Contest, which is similar to a scavenger hunt where students develop higher-level thinking while doing controlled research on the internet and interacting with each other.

Furthermore, learners sometimes feel bored with routines and topics from earlier foreign language learning experiences. Teachers should aim to prevent that by focusing on the learners' motivation (Riemer, 2017: 19). List agrees that motivation can be initiated if the teacher arouses the learner's curiosity with uncommon and surprising perspectives on the target language (List, 2002: 10). Music helps to achieve this. Additionally, if the material is relevant to the learner, it cultivates interest. Teachers have to find out their students' individual interests even if it is difficult due to heterogeneity in class and class size variations. Once they know their students' interests, it is quite easy to choose the right song for a class. This leads me to the next part of this chapter, where I present practical advice on how to choose a song and ideas for assignments and activities.

Choice of song

As no authentic song is tailored to *ab initio* students, the teacher's choice is very important. They have to consider the song's (linguistic) quality and any problematic aspects of the lyrics, the music genre, the song's rhythm and length, as well as aspects such as the quality of the singer's pronunciation, chorus, any cultural information referred to by the song and the learners' age, language level and so on. Teachers should try to decide why a song might be interesting for their students, perhaps considering its topic, grammar or language, and ensure that neither they nor the students will be bored by listening to the song repeatedly (Esa, 2008: 4). They also have to think about the learning objectives for the use of a particular song (Rodríguez Cemillán, 2000).

Oebel suggests letting the learners choose the song (Oebel, 2002: 5). However, that may be difficult for *ab initio* courses as their knowledge about German songs might be quite limited at the beginning of a course. Generally, even rap music is feasible because its poetry/lyrics are similar to everyday language (Perner, 2014: 324), for example, omitting word endings. However, for beginners, it may make sense to use slower songs to support a sense of achievement, and it is more important that the songs are motivating and that the topics are interesting for the class. In that respect, I would be careful not to use children's songs.

Below, I list examples of songs conventionally used in German foreign language classrooms. Considering that teachers can find a lot of material online and new songs are continuously being released, I mention just a few, which are also useful for more advanced courses. The following choice focuses mainly on grammar structures in the songs' lyrics because of their frequent occurrence. Even though teachers should not pick songs solely for their grammar, grammar (and vocabulary) will very often be a deciding factor:

- 'Seite an Seite' by Christina Stürmer (perfect tense);
- 'Krieger des Lichts' by Silbermond (imperative);
- 'Müssen nur wollen' by Wir sind Helden (modal verbs);
- 'Ich wollt' ich wär' ein Huhn' by Comedian Harmonists (subjunctive);
- 'Nur für dich' (and many others) by Wise Guys (e.g., past tenses);
- 'Oft gefragt' by AnnenMayKantereit (separable prefix verbs with perfect tense);
- 'Wir trafen uns in einem Garten' by 2raumwohnung (two-way prepositions).

Some didactisations for these can be found on websites listed at the end of this chapter. However, teachers should feel encouraged to didacticise songs to their own and their students' wants and needs. If there is more advanced grammar in the song, the teacher is able to guide the students' focus to the grammar phenomenon they want to discuss and ignore the advanced grammar structures for the time being. Using a song for its grammar potential does not limit the teacher from talking about other aspects of the song such as its content or vocabulary and vice versa.

Popular songs chosen for their vocabulary are 'MFG' by Die fantastischen Vier (common abbreviations in German) or '194 Länder' by Mark Forster (travelling, cities and countries). Songs with words from other languages should also be part of the selection here as they present opportunities to include the learners' first language(s) into the class and, therefore, their personal interest. Using a video that accompanies a song may help understanding (such as 'Nein Mann' by Laserkraft 3D) or to support the message of the song (as in 'Sowieso' by Mark Forster). At other times, teachers might solely choose a song for its content, origin, or wider reception, for example, history, politics or regional aspects such as 'Ermutigung' by Wolf Biermann (GDR protest song), 'Baun' by Sigrid Horn (2019 winner of the protest song contest in Austria) or 'Der letzte Kaiser' by Wiener Blond (a song about Vienna). If a teacher would like to focus on cultural aspects, commercials with songs are useful, too. Recently, supermarkets have been using catchy songs in their commercials such as Hofer's 'Preis Song' or Edeka's 'Supergeil'. In any case, these songs can be used for practising vocabulary related to shopping.

When considering the learning objectives, teachers not only have to think about why they are using the song but also how they want to use it. For example, they have to decide if the learners watch the music video or other visual material, too. A music video, official or fan-made, is authentic material that can also lead to speaking or writing prompts. However, teachers must ensure that the visual material does not differ too much from the lyrics to help the learners focus. Otherwise, they might be distracted, and beginners in particular might quickly stop listening and be frustrated by the lyrics if they feel they cannot follow them.

Listening comprehension and other assignments and activities

Listening comprehension involves distinguishing sounds, activating prior knowledge and expectations, connecting known with unknown information and interpreting something heard (Badstübner-Kizik, 2010b: 1598). Teachers decide how the learners have to listen and create tasks accordingly.

Listening assignments should be manageable, achievable, targeted and purposeful. Traditional listening tasks include multiple choice or comprehension questions, which are rarely based on real purpose because they are not authentic questions. Authentic listening tasks are used to gain information learners find relevant. These tasks have to be interesting to keep the listeners' attention even if they listen repeatedly. Therefore, they should align with the communicative interest of the learner, that is, what they would want to listen for. It is essential that teachers prepare the learners to listen for specific information because beginners tend to try to understand every single word. Avoid giving instructions such as: 'just listen closely' (Oebel, 2002: 3, 5).

In the literature, different didactisation models can be found. For example, Esa suggests three phases for the didactisation of a song,[5] which is essential for making it accessible to learners. The third phase, development, is the most important and laborious of the didactisation process and consists of three parts: first, teachers develop lexical and illustrative exercises to introduce the vocabulary and content step by step before ever listening (or sometimes even saying that they are going to listen) to a song. Then, teachers create comprehension exercises to help the students know what they are listening for. Lastly, teachers design application exercises so the students can apply their knowledge (Esa, 2008: 4–5).

These activities can also be categorised as pre-listening activities, while-listening activities and post-listening activities. I base the following activities on my own training as a teacher of German as a foreign language and my personal teaching experience. They should be seen as suggestions as there is no one-size-fits-all approach in language learning.[6]

Teachers use pre-listening activities to introduce learners to the topic. They build up the learners' motivation and expectation, and activate their prior linguistic, cultural and music-related knowledge. The information provided should be relevant to the learners and the listening objective (Rodríguez Cemillán, 2000). I list possible activities and instructions here; teachers may:

- Ask students about their expectations of a specific topic, create an associogram or mind map, gather vocabulary specific to the topic or introduce vocabulary from the lyrics:
  - Name at least three emotions in German. Are they considered positive, negative or neutral? When do people feel happy? How do we express positive emotions? ('Auf uns' by Andreas Bourani)

- What musical instruments do you know in German? ('Millionen Lichter' by Christina Stürmer)
- What are some of the landmarks in Vienna? What is Vienna known for? ('Der letzte Kaiser' by Wiener Blond)
- Use visual stimuli such as illustrations, pictures, photos or videos – either relevant to the topic, taken from the music video or representing the artist, and let the learners guess what genre the song might belong to; show the music video without sound, or ask the learners to tell a story based on pictures:
  - What do you see on the picture/in the video? Write down the words with their article and plural! ('Oft gefragt' by AnnenMayKantereit)
  - What musical instruments do you see in the video? ('Millionen Lichter' by Christina Stürmer)
- Use audio stimuli such as sounds, music or voices; ask the students to close their eyes while listening for the first time to focus their perception:
  - Describe what you hear. Can you distinguish the instruments?
- Use parts of the lyrics such as the song title or only singular words (asking the learners to tell/write a story with these); let the learners restore the text (jumbled-up stanzas), read the lyrics and explain any unfamiliar words:
  - Who is the 'we' from the title? Why are they in a garden? Tell a story about what happened in the garden using the *Perfekt*. / Write a story about what happened in the garden using the *Präteritum*. ('Wir trafen uns in einem Garten' by 2raumwohnung)
  - Describe the German teacher who the song is about. What makes a good or bad teacher? ('Meine Deutschlehrerin' by Wise Guys)
- Use other texts about the artist or the topic
- Ask learners to match pictures with text or text with text
- Let the students anticipate and hypothesise based on the title or the first few notes of the song:
  - What could be these questions that are often asked? ('Oft gefragt' by AnnenMayKantereit)
  - What could be the best time of someone's life? What was the best time of your life so far? ('Schönste Zeit' by Bosse)
  - Why would the singer like to be a chicken? Would you like to be a chicken or another animal? Why (not)? ('Ich wollt' ich wär' ein Huhn' by Comedian Harmonists)

○ What do children have to do? What are they supposed to do? What do they want to do? ('Immer muss ich alles sollen' by Gisbert zu Knyphausen)

While-listening activities focus on the comprehension of details, distinction and identification of information and comparison of expectation with the actual song (lyrics). If the teacher uses music without lyrics or wants to focus solely on the music, the learners could describe or draw the rhythm or the melody or identify the instruments and their impact. If the teacher uses the lyrics, they could ask the students to perform one of the following activities:
- Correct the text or its order
- Fill gaps in a text
- Anticipate the title if they do not know it yet
- Note down colours, smells, feelings, impressions that come to mind
- Match pictures with text or text with text
- Compare new information with information gathered before listening
- Perhaps sing along (but no one should feel uncomfortable)
- Gather vocabulary for a specific topic, or all the words learners understand, or how often a specific word appears; a list could be provided for weaker learners, and they have to circle the words they hear (or the infinitives to verbs used in the lyrics), or they have to mark words that fit with the song (adjectives), for example, bingo:
  ○ Listen for words related to happiness. ('Auf uns' by Andreas Bourani)
  ○ How many times do you hear the word 'Zuhause'? ('Oft gefragt' by AnnenMayKantereit)
  ○ List all the instruments you see in the video. ('Millionen Lichter' by Christina Stürmer)
  ○ Write down any grammar mistakes you notice while listening. ('Meine Deutschlehrerin' by Wise Guys)

For *ab initio* students, it is generally a good idea to provide text as they will not be able to understand everything by listening. In this respect, also think about using captions if you are showing the music video. This will help students with hearing difficulties and enable them to take part in the activities.

Post-listening activities are usually used to determine if the learners understood the text according to the respective listening objectives. This is also important as a base for further activities with or based on the song.

Teachers have to be flexible if the original listening objective has not been achieved. They will then have to come up with new objectives. Therefore, it is useful to prepare multiple differentiated listening tasks to keep the students' focus and motivation (Oebel, 2002: 5). Tasks in this phase can either focus on the lyrics or further (creative) activities or both, for example:

- Organise lyrics or pictures in a specific manner
- Fill gaps in a text or table
- Answer questions about the text (w-question words), multiple choice, true or false:
  - Who is the singer? Who do they sing to ('du')? Where are they? When is this taking place? What is happening? Why do they do what they do?
- Summarise (including a specific task):
  - Summarise the content of the song by using coordinating conjunctions.
- Translate:[7]
  - Translate the chorus of the song literally. Then decide what needs to be changed to make it sound more like a song.
- Compare what has been heard to hypotheses prior to listening:
  - What did you get right? How did you know? What did you get wrong? What is correct?
- Do vocabulary exercises, for example, look for words related to 'X', or synonyms and antonyms, or create compound nouns:
  - Look for words and phrases expressing happiness. ('Auf uns' by Andreas Bourani)
  - How does the singer describe their relationship to the person addressed in the song? What kind of relationship could this be? ('Oft gefragt' by AnnenMayKantereit)
- Do grammar exercises, for example, changing tenses or personal pronouns, or look for a specific grammar phenomenon:
  - Find all prepositions in the song and write down which case they take. ('Wir trafen uns in einem Garten' by 2raumwohnung)
  - Switch 'ich' and 'du' and correct the verb conjugation accordingly. ('Oft gefragt' by AnnenMayKantereit)
  - Correct the grammar mistakes in the lyrics. ('Meine Deutschlehrerin' by Wise Guys)
- Match pictures with text or text with text
- Add punctuation
- Discuss the topic of the song (in its historical and political context); this might only be possible with students who already have some

background knowledge about German-speaking countries, but this discussion does not necessarily have to be in German:

- How would you describe your relationship with your parents? What do parents have to do for their children? What are children expected to do for their parents? ('Oft gefragt' by AnnenMayKantereit)
- What is *Heimat* and how do we feel about it? ('Hallo Hometown' by Bosse)
- What do people consider the best time of their life? What does that say about their values? ('Schönste Zeit' by Bosse)
- How important is work for you? Would you prefer to never work? ('Ich wollt' ich wär' ein Huhn' by Comedian Harmonists)
- What are ways of protesting? What are people protesting? How safe is it to protest? What protest has an impact? ('Baun' by Sigrid Horn)
- What do you learn about Vienna and its citizens? How are they being portrayed in this song? Is this a city you would like to visit? Why (not)? ('Der letzte Kaiser' by Wiener Blond)
- What is important in a relationship? Why do relationships end? / How does the song portray gender roles? ('Nur für dich' by Wise Guys)
- Do research on the internet, for example, about the artist, depending on your objective, this could also be in the students' first language:
  - Plan a trip to Vienna. Where would you go? What would you see? ('Der letzte Kaiser' by Wiener Blond)
- Express and describe personal feelings and opinions about the song.

The last activity on this list should always be feasible. Even if the learners do not understand anything, they will be able to feel or think something when they listen to the music. Teachers usually teach them simple adjective phrases such as *gut* or *nicht so gut* during the first week of class when questions like *wie geht's?* are introduced. Therefore, students are able to express their opinion on the song and thus at least one activity is possible (in speaking or writing), especially if the other objectives have not been met, for whatever reason.

Creative post-listening activities include tasks such as:

- Writing dialogues or role plays
  - How did they meet? Imagine the dialogue of the two people in the garden. ('Wir trafen uns in einem Garten' by 2raumwohnung)

- The couple is celebrating their anniversary. Imagine a dialogue between the two. ('Seite an Seite' by Christina Stürmer, 'Eins sein' by Wilhelmine)
- Coming up with a new ending, new title, new lyrics or with alternatives starting somewhere in between:
  - They decide to get back together. Imagine a dialogue between the two. ('Wir trafen uns in einem Garten' by 2raumwohnung)
- Recounting or retelling the story or situation
- Creating pictures, photos, collages, music videos, or writing a song
- Using writing prompts such as writing fan mail, a (critical) review, an interview with the artist, or an answer to a comment on YouTube underneath the song (in this case, teachers should choose appropriate comments beforehand or adapt them), or writing a story using only the words they comprehended while listening.

Referring to the last point on the list, Waychert explains that even *ab initio* students should be able to write short (internet) comments. Furthermore, he suggests the students could fill in a form to simulate a concert ticket reservation, as this is one of the can-do statements for beginners according to the CEFR (Waychert, 2015: 52).

Finally, beginners should also have the option to compare results with classmates to check and gather information while working on the tasks. Teachers should not use music for tests in order to maintain the benefit of music being associated with an atmosphere free from fear or stress. In that sense, cooperative writing might be considered here, too.

There are many different activities incorporating the use of music in the classroom, and also plenty of resources for teachers to draw upon. They may look for songs on YouTube or blogs that can easily be found on the internet. When using links to music videos, ensure they are still working and that they are accessible in class. Check any lyrics taken from the internet and be aware of potential copyright issues. The Goethe Institut also offers materials on the German music scene. Morgret lists materials produced by publishers, too (Morgret, 2015: 77–9).

Conclusion

I use music in my courses regularly and believe this topic can be of interest for other *ab initio* teachers who want to use authentic materials and encourage their students to become interested in the culture of German-speaking countries. Essentially, considering the literature and my personal experiences, using music in class is attractive because it is a form of learner-centric teaching. Activities with music are easily adaptable for online teaching, too.

I have written about the benefits of music, that using songs trains language skills, teaches cultural aspects, and facilitates pronunciation, and as nicely summarised by Stansell: '[m]usic positively affects language accent, memory, and grammar as well as mood, enjoyment, and motivation' (Stansell, 2005: 3). Nevertheless, it would be desirable to have more studies on music in the foreign language classroom, especially with adult learners (such as the students at UK universities).

Ab initio students do not have to understand every detail of a song in order to become active, productive, and creative learners. But they need clear learning objectives when teachers use songs as part of a lesson, in any phase during the class, and of an overall course concept. Music is neither the solution to the problem of unmotivated students nor a guarantee for language learning success, but we can use it for much more than a simple listening exercise.

Notes

1 For a more detailed analysis of characteristics of different learner generations, see Chapter 3, this volume.
2 For an overview of studies focusing on memory performance, see Morgret (2015).
3 For an overview of textbooks using music and didactic songs, see Morgret (2015, especially 77–9) and Waychert (2015, especially 43–7).
4 For more detailed information on this project, see Mericka (2018).
5 For a more detailed description and a concrete example, see Esa (2008).
6 For a typology of exercises, see Badstübner-Kizik (2007).
7 For examples of activities including the translation of lyrics, see Pleß (2014).

Internet links

https://deutschmusikblog.de/
https://www.goethe.de/ins/cn/de/spr/unt/kum/arbeitsblaetter.html
https://www.goethe.de/ins/fr/de/spr/unt/kum/jug/utm.html
https://www.goethe.de/prj/stg/de/mat/mmu.html
https://landeskunde.wordpress.com/musik-und-daf/
https://lyricstraining.com/
https://p.dw.com/p/3Hi8N
https://sites.google.com/site/dafmusik/

References

Badstübner-Kizik, C. (2004) 'Wortschatzarbeit, Schreiben, Hörverstehen … und was noch? Anmerkungen zur Rolle von Kunst und Musik im Fremdsprachenunterricht'. *ÖDaF Mitteilungen* 1, 6–19.

Badstübner-Kizik, C. (2007) *Bild- und Musikkunst im Fremdsprachenunterricht. Zwischenbilanz und Handreichungen für die Praxis*. Frankfurt am Main: Peter Lang.

Badstübner-Kizik, C. (2010a) 'Musik in Lehrwerken für den Fremdsprachenunterricht – was will und was kann sie (nicht)?' In *Der Einsatz von Musik und die Entwicklung von audio literacy im Fremdsprachenunterricht*, edited by G. Blell and R. Kupetz, 109–20. Frankfurt am Main: Peter Lang.

Badstübner-Kizik, C. (2010b) 'Kunst und Musik im Deutsch als Fremd- und Zweitsprache-Unterricht'. In *Deutsch als Fremd- und Zweitsprache. Ein internationales Handbuch. Band 1*, edited by H. Krumm, C. Fandrych, B. Hufeisen and C. Riemer, 1597–601. Berlin and New York: De Gruyter.

Blell, G. (2010) 'Audio Literacy/Musik'. In *Metzlers Lexikon: Fremdsprachendidaktik: Ansätze – Methoden – Grundbegriffe*, edited by C. Suhrkamp, 226–9. Stuttgart: Metzler.

Blell, G. and Hellwig, K. (1996) 'Zur Einführung: Bildende Kunst und Musik im Fremdsprachenunterricht'. In *Bildende Kunst und Musik im Fremdsprachenunterricht*, edited by G. Blell and K. Hellwig, 7–13. Frankfurt am Main: Peter Lang.

Buttner, A. (2012) *100 Methoden für den Englischunterricht: Ideen zur Förderung der mündlichen und schriftlichen Sprachkompetenz*. Mülheim an der Ruhr: Verlag an der Ruhr.

Christiner, M. and Reiterer, S.M. (2015) 'A Mozart is not a Pavarotti: Singers outperform instrumentalists on foreign accent imitation'. *Frontiers in Human Neuroscience* 9:482, 1–8.

De Florio-Hansen, I. (2014) *Fremdsprachenunterricht lernwirksam gestalten. Mit Beispielen für Englisch, Französisch und Spanisch*. Tübingen: Narr Verlag.

Esa, M. (2008) Musik im Deutschunterricht: Der gezielte Einsatz. *Die Unterrichtspraxis / Teaching German* 41:1, 1–14.

Karyn, A. (2006) 'Lieder und Musik in DaF-Lehrwerken. "Wenn ihre Schüler Spaß am Rap haben, werden sie wissen, was zu tun ist"'. *Info DaF* 33:6, 547–56.

List, G. (2002) 'Motivation im Sprachenunterricht'. *Fremdsprache Deutsch* 26, 6–10.

Mericka, K. (2018) 'LipDub: A technology-enhanced language learning project with music'. In *Innovative language Teaching and Learning at University: Integrating informal learning into formal language education*, edited by F. Rosell-Aguilar, T. Beaven and M. Fuertes Gutiérrez, 59–65. Voillans: Research-publishing.net. https://doi.org/10.14705/rpnet.2018.22.776 (accessed 4 July 2022).

Morgret, S. (2015) *Die Förderung phonetischer Kompetenzen durch den aktiven Einsatz von Musik im Unterricht DaF. Eine empirische Studie am Beispiel von arabischen Studierenden in der Grundstufe (Sprachniveau A2)*. Online. https://kobra.bibliothek.uni-kassel.de/bitstream/urn:nbn:de:hebis:34-2015120149469/10/DissertationStefanieMorgret.pdf (accessed 6 January 2021).

Oebel, G. (2002) *Deutsche Populärmusik im DaF-Unterricht*. Online. www.lernen-durch-lehren.de/LDL_ALT/material/berichte/daf/oebel.pdf (accessed 20 January 2021).

Perner, M. (2014) 'Musik im DaF-Unterricht: Von der Sprache zur Musik – und zurück'. In *Ästhetisches Lernen im DaF-/DaZ-Unterricht: Literatur – Theater – Bildende Kunst – Musik – Film*, edited by N. Bernstein and C. Lerchner, 313–33. Göttingen: Universitätsverlag Göttingen.

Pleß, U. (2014) 'Übersetzen von Liedern im DaF-Unterricht'. In *Ästhetisches Lernen im DaF-/DaZ-Unterricht: Literatur – Theater – Bildende Kunst – Musik – Film*, edited by N. Bernstein and C. Lerchner, 151–64. Göttingen: Universitätsverlag Göttingen.

Riemer, C. (2017) 'Affektive Faktoren im L2-Erwerb: Zur Rolle von Einstellungen, Motivation und Angst'. Keynote speech presented at the ÖDaF-Jahrestagung, Vienna, 18 March 2017.

Rodríguez Cemillán, D. (2000) *Internet-Dossier: Musik im Unterricht (Teil 3): Was kann Musik im Fremdsprachenunterricht leisten*. Online. www.deutsch-als-fremdsprache.de/infodienst/2000/daf-info1-00.php3#1 (accessed 10 January 2021).

Rodríguez Cemillán, D. (2014) 'Lieder, die ein Deutschlehrer braucht'. *Magazin/Extra* 1, 53–7.

Sposet, B. (2008) *The Role of Music in Second Language Acquisition. A bibliographical review of seventy years of research, 1937-2007*. Lewiston, NY: The Edwin Mellen Press.

Stansell, J.W. (2005) 'The use of music for learning languages: A review of the literature'. Online. http://writingthetrueself.com/pdfs/Jon_Stansell_The_Use_of_Music_for_Learning_Languages.pdf (accessed 10 January 2021).

Waychert, C. (2015) 'Deutschsprachige Musik auf der Niveaustufe A'. In *IDT 2013, Band 2.2 – Kognition, Sprache, Musik: Sektionen A2, A4, A5*, edited by C. Badstübner-Kizik, A. Bakuradze, R. Koroschetz Maragno, F. Missaglia, M. Möllering and S. Winklbauer, 43–56. Bozen: Bozen-Bolzano University Press.

Waychert, C. (2017) 'Einstieg ins Thema'. Online. https://sites.google.com/site/dafmusik/arbeitsfelder/einstieg-ins-thema (accessed 10 January 2021).

Wild, K. (2014) 'Neue Töne im Ausspracheunterricht'. In *Ästhetisches Lernen im DaF-/DaZ-Unterricht: Literatur – Theater – Bildende Kunst – Musik – Film*, edited by N. Bernstein and C. Lerchner, 335–49. Göttingen: Universitätsverlag Göttingen.

6
Grammar teaching and learning in the German *ab initio* classroom
Birgit Smith

Introduction

Grammar?! Students up and down the country studying grammar at any level often sigh when they hear that they are required to learn grammar. Teachers sometimes also struggle with teaching structures if they have not been explicitly exposed to these during their language degree. The study of grammar can suffer from a poor reputation. Misconceptions exist such as: grammar is an arbitrary set of rules, grammar does not have to be taught, learners acquire the rules by themselves or, if taught, lessons are boring. Grammar is not the be-all and end-all, but we should not avoid teaching it. It forms an integral part of language and an integral part of the language learning process.

In order to attempt to address the above mentioned issues, I will evaluate in this chapter the role of explicit grammar teaching in the tuition of *ab initio* German. The chapter starts with an overview of how grammar was taught historically. It then moves on to evaluate how native speakers produce and understand an infinite number of utterances, including many that are new which shows that, for them, implicit grammatical knowledge is acquired without instructions. Learners who learn a second/foreign language later in life are not so fortunate, as many will have to acquire this linguistic competence explicitly in the language classroom.

I will then demonstrate how adult learners can use their first language (L1) as a resource and how their cognitive development allows for greater problem-solving skills including memory strategies, cognitive strategies for understanding and producing language and compensation strategies for using the language despite gaps in their knowledge. Grammar-focused teaching improves accuracy. Research has shown that explicit second language (L2) instruction brings substantial gains in the learning of target structures in comparison with implicit instructions whereby learners have to induce rules from examples given to them (Ellis, 1994; Rebuschat, 2015; Ellis, Romer and O'Donnell, 2016). Grammatical competence is one of the communicative competences. This involves knowing how to use the grammar and vocabulary of German to achieve communicative objectives. Finally, I will argue that the debate should move on from discussions of *whether or not* grammar should be taught to *how* grammar should be taught. With examples showing how grammar could be integrated in the classroom, I will claim that explicit teaching of grammatical forms should be part of any *ab initio* German syllabus, using a combination of focus on form instructions and meaningful communication.

Grammar teaching over time

The issue of grammar teaching has been divisive, partly because arguments may have been founded on political or ideological views. Within the wider context of educational reforms, the debate about grammar has been less about grammar than 'the particular values and standards the idea of grammar has been made to symbolise' (Cameron, 1995: 28). Has it always been like that? Up until the 1960s, the language curriculum was based on the teaching of literature and explicit grammar teaching, although language learning was reserved for the upper classes (McLelland, 2018: 9). Until the 1960s Latin had always been the language of choice for the educated classes, as it was thought that Latin developed intellectual abilities and that the study of Latin grammar was an end in itself (Howatt and Smith, 2014: 80). Thus, languages were not seen as a tool for communication as they are today.

A fundamental reorganisation of the British school system took place with a change to a comprehensive education system. While in 1965, 20 per cent of children were educated in comprehensive schools, this number had risen to over 70 per cent by the mid-1970s. Teachers found themselves having to teach foreign languages to students possibly less able than previously encountered in the grammar schools. Teaching grammar was seen as demotivating to the less-able pupil and the main concern was to make the learning of foreign languages more relevant to pupils' lives. With the introduction of the National Curriculum in 1988, the content of the language curriculum became more centralised with the government taking more control of the curriculum and examination boards set their requirements subject to the National Curriculum (McLelland, 2018: 9). The ability to hold a conversation, comprehend spoken and written language and the ability to write in the language was seen as more important than the ability to translate into and from the language (McLelland, 2018: 11).

With the development of new methodologies in language learning, communicative teaching methods gained in popularity with their focus on communication and less emphasis on grammatical accuracy. In the twenty-first century, teaching of the spoken language is still very much at the heart of language teaching methods, which assume implicitly that speaking comes first and use grammar as a support for written tasks rather than as the main focus (Cook, 2005: 20).

Language policies changed again from 2004 onwards with languages now only being compulsory at primary school level between the ages of 7 and 11. However, languages are not a compulsory subject at GCSE and A-level, as languages were, and are, still seen as difficult and fewer pupils than ever before are taking languages at these levels (Ofsted, 2021: 4). German GCSE entries dropped from 43,260 in 2018 to 37,035 in 2021. With 2,525 studying German at A-level in England, entries saw an 8 per cent decline in 2021 compared with 2020 (Government/Ofqual, 2021).

As fewer pupils in schools now study German up to A-level, universities tried to remedy this by offering *ab initio* courses, either in addition to their main language degree courses or as part of an undergraduate degree to improve the language learning environment in the UK when compared to continental Europe. In 2016, only 32 per cent of UK 15–30-year-olds felt confident reading and writing in two or more languages, compared to 79 per cent in France, 91 per cent in Germany and 80 per cent on average across EU member states (Eurostat, 2016: 42). A British Council report issued in 2019 highlighted the ongoing concern about the level of participation in language learning since the subject was removed from the compulsory curriculum at Key Stage 4 in 2004 (Tinsley, 2019: 2–3).

Why are British children and young adults so disinclined to learn a foreign language? In a study by Clark and Trafford (1996: 47), many pupils expressed their opinion that foreign languages are more demanding than other GCSE subjects. This was corroborated by Fisher (2001: 35) who found that 60 per cent of pupils preferred other subjects. In addition to this 'climate of negativity', as McPake and colleagues (1999: 71) label it, their study into the decline in uptake of foreign languages in Scotland found that students did not see material gains for themselves in learning a foreign language. Competence in a modern language was not seen by students as an essential skill in achieving their goal of entry into higher education or into a career. Does teaching methodology play a role in this lack of popularity of languages?

Communicative skills, communication and the language learner

The National Curriculum assumes that German language teaching is 'based on a sound foundation of core grammar and vocabulary', and students should be taught to 'use accurate grammar, spelling and punctuation' (2013: 2). However, it does not specify how the language should be taught. Grammatical accuracy and linguistic sophistication are only stipulated assessment criteria for the higher grades, but measures of accuracy and sophistication do not exist. Many teachers take the view that communicative foreign language learning requires the use of as much target language as possible, and students doing as much oral work as possible with little formal teaching of grammar (Coleman, 1996: 34). Students are thus exposed to the sounds of the foreign language and have to reproduce them, but it is not clear how, and to what effect, teachers correct incorrect utterances. Classroom data from a number of studies support the view that corrective feedback and form-focused instruction is more effective in promoting second language learning than programmes which are limited to emphasis on fluency (Lightbown and Spada, 1999: 443). This poses the question of the role of explicit grammar teaching in the curriculum of any language learning setting.

This focus on communicative skills has led to a shift away from the teaching of accuracy to a content-based curriculum. McCulloch criticises this as 'students who have discussed urban pollution do not know the plural of *Stadt*; students who have discussed the political parties, do not know the gender of *Partei*. At the end of the day, the linguistic expectation is so limited …' (1995: 18). I therefore argue that we need to expect students to learn the gender of German nouns right from the beginning of their *ab initio* language learning journey.

However, the emphasis on communicative skills was, and still is, thought to be more motivating for learners, in that they learn early in the course to say words and sentences in the foreign language, thus increasing the positive learning experience. Language as a form of communication is therefore often seen as more important than grammatical accuracy. Early success in language learning is key in encouraging the learning of the language, as it is seen to have positive motivational effects on the language learner. In this sense, high levels of motivation are a result of success, not vice versa. Language learners want to see quick progress. As a result, one could say 'just learn the two thousand most common words and you know the language' as was suggested in June 2021 by the Governmental Curriculum Research Review: Languages (2021: 11).

However, while learners learn vocabulary one word at a time, sentences are not learned in this way. Rather than memorising large chunks of language, learners need to know the rules of the language to form sentences themselves. By knowing the rules in conjunction with vocabulary, they have an infinite number of sentences at their fingertips. The next section will explore further how the *ab initio* learner can acquire grammatical concepts.

The role of grammar in language learning

Although the L1 proficiency of native speakers varies considerably based on their education, literacy and so on, they can produce and understand a non-finite number of utterances, including many that are new and unfamiliar (Hulstijn, 2015: 16). Unless they have undergone formal instruction in grammar, they are typically not consciously aware of explicit grammatical rules. However, while the grammatical knowledge of a native speaker is for the most part implicit, learners who learn a second language later in life learn in a different way. They will have to acquire this linguistic competence explicitly, as the capacity to understand the grammar of a second language, using the intuition of a child learning his or her first language, is typically lost in late childhood (Hartshorne, Tenenbaum and Pinker, 2018: 268).

The native language may influence learners' understanding of language as well. Sheppard suggests that 'a grasp of formal English grammar can actually help people acquire foreign languages more rapidly, more securely and to a more sophisticated level' (1993: 9). However, the transfer of patterns of the first language is one of the major sources of errors in learner language, as Lightbown and Spada (1999: 165) state.

Nevertheless, correctness of grammar is indeed relative. While most grammar resources aim to be as comprehensive as possible in their analyses of a language, there is no single set of regulations that could be considered authoritative. Evaluations are often made by the authors themselves, who sometimes disagree about the acceptability of a language form. Creativity is a hallmark of human language, and language changes over time. This does not make one form of grammar more correct than others, nor should the language of native speakers be taken as the yardstick to measure the language competency of a learner.

First Language Acquisition (FLA) is part of a child's cognitive and social development. The cognitive differences between a child and an adult learner suggest that teaching methods have to be different. Implicit linguistic knowledge is acquired by the age of seven, and Bialystok suggests a second component, namely control of linguistic processing, which she defines as 'the ability to control attention to relevant and appropriate information and to integrate those forms in real time' (1990: 125). Thus, when students learn German at university level, they already have acquired linguistic concepts that are available for Second Language Acquisition (SLA). However, for SLA new notions such as referential concepts or linguistic categories may have to be learned, or concepts might have to be modified, which may prove to be a difficult task for the SLA German learner.

When considering the needs of the *ab initio* German learner, it is necessary to take individual intellectual background, prior knowledge, interests and objectives of the learner into account. These L2 learners can communicate effectively and do not need to learn a foreign language in the same manner as they learned their first language. They can use their L1 as a resource to analyse, or express, meaning and their cognitive development allows for greater problem-solving skills. This orientation towards the needs of the learner is also central to the question of the relationship between spontaneous, unguided foreign language learning (when one is immersed in an environment where the L2 is spoken) and classroom-based language learning. Normally, in the UK higher education context, acquisition happens through formal teaching where the L2 is not spoken outside the classroom. This has implications on how we need to teach *ab initio* German.

Language acquisition, teaching and learning strategies

Not only does the learner's background play a part in language acquisition, the strategies teachers employ to teach the language also have a role to play. These methods have to be meaningful to the learners themselves, and so possibly may be different from one learner to the next, depending on the individual learner's background, experiences and preferences. Learners develop direct and indirect strategies to make learning easier. The direct strategies include mnemonic techniques to remember and retrieve information, cognitive strategies for understanding and producing language and compensation strategies for using the language despite gaps in knowledge. However, indirect strategies feature metacognitive strategies to co-ordinate the learning process, affective strategies to regulate emotions and social strategies to learn with others (Oxford, 1990: 14–16). Tutors should support *ab initio* learners to become aware of these strategies and help them to develop the ones they already have based on their own language learning experiences.

On the plus side, students studying *ab initio* German at English universities are normally motivated to learn, as they have chosen this subject. International students in the UK are often studying German as a third or fourth language, thus bringing with them a wealth of language-learning experience. They are aware of their L1 structures in comparison to the grammatical rules of German and can thus deduct patterns (Oxford, 1990). Their quick uptake of the structures can be a bonus for the English native learner who might be more motivated to keep up with the pensum, but it could also be a distraction and demotivating factor for struggling students. The teacher therefore has to take different abilities into consideration and ensure that differentiated instruction caters to the learners' needs.

What is clear is that there is a wide variation among *ab initio* learners in terms of their ability to achieve a very high level of competence. Following a communicative methodology, 'learners often failed initially to produce correct sentences and instead displayed language that was markedly deviant from target language norms' (R. Ellis, 1994: 15). Birdsong complains that the 'failure to acquire the target language grammar is typical' (1992: 706). This failure has been of concern for decades, and to date, a successful way to remedy this problem, if there is one, has not been found. Numerous theories of how learners learn languages have been put forward, but there is not one theory that has all the answers. The next section will explore the role of explicit grammar teaching in the classroom.

Explicit grammar teaching at *ab initio* level

Many SLA classroom studies have demonstrated that focusing students' attention on form gives better results than implicit learning. Lightbown and Spada (1999: 439) and R. Ellis (2001: 6) have shown that explicit teaching improves grammatical accuracy with Roehr suggesting that German learners' linguistic and metalinguistic knowledge are strongly correlated (2008: 173).

Schmidt argues that 'you can't learn a foreign language (or anything else, for that matter) through subliminal perception' (1990: 142) and that noticing differences between L1 and the target language is the necessary condition for converting input into intake (1990: 160). Schmidt also discusses several factors affecting noticing such as expectation, frequency, skill level, and task demands. He suggests that 'those who notice most, learn most' (Schmidt, 1990: 144). Hence, in order to facilitate the learning of *ab initio* German students, we should make them explicitly aware of the structures of German so that they notice new linguistic features that they encounter and which they may find difficult. Winne states that learners who know how to learn

> set goals for extending knowledge and sustaining motivation. They are aware of what they know, what they believe, and what the differences between these kinds of information imply for approaching tasks. They have a grasp on their motivation, are aware of their affect, and plan how to manage the interplay between these as they engage with a task. They are also deliberate about small-grain tactics and overall strategies, selecting some instead of others based on predictions about how each is able to support progress toward chosen goals. (Winne, 1995: 173)

Swain also found that communicative language teaching is not enough for students to acquire form. Extensive research on learning outcomes in French immersion programmes showed that, despite long-term exposure to the language, the learners did not achieve accuracy in some grammatical forms (Swain and Lapkin, 1989: 158). Thus, communicative language teaching on its own was found to be inadequate. In addition, Skehan (2003: 7) indicated that language learners cannot process the target language input for both meaning and form at the same time. If the learner fails to notice target forms in the input, he or she will fail to process and acquire them. Therefore, we need to give *ab initio* learners every chance to grasp new structures when they are first presented to them.

A large number of classroom studies have shown that grammar-focused teaching or form-focused instruction improves accuracy (Schmidt, 1990, 2001; Doughty and Williams, 1998; Lightbown and Spada, 1999). Several studies have shown that corrective feedback of learner errors together with the teaching of specific target forms has a positive effect on accuracy (Lightbown and Spada, 1999; Doughty, 2001; R. Ellis, 2001, 2002). Norris and Ortega also found in a meta-analysis of 49 studies on the effectiveness of L2 instruction that explicit instruction brings substantial gains in the learning of target structures in comparison with implicit instructions (2000: 480).

Therefore, the debate should move on from discussions of *whether or not* grammar should be taught to *how* grammar should be taught. *Ab initio* German learners sometimes experience problems with transferring knowledge from controlled practice to communicative practice. Mechanical exercises and drills such as rewriting, gap-filling and transformation exercises applied in the grammar-translation or audiolingual method tend to fail the learner as they lack meaningful context. Rogers suggests that the 'reinstatement of grammar as part of the communicative competence need not lead back to syllabuses which are driven by wholly formal considerations, nor to teaching methods which return to decontextualised rote learning' (1996: 38). Therefore, I certainly do not advocate returning to the old methods of practising declension tables nor grammar translation methods. However, there have been a number of suggestions on how to integrate grammar teaching in the curriculum. R. Ellis suggests that explicit teaching of grammatical forms should be part of a communicative syllabus, and he recommends a combination of focus on form instructions and meaningful communication (2002: 169). Learners need to notice and produce structures that have been presented to them either explicitly in a grammar lesson or implicitly through frequent exposure (Swain, 1995; Swain and Lapkin, 2001; N. Ellis, 2002; R. Ellis, 2002, 2003). Moreover, Altun and Dinçer found that students who were taught explicitly outperformed those who were taught implicitly by a wide margin in grammar and writing (2020: 102).

VanPatten suggests one way of teaching grammar is through what he calls 'processing instruction' (2002: 758). An initial exposure to explicit instruction is combined with a series of activities that consist mainly of tasks that encourage comprehension of the target structures rather than their production. How could this work in practice? In task-based language teaching (TBLT), the tasks are viewed as 'mediators of language learning and a reference point' to make sense of the language, so the focus is on meaning, not form (Bygate, 2016: 385). Language is a tool rather than an object. In this way, TBLT is far more connected to real life interaction than previous teaching approaches, and in this way, according to Bygate, 'goes counter to traditions of language teaching everywhere, both East and West' (2016: 385). The heart of the language learning process, according to Ellis (2017: 520), is the fact that while the learner is primarily focused on meaning, they can simultaneously have their attention drawn to linguistic features as they arise within a context. In Ellis's view, all versions of TBLT allow for attention to grammar through focus on form at some stage in a task-based lesson (2017: 515). Students seem to value teaching that is focused on understanding meaning and the use of grammatical structures (Fujino, 2019: 12).

Therefore, though grammar in itself may not have a central place in TBLT, it is certainly important and should be included in all TBLT lessons. In the following section I will suggest some practical solutions on how to integrate grammar in the *ab initio* classroom.

Integration of grammar in the *ab initio* German curriculum

How can we make the most of the *ab initio* learners' experiences and integrate grammar into their daily language learning? The *ab initio* German module that I have been teaching for years employs various methods. The main starting point is the deductive approach by explaining the grammatical structures to be learned and then giving the students a selection of written and listening materials to recognise the patterns before practicing these structures actively in oral conversations and written tasks. Alternatively, we switch it round with the inductive approach by asking students to explore patterns for themselves first in written materials before giving them the formal explanation. Exposing students to different teaching methods allows them to explore their own learning styles and they can then build on their strengths.

The flipped classroom whereby students acquire knowledge before a seminar and thus have time to practise and apply concepts in class (Stickler and Hampel, 2015: 64) is also one of the approaches that we tried and tested for explicit grammar teaching. Traditionally, grammar is taught by lecturing in a face-to-face context about a grammatical aspect whereby learners are expected to passively absorb and synthesise the information. However, these grammar lectures lend themselves to be moved out of the classroom to online mini presentations plus exercises that the student can work on and understand in their own time, thus gaining more confidence in their abilities by having a solid grasp of the structures. This then increases classroom time for interactive activities that facilitate language development.

Another approach is the application of corpora in language learning. Corpora are a 'text collection which is large, computer-readable and designed for linguistic analysis' (Stubbs and Halle, 2012: 1). On the one hand, corpora are a useful resource for the teacher in that they can aid in devising materials. For example, they have helped to develop language-teaching materials and have an influence on syllabus design. On the other hand, a corpus is a resource for the learner as a means of data-driven and discovery learning (Johns, 1991; Burnard and McEnery, 2000). Johns argues that 'the data-driven learning approach is the attempt to cut out the middleman … and give direct access to the data so that the learner can take part in building up his or her own profiles of meaning and use' (1991: 30). Corpora and corpus-based exercises can be useful as they 'favour learning by discovery. The study of grammar (or vocabulary, or discourse, or style) takes on the character of research, rather than spoon feeding or rote learning' (Tribble and Jones, 1990: 12). One such corpus is the *Digitale Wörterbuch der deutschen Sprache* (*DWDS*), an electronic corpus of German of the twentieth and twenty-first centuries, developed, published and maintained by the Berlin Academy of Science. It is a large, representative, free and publicly available corpus of German with a built-in corpus search and analysis tools. Moreover, the corpus is annotated for parts-of-speech (POS) and lemmata. In other words, it allows searches not only for specific word forms but also for word classes (for example, past participles) and all inflected forms of one base form, or lemma (such as the forms *gehe, gehst, ging, gegangen…* of the lemma *gehen*). Another corpus worth considering is the COSMAS corpus maintained by the Institute for German Language and is the largest German corpus containing classic texts, newspapers and also transcribed spoken language.

German language corpora are large in size and give the learner plenty of opportunities to explore the language. These corpora are not useful for teaching grammar per se, as they were not designed with this purpose in mind. However, by exposing the learner explicitly to a point of grammar, for example the perfect tense, the learner could then explore how this tense works by processing sentences and building up their own bank of examples that are relevant to them and their stage of learning. Corpora can help tutors and students to make a mental transition from conceptualising grammar as a collection of rules toward understanding language as a meaning-making resource. In addition, working with a corpus puts the students in charge of their own learning, which leads away from teacher-focused activities to learner-focused tasks. This shift from a deductive to an inductive teaching environment changes the role of the learner from an often-passive recipient of teachers' knowledge into the driving force behind their own learning. They have to actively engage with a text at word level and devise rules for themselves in order to describe the grammatical feature. The step-by-step analysis of language structures enables the student to produce a correct-item response. This systematic analysis of input for the purpose of deducing generalisations seems to reflect the controlled problem-solving processes which then result in skill acquisition.

Conclusion

As tutors we need to enable the *ab initio* German language learner to acquire knowledge of, and about, the language as well as advancing their skills of using the language. Practising a structure explicitly does not guarantee that the learner will be able to use this structure in communicative conditions. When the learner moves to a meaning-focused activity, they seem to revert to their own resources and often do not seem to pay attention to the linguistic rules they have practised previously, thus indicating that they have not acquired a full understanding of these rules. As discussed above, German learners can benefit from a focus on form approach that helps them to recognise patterns and facilitates their understanding of how the target grammatical structures work in context.

Moreover, students need to be exposed to explicit grammatical rules in their early studies. While learners will always make mistakes and learn from these, learning language that is correct from the start reduces the need to modify language later. This has implications for the content of the syllabus and assessment of school-based examinations such as GCSE and also for *ab initio* courses at higher education level. I therefore suggest that from the very beginning of any German course, more emphasis is placed on grammatical accuracy by teaching structures explicitly, but we also need to raise awareness of correct structures by exposing students to authentic materials with the aim that students can deduce explicit rules for themselves, helped by the tutor. By not exposing the learner explicitly to the rules of German, we might be doing some learners a disservice by not giving them the tools to analyse language. Right from the start, grammar should be embedded explicitly in the teaching of German so that the learner commits correct structures of language to long-term memory, structures that are then practiced in written and oral form so that they can become automatic. Students should thus be made aware of the value of learning structures so that they are able to construct their own language without too many errors.

Explicit teaching of grammatical rules is insufficient, the learner needs to be given authentic materials to deduce patterns and practice patterns before their knowledge can become implicit automatic knowledge. Students need to learn as well as acquire when there are only a few hours a week available for tuition. Different learning strategies such as pattern recognition and making associations with the shared L1 and other structures are also beneficial. We as tutors need to emphasise the positive aspects of why grammar is useful for language learners, we need to make grammar exciting to learn by introducing the learner to different teaching and learning methods and thus enable our students to be masters of their own language-learning future.

References

Altun, L. and Dınçer, R. (2020) 'A comparison of implicit and explicit teaching in terms of grammar and writing skills of intermediate learners'. *Bartin University Journal of Faculty of Education* 9:1, 96–105.

Berlin-Brandenburgische Akademie der Wissenschaften/Berlin Academy of Science. Online. www.dwds.deIt www.linguistik.hu-berlin.de/en/institut-en/professuren-en/korpuslinguistik/links-en/korpora_links (accessed 15 July 2021).

Bialystok, E. (1990) *Communication Strategies*. Oxford: Blackwell.

Birdsong, D. (1992) 'Ultimate attainment in second language acquisition'. *Language* 68, 706–55.

Burnard, L. and McEnery, T. (eds) (2000) *Rethinking Language Pedagogy from a Corpus Perspective*. New York: Peter Lang.

Bygate, M. (2016) 'Sources, developments and directions of task-based language teaching'. *Language Learning* 44:4, 381–400.

Cameron, D. (1995) *Verbal Hygiene*. London: Routledge.

Clark, A. and Trafford, J. (1996) 'Return to gender: boys' and girls' attitudes and achievements'. *Language Learning Journal* 14:1, 40–9.

Coleman, J. A. (1996) *Studying Languages: A survey of British and European students*. London: CILT.

Cook, V.J. (2005) 'Written language and foreign language teaching'. In *Second Language Writing Systems*, edited by V. Cook and B. Bassetti 421–67. Clevedon: Multilingual Matters.

COSMAS Corpus Online. www.ids-mannheim.de/cosmas2/ (accessed 15 May 2021).

Digitales Wörterbuch der deutschen Sprache/Digital Dictionary of the German Language DWDS. Online. www.dwds.de/ressourcen/korpora/ (accessed 15 May 2021).

Doughty, C. (2001) 'Cognitive underpinnings on focus on form'. In *Cognition and Second Language Instruction*, edited by P. Robinson, 206–57. New York: Cambridge University Press.

Doughty, C. and Williams, J. (eds) (1998) *Focus on Form in Classroom Second Language Acquisition*. New York: Cambridge University Press.

Ellis, N.C. (2002) 'Frequency Effects in Language Processing: A Review with Implications for Theories of Implicit and Explicit Language Acquisition'. *Studies in Second Language Acquisition* 24, 143–188.

Ellis, N., Romer, U. and O'Donnell, M. (2016) 'Construction and usage-based approaches to language acquisition'. *Language Learning* 66:1, 23–44.

Ellis, R. (1994) *The Study of Second Language Acquisition*. Oxford: Oxford University Press.

Ellis, R. (2001) 'Investigating form-focused instruction'. *Language Learning* 51:1, 1–46.

Ellis, R. (2002) 'Grammar teaching – practice or consciousness raising?' In *Methodology in Language Teaching*, edited by J. Richards and W. Renandya, 167–74. Cambridge: Cambridge University Press.

Ellis, R. (2003) *Task-Based Language Learning and Teaching*. Oxford: Oxford University Press.

Ellis, R. (2017) 'Position paper: Moving task-based language teaching forward'. *Language Teaching* 50:4, 507–26.

Fisher, L. (2001) 'Modern foreign languages recruitment post-16: The pupils' perspective'. *Language Learning Journal* 23:1, 33–40.

Foreign Language Learning Statistics, (2016) Eurostat. Online. https://ec.europa.eu/eurostat/statistics-explained/index.php?title=Foreign_language_skills_statistics (accessed 15 May 2021)

Fujino, H. (2019) 'L2 learners' perceptions of grammar: The case of JFL learners in the UK'. *Language Learning Journal* 19:3, 1–15.

Government/Ofqual (2021) 'Entries for GCSE, AS and A Level Summer 2021: Provisional entries for GCSE, AS and A-level: summer 2021 exam series'. Online. www.gov.uk/provisional/statistics/provisional-entries-for-gcse-as-and-a-level-summer-2021-series (accessed 15 July 2021).

Hartshorne, J., Tenenbaum, J. and Pinker, S. (2018) 'A critical period for second language acquisition: Evidence from 2/3 million English speakers'. *Cognition* 177, 263–77.

Howatt, A.P. and Smith, R. (2014) 'The History of teaching English as a foreign language, from a British and European perspective'. *Language & History* 57:1, 75–95.

Hulstijn, J. (2015) *Language Proficiency in Native and Non-Native Speakers: Theory and research*. Amsterdam: John Benjamins.

Johns, T. (1991) 'Should you be persuaded – two samples of data-driven learning materials'. *English Language Research Journal* 4:1, 1–16.

Lightbown, P.M. and Spada, N. (1999) *How Languages Are Learned*. Oxford: Oxford University Press.

McCulloch, D. (1995) 'Where has all the grammar gone? An "accusative" search'. *German Teaching* 12, 13–18.

McLelland, N. (2018) 'The history of language learning and teaching in Britain'. *Language Learning Journal* 46, 6–16.

McPake, J., Johnstone, R., Low, L. and Lyall, L. (1999) *Foreign Languages in the Upper Secondary School: A study of the causes of decline*. Glasgow: Scottish Council for Research in Education.

National Curriculum (2013) Online. https://assets.publishing.service.gov.uk/government/uploads/system/uploads/attachment_data/file/239083/SECONDARY_national_curriculum_-_Languages.pdf Reference: DFE-00195-2013 (accessed 13 May 2021).

Norris, J. and Ortega, L. (2000) 'Effectiveness of L2 instructions: A research synthesis and quantitative meta-analysis'. *Language Learning* 50, 417–28.

Ofsted (2021) 'Curriculum research series: Languages'. www.gov.uk/government/publications/curriculum-research-review-series-languages (accessed 15 July 2021).

Oxford, R. (1990) *Language Learning Strategies in Second Language Acquisition*. Cambridge: Cambridge University Press.

Rebuschat, P. (ed) (2015) *Implicit and Explicit Learning of Languages*. Amsterdam: John Benjamins.

Roehr, K. (2008) 'Metalinguistic knowledge and language ability in university-level L2 learners'. *Applied Linguistics* 29, (2), 173–99.

Schmidt, R.W. (1990) 'The role of consciousness in second language learning'. *Applied Linguistics* 11:2, 129–58.

Schmidt, R. (2001) 'Attention'. In *Cognition and Second Language Instruction*, edited by P. Robinson, 3–32. Cambridge: Cambridge University Press.

Sheppard, R. (1993) 'Getting down to brass syntax: German teaching and the great standards debate'. *German Teaching* 8, 2–10.

Skehan, P. (2003) 'Task-based instruction'. *Language Teaching* 36:1, 1–14.

Stickler, U. and Hampel, R. (2015) 'Transforming teaching: new skills for online language learning spaces'. In *Developing Online Language Teaching*, edited by R. Hampel and U. Stickler , 63–77. London: Palgrave Macmillan.

Stubbs, M. and Halle, D. (2012) 'Corpus linguistics: Overview'. In *The Encyclopaedia of Applied Linguistics*, edited by C.A. Chapelle, 1377–9. Oxford: Blackwell.

Swain, M. (1985) 'Communicative competence: Some rules of comprehensible input and comprehensible output in its development'. In *Input in Second Language Acquisition*, edited by S. Gass and C. Madden, 235–53. Rowley, MA: Newbury House.

Swain, M. (1989) 'Canadian immersion and adult second language teaching – what's the connection?' *Modern Language Journal* 73, 150–9.

Swain, M. and Lapkin, S. (2001) 'Focus on form through collaborative dialogue: Exploring task effects'. In *Researching Pedagogic Tasks: Second language learning, teaching and testing*, edited by M. Bygate, P. Skehan and M. Swain, 99–118. Harlow: Pearson Education.

Tinsley, T. (2019) 'Language trends 2019'. British Council. Online. www.britishcouncil.org/research-policy-insight/research-reports/language-trends-2019 (accessed 5 May 2021).

Tribble, C. and Jones, G. (1990) *Concordances in the Classroom*. Harlow: Longman.

VanPatten, B. (2002) 'Processing instruction: An update'. *Language Learning* 52, 755–803.

Winne, P.H. (1995) 'Inherent details in self-regulated Learning'. *Educational Psychologist* 30:4, 173–87.

7
Selecting the right resources for beginners' level: a textbook evaluation
Christian Mossmann

Introduction

Selecting materials is one of the most important decisions that a language teacher makes when designing a course. Choosing a textbook that is well suited to the intended learning outcomes, learner needs and interests and the context of the teaching programme is key to the success of any course. This is particularly true for *ab initio* language teaching, where textbooks, if chosen and adapted well, can provide a map for both teachers and learners that gives coherence to individual lessons and the course as a whole (Richards, 2015: 594).

For the context of German *ab initio* teaching, practitioners can choose from a wide range of textbooks, but only few specifically target university students and, to my knowledge, no textbook currently on the market was developed specifically for use in a British university context. Language teachers therefore have to adapt materials to their particular teaching and learning context. With publishers regularly releasing new series and new editions, staying abreast of the latest textbooks and evaluating their usefulness for a particular course can be challenging. A textbook evaluation with clearly defined criteria based on a particular teaching and learning context enables the practitioner to make an informed decision.

This chapter discusses approaches to textbook selection and evaluation and proposes a set of criteria for the *ab initio* context. It then applies this framework to two *ab initio* textbooks (*DaF kompakt neu* and

Neue Horizonte) to demonstrate how to go about the evaluation of these teaching and learning tools.

The role of the textbook in the *ab initio* classroom

While it is common for language teachers at universities to create their own materials for higher levels, in the context of *ab initio* teaching it is rare to design a course without a textbook taking on a central role. Hotho (1996: 19) stresses that particularly at *ab initio* level, a well-chosen textbook can be an invaluable practical and pedagogic resource, provided it is used flexibly and with the needs of the learners as a guiding principle. Crucially, textbooks should not only provide a range of texts but cover the whole spectrum of language teaching and learning, including pronunciation, lexis, vocabulary and grammar, as well as offering variety in the exercises they provide (Rösler and Schart, 2016: 485). Modern textbooks therefore need to integrate a multitude of factors related to the teaching and learning process, while striking a balance between the requirements of a systematic presentation of the subject matter, its progression and its complexity (Neuner, 1989: 241).

For all that the textbook tends to take on a prominent role in the *ab initio* language classroom, it is important not to let it determine the syllabus. As Cunningsworth points out, the textbook should be at the service of teachers and learners and not be the arbiter of course content and teaching methods: 'Coursebooks are best seen as a resource in achieving aims and objectives that have already been set in terms of learner needs. They should not determine the aims themselves or *become the aims*' (Cunningsworth, 1995: 5, his emphasis). It is thus essential to remain critical of the role of the textbook in the language classroom, both when designing a course and while it is running.

The textbook can fulfil many functions for the teacher and, even more so, for the learners. It can serve as a resource for presentation material, provide activities for practice and interaction, act as a reference for grammar and vocabulary, and as a source of ideas for classroom activities (Cunningsworth, 1995). Working with a well-chosen textbook can significantly enrich the teaching and learning experience. It can also provide a clear structure of activities, especially when teachers adopt a critically selective and creative approach and shape the content to learners' needs (McGrath, 2016: 16).

Language teaching materials should reflect the reality of language use and help learners to develop intercultural awareness and sensitivity

(Tomlinson, 2003: 22). The textbook therefore serves not only as the interface between learner and language, but also between learner and foreign cultures and societies (Hotho, 1996: 20). In the case of German as a foreign language, this means the full spectrum of German-speaking countries, their cultures and societies. While there has been progress among publishers to ensure that textbooks avoid social bias and ethnocentrism (Richards, 2015: 614), not all modern textbooks are exemplary when it comes to diversity, making this one of the key areas to consider in textbook selection (see Funk, 2004, for a summary of common didactic-methodological and pedagogical shortcomings of textbooks). Ultimately, any textbook should enable learners to develop intercultural communicative competence (as described by Byram, 1997).

What to consider in textbook selection for the *ab initio* classroom

Language practitioners in charge of designing language modules in higher education usually have the freedom to adopt any materials they consider the best fit for their particular teaching and learning situation. Arguably, this freedom is greater than ever, with the language teaching community no longer being restricted by often limiting discussions about the best method of teaching languages. Teaching in the 'postmethod condition' empowers educators to develop a pedagogy that is local and context-sensitive and informed by principled pragmatism (Kumaravadivelu, 2006: 67). In order to adopt and adapt materials successfully, teachers who choose a textbook therefore need to possess detailed knowledge of the target group and the teaching objectives, an awareness of suitable teaching materials available for their context, and the ability to analyse these materials (Rösler, 1996: 38).

An *ab initio* language programme at university level, in particular as part of a language degree programme, generally requires students to acquire a wide range of linguistic forms, vocabulary and communicative skills within a short period, often allowing only little time for application and placing significant emphasis on performance and performance testing (Hotho, 1996: 10). In order to scaffold this accelerated pace of learning, working with materials that support learners in making progress quickly and sustainably is key. In the light of different needs and preferences of individual learners, any chosen materials also need to do justice to a variety of learning styles (see, for instance, Ünsal, 2018, on the importance of learning styles in language teaching).

Since *ab initio* courses are often front-loaded with a large amount of grammatical input, this tends to favour more analytical learning styles over more affective approaches to learning. Thus it comes as no surprise that conventional language textbooks designed for beginners 'tend to be biased towards the learning preferences of analytic, left brain learners at the expense of more experiential, right brain learners' (Islam, 2003: 261). To ensure that all learners have equal learning opportunities and chances to succeed, teachers need to be aware of such shortcomings in textbooks and mitigate them by making use of supplementary activities, materials and resources.

As Islam reminds us, the language acquisition process can be enhanced 'when language input is relevant, significant, salient, engaging and of interest to the learner' and teachers and learners generally prefer topics that allow for imagination, creation and affective engagement in addition to topics that cover everyday survival language (Islam, 2003: 258). *Ab initio* textbooks are not simply a tool that enables learners to deal with basic everyday situations. They also have to engage learners by offering them a variety of topics, texts and activities.

Monolingual versus bilingual textbooks

A key decision to be made when selecting a textbook for language courses is whether to adopt a monolingual textbook, using only the target language, or a textbook that draws upon both the target language and English as languages of instruction. Rösler and Schart (2016: 486) argue that while the linguistic and cultural background of learners plays a significant role in the learning process, monolingual textbooks tend to ignore these factors due to economic considerations or a dogmatic monolingualism. Yet they stress that even if the learners' linguistic and cultural background is taken into account, this is not necessarily a sign of quality in itself. Of more importance is the effective use of this background and its integration into the concept that underlies the textbook (Rösler and Schart, 2016).

The main argument for choosing a monolingual textbook is that it provides an immersive language environment by exposing the learner solely to the target language. This helps to encourage students to negotiate different language situations in the target language from the very start of their exposure to it. Monolingual textbooks further engage students in additional target language reading practice through numerous instructions and expose students frequently to certain grammatical forms, such as the imperative. Working with a monolingual textbook therefore entails certain advantages and for the context of German *ab initio* offers a considerably larger range of textbooks to choose from.

Since all learners in the *ab initio* classroom at British universities tend to be proficient in English, adopting a textbook that draws on both German and English as languages of instruction is another option. This allows the textbook to adopt a contrastive approach, highlighting key lexical and syntactical differences between English and German in an attempt to draw attention to common pitfalls in language production. A bilingual textbook can also help to ensure that learners are able to comprehend all instructions from the beginning. This can be particularly relevant for intensive *ab initio* courses, which expect learners to make progress quickly and to complete a substantial number of activities autonomously.

For intermediate and advanced levels, the benefits of using a monolingual textbook are compelling. However, for the *ab initio* language teaching context, a textbook that also draws on English can help in implementing a syllabus built on fast progression, particularly at the early stages of the course. Ultimately though, it depends on the preference and teaching methodology of the practitioner in charge of designing the course which option represents a better choice for their course.

Ab initio textbooks in use at British universities

The market for German beginner textbooks is constantly evolving, with new textbooks being published on a regular basis. Information gathered through a German *Ab Initio* Network meeting in 2017 indicates that a wide range of German beginners' textbooks is in use at *ab initio* courses at universities in England, Scotland and Wales. The list, which aims to give an idea of textbooks in use and is not exhaustive, includes the following textbooks, with number of institutions reporting use of textbook in brackets (see reference list for full bibliographical details): *Begegnungen* (1), *DaF Kompakt* (2), *Delfin* (1), *Menschen* (1), *Motive (4)*, *Neue Horizonte* (2), *Studio D* (1), *Themen aktuell* (2), *Wie geht's?* (1), *Willkommen* (2).

The list suggests that most language courses work with monolingual textbooks from German publishers. Three of these textbooks use both German and English as languages of instruction, two of them from American publishers (*Neue Horizonte* and *Wie geht's?*) and only one from a British publisher (*Willkommen*). It is perhaps not surprising that there does not seem to be a clear favourite beginners' German textbook for use at British universities since there is no textbook that specifically targets British university students. This also helps explain the use of American textbooks *Neue Horizonte* and *Wie geht's?*, which are more directly targeted at college and university students. While textbooks in printed form or as e-books from established publishers still represent the most commonly adopted teaching and learning resources together with the multimedia resources and materials for virtual learning environments they provide, it remains to be seen how new technology may affect this in the future (see Chapter 12, this volume, for a discussion of app-based learning and the potential of virtual and augmented reality for language learning).

Adopting a textbook evaluation approach

The previous sections have highlighted some key considerations for selecting a textbook. Given the numerous factors that need to be considered, it is helpful to adopt a systematic approach that reduces the pitfall of personal subjectivity. Using a textbook evaluation to select suitable materials has been a long-established approach in this respect and a multitude of guidelines and checklists for evaluating textbooks for language teaching have been developed (see, for instance, Cunningsworth, 1995; Funk, 2004; Bernstein and Guadalupe García Llampallas, 2015). Referring to existing checklists is useful, but inevitably these lists of criteria need to be adapted to the particular teaching and learning situation. It can be a challenge to create a checklist short enough to be workable in a real-world context, yet detailed enough to allow for a meaningful evaluation. Importantly, any textbook evaluation should assess the textbook from the perspective of the learners rather than analysing a textbook as a printed product (Rösler, 2012: 48).

Textbook evaluations should not be limited to impressionistic approaches or based on ad hoc lists of subjective criteria, but be driven by a set of principles that allows for greater validity and reliability and requires teachers to engage with their own theory of teaching and learning (Tomlinson, 2003: 17–18). Using a criterion-referenced evaluation helps to reduce subjectivity and makes an evaluation more principled, rigorous, systematic, and reliable (Tomlinson, 2003: 23). The arrangement of individual criteria into categories facilitates focus and enables generalisations to be made, while giving a score for each criterion allows some sets of criteria to be weighted more heavily than others (Tomlinson, 2003: 30–2). This process allows practitioners to decide which aspects they consider particularly important.

A useful approach is to combine a first impressionistic assessment with a more detailed one based on differentiated criteria, as this tends to identify both the strengths and shortcomings of a textbook (Niewalda, Schmidt and Sakamoto, 2016: 630). An impressionistic overview can provide a useful general introduction to the material and be particularly appropriate to compiling a shortlist for more detailed analysis or looking at new material that teachers may consider adopting at a later stage (Cunningsworth, 1995: 1). Combining an impressionistic overview with a more in-depth examination of a representative sample of the textbook, such as one or two units, can yield particularly useful insights into the balance of activities and skills, the potential for learner participation, the amount of new language that is introduced as well as opportunities for consolidation (Cunningsworth, 1995: 2).

Example of how to conduct an *ab initio* textbook evaluation

Since each teaching and learning context is unique, it is only the language teaching professional in charge of the course who can make an informed decision on the most suitable materials for their learners and their teaching methodology. This chapter can therefore not make any general recommendations on the best textbook for an *ab initio* language module. What it can provide, however, is a set of criteria that is particularly relevant for *ab initio* language courses at British universities and apply it to a selection of textbooks with the aim of demonstrating how to conduct a textbook evaluation that is both insightful and manageable.

This set of criteria, which I present below, is in parts informed by criteria put forward elsewhere. A key influence has been a checklist for evaluation and selection developed by Cunningsworth (1995: 3–4) that is organised in a manageable set of relevant criteria. The list generally holds up well even if it was published over 25 years ago, but one needs to bear in mind that the area of interculturality is largely missing. The first two categories of my criteria 'aims and approaches' and 'design and organisation' are direct borrowings from Cunningsworth (1995: 3) while the individual criteria of these categories differ as I tailored them to the *ab initio* context.

My third category of 'systematic development of language skills' and fourth category of 'interculturality' were informed by Bernstein and Guadalupe García Llampallas (2015: 108). They present a list of criteria that they developed for use at language centres in particular, consisting of

13 categories and 119 individual criteria. Applying their comprehensive list has the potential to subject a textbook to a deep analysis, so would be useful for those looking for a detailed list that also allows for weighting criteria according to their relevance for the particular learning and teaching context. To include interculturality as a category was further inspired by Neuburg and Ott (n.d.: 2) who include this aspect in their category 'Landeskunde & Interkulturalität', along with four other categories (grammar, vocabulary, texts & content, learner orientation) and four further dimensions of analysis (pronunciation and listening comprehension, visual design, available media, external factors). While their checklist provides useful criteria for the evaluation of grammar and vocabulary in particular, assessing the development of the four skills could be more systematic (see Funk, 2004, for a more systematic presentation of the four skills). As a fifth category I added 'progression and learning styles' since a fast progression and fostering autonomous learning constitute particularly pertinent features to many *ab initio* higher education courses.

Overall, the checklist I put forward here contains 20 individual criteria grouped in five categories:

1. **Aims and approaches**
1.1 Target audience
1.2 Transparent presentation of intended learning outcomes
1.3 Methodological and theoretical approaches
1.4 Adopting a contrastive approach that addresses key linguistic differences between German and English
1.5 Clear reference to the Common European Framework of Reference for Languages (CEFR)

2. **Design and organisation**
2.1 Choice of topics that are engaging and motivating for university students
2.2 Clear and systematic structure of units
2.3 The use of different registers and, where appropriate, use of authentic language
2.4 Available components and supplementary materials
2.5 Provision of multimedia resources that can support a blended learning approach

3. **Systematic development of language skills**
3.1 Covering all four skills in an integrated manner with sufficient opportunities for practice and consolidation

3.2 Systematic introduction of relevant vocabulary in context and with a range of suitable exercises

3.3 Systematic development of grammatical competence that introduces grammar topics in context and offers sufficient opportunity for practice and consolidation

3.4 Integrated pronunciation exercises, covering pronunciation, intonation and prosody

3.5 Systematic development and practice of communicative and pragmatic skills

4. Interculturality

4.1 Embedding content in cultural context and conveying relevant cultural knowledge, without fostering stereotypes

4.2 Fostering intercultural awareness and raising awareness of learners' perception of their own cultural background

5. Progression and learning styles

5.1 Support of fast progression with sufficient opportunities for revision and consolidation

5.2 Fostering of autonomous learning

5.3 Activation of different learning styles

These criteria are applied to a selection of two German *ab initio* coursebooks: *DaF kompakt neu* and *Neue Horizonte*. Both titles represent textbooks produced for young adult learners attending courses with a fast progression. They differ in that one is monolingual and by a German publisher (*DaF kompakt neu*) while the other is bilingual and by an American publisher (*Neue Horizonte*).

The textbook evaluation in Table 7.1 shows that while the two textbooks cover comparable topics, they adopt different approaches in the way they present and structure materials and learning activities. The task-based approach of *DaF kompakt neu* provides ample opportunities to develop receptive skills and encounter different registers and authentic language. It is clearly mapped to CEFR levels, can be used flexibly and provides useful supplementary materials. For use in fast-paced university courses, teachers might need to supplement this textbook with materials to develop the productive skills more effectively, more systematic grammar overviews as well as additional video and interactive online materials.

Neue Horizonte follows a contrastive approach, presenting grammar topics systematically in English, with regular opportunities for revision

Table 7.1: Textbook evaluation results of *DaF kompakt neu* and *Neue Horizonte*. Source: Author

	DaF kompakt neu A1–B1 (Kursbuch and Übungsbuch)	*Neue Horizonte (including Student Activities Manual)*
1. Aims and approaches		
1.1	The book is targeted at university students and young professionals who plan to spend time in a German-speaking country, either studying or working.	The primary target audience is college and university students.
1.2	The table of contents provides an overview of productive and receptive language goals ('*Sprachhandlungen*') and grammar topics of each unit. The former are reinforced at the top of pages within units to remind learners of intended learning outcomes.	Each unit outlines the content at the beginning, including communicative functions and cultural topics. At the end of each unit, learners are invited to reflect on their mastery of the unit's intended learning outcomes.
1.3	The focus is on a communicative approach, preparing learners linguistically and culturally for topics and situations they might encounter. Grammar topics are derived from each unit's topics and speech acts.	Diversified methodology, with a focus on functional grammar-based learning, complemented with a communicative approach and some translation tasks.
1.4	As a monolingual textbook produced for an international market, a contrastive approach is not adopted, but the *Übungsbuch* encourages reflections on differences between German and other languages.	The book follows a contrastive approach, including regular English instructions, grammar explanations and translation exercises. This can be useful in an accelerated learning approach, but the book misses a chance in not utilizing more German meta language for instructions in later units.
1.5	The book is clearly mapped onto CEFR levels A1, A2 and B1 and aims at preparing students for official B1 exams.	There is no reference to CEFR levels.
2. Design and organisation		
2.1	Topics are generally based around university and work life. The task-based approach focuses on conveying factual knowledge and application of the language.	The topics in the first units are of a general nature, but later units include university life and more cultural topics.
2.2	Clear structure, with each chapter consisting of three sub-units that guide learners through a wide variety of communicative exercises. Each unit ends with an overview of vocabulary, useful expressions for speech acts and grammar structures.	Clear structure of units, with each unit following a similar approach, leading learners from initial dialogues through a presentation of vocabulary and grammar topics to longer reading passages.

2.3	The book covers different registers, ranging from colloquial to formal bureaucratic language, and uses authentic language convincingly. Learners are made aware of language variations among German-speaking countries.	A range of registers is used for both spoken and written language. Authentic language is mostly used in reading texts. The introduction of modal particles from the start aims to foster authentic language use, but may confuse students at this early stage.
2.4	The textbook can be purchased as separate books for CEFR levels A1 to B1, with each book including both the *Kursbuch* and the *Übungsbuch*. Alternatively, you can opt for a standalone *Kursbuch* for each of the three CEFR levels and a separate *Übungsbuch*. You can also purchase an interactive e-book version. An additional *Intensivtrainer Wortschatz und Grammatik* is available for each of the three levels.	For use at British universities, the international edition of *Neue Horizonte* is most suitable. The *Student Activities Manual* complements the textbook with exercises for each unit and for further revision.
2.5	The *Klett Augmented App* provides access to all audio files for listening comprehension exercises, which you can also access in the digital version of the textbook. The website offers an answer key to exercises and grammar explanations in English as well as some interactive exercises for A1 level. The digital version of the book is a useful tool in blended learning, but it would be helpful if video materials and more interactive activities were also supplied.	The textbook website provides a range of interactive online materials, some freely accessible and some only available to premium users. At present, some of the online resources seem somewhat outdated.
3. Systematic development of language skills		
3.1	The focus of the *Kursbuch* is on receptive skills with many reading and listening exercises throughout all units. The reading texts in each unit are of different types and mostly focus on practical and factual situations. Longer types, e.g. drawing on literary texts, are rare. There could be a greater variety of tasks to develop the productive skills, especially with regards to freer forms of oral communication.	The focus lies more on grammar and vocabulary acquisition and consolidation than covering all four skills. There are regular writing exercises and a suitable range of text types, but reading comprehension exercises lack variety. Some speaking exercise topics seem random and lack scaffolding for freer speaking, while others are too grammar-focused. Listening comprehension is confined to a separate section in the activity manual, with exercises based on videos that are not very engaging for university students.

3.2	The book introduces vocabulary in context and the *Übungsbuch* provides a good range of engaging exercises for consolidation. At the end of each unit, there is an overview of new vocabulary, but this would benefit from providing grammatical information on separable verbs as well as strong and irregular verb forms.	Each unit has two clearly marked sections that introduce new vocabulary complete with an English translation. Vocabulary is relevant and practiced in both the textbook and the activity manual, with scope for more engaging exercises.
3.3	Grammar topics are integrated well into the units and introduced in an inductive way, inviting learners to derive the rules themselves from examples. While this can be an effective approach, it might become time-consuming when applied to up to six grammar topics per unit. Each unit ends with an overview of grammar, but with little explanation added.	There is a strong focus on developing grammatical knowledge and competence in a deductive manner. Presentation of grammar topics is clear. However, with up to seven grammatical topics per unit and grammar topics not always well-integrated within the wider context of the units, this volume might overwhelm some students. The *Student Activities Manual* includes regular 'Summary and Review' sections that are helpful for revision and consolidation.
3.4	In the *Übungsbuch* there are pronunciation and intonation exercises for each unit, which makes them feel more like an add-on, rather than being integrated into the core *Kursbuch*. The exercises as such are engaging and comprehensive, covering a wide range of pronunciation and intonation topics. The inclusion of the affective dimension around emotions is exemplary.	Pronunciation exercises are confined to the lab manual section of the activities manual. Accompanying audio files are only accessible in the premium part of the website.
3.5	The task-based approach focuses on enabling learners to deal with the communicative demands of everyday student and working life in an appropriate manner, raising awareness of how to adjust speech acts in line with the speaker's communicative intents.	Communicative goals tend to be integrated into grammar practice exercises in ways that are not always conducive to the development of communication skills embedded in a variety of social contexts. There is some helpful guidance on what to pay attention to in written forms of communication.

4. Interculturality		
4.1	From the start, the integrated approach embeds content well in its cultural context. The full range of German-speaking countries is covered, but the focus is on fairly bite-sized, factual information, with scope for deeper insights and addressing more affective dimensions.	Reading texts and writing tasks are embedded well within cultural contexts. Each unit includes an almanac with cultural information. The themes of units ten to 15 focus on cultural topics, dealing with Germany past and present as well as Switzerland and Austria, with the last unit being dedicated to cultural diversity. While it is good to see diversity included, it would be preferable to see this more integrated throughout the units.
4.2	Intercultural awareness is fostered through reflections in the *Kursbuch* and from A2 level increasingly in the *Übungsbuch*, inviting learners to reflect on their own cultural background and intercultural differences.	The focus is more on conveying cultural knowledge. At times, students are invited to reflect on intercultural differences, but not in a very systematic manner.
5. Progression and learning styles		
5.1	The book has been designed for fast progression at a manageable pace. This is aided by the integration of tasks, although more opportunities for revision and consolidation would be beneficial.	There is a fast progression covering a large number of grammatical topics. Scaffolding this through the use of English for explanations and consolidation exercises is helpful for learners.
5.2	Autonomous learning is mostly fostered in the *Übungsbuch* from A2 level by inviting learners to do their own research on topics or engage in project-based learning. The inclusion of answer keys to all exercises and transcripts for listening tasks is helpful in allowing learners to complete these tasks independently.	Autonomous learning is fostered through regular revision sections in the activities manual and on the textbook website.
5.3	There is a focus on analytical, cognitive, and auditory ways of learning, with scope for more kinaesthetic learning styles.	There is a focus on analytical, cognitive learning, with scope for addressing more auditory and kinaesthetic learning styles.

and consolidation while also providing longer reading passages in authentic language, including from literary sources. Unfortunately, it provides little variety in the exercises it includes for reading comprehension and the tasks intended to develop communicative skills tend to be too grammar focused in their design. For effective use in *ab initio* university courses, teachers might need to provide supplementary materials to develop students' listening comprehension skills and work on pronunciation and intonation, in particular.

Conclusion

Acknowledging that the ideal textbook does not exist is a truism in language education but arguably the current choice of textbooks has improved in recent decades since Rösler (1996: 38) lamented in the mid-1990s: 'the question is how to choose from the large number of available textbooks those which are the least unsuitable for a specific target group and its teaching objectives'. Language practitioners today can choose from a range of textbooks for the *ab initio* German classroom, and modern textbooks tend to reflect the developments in language teaching, putting an increased focus on the authenticity of language content as well as links to international benchmarks and standards (Richards, 2015: 599).

However, with a lack of textbooks designed for the particular context of *ab initio* language courses at British universities, selecting the most appropriate textbook is not a straightforward process. As the example of the textbook evaluation of two *ab initio* textbooks has shown, each textbook adopts different approaches and puts different emphasis on the development of individual skills. The identification of strengths and weaknesses of textbooks is key not only in selecting the most appropriate textbook, but also in identifying how to adapt and supplement it for best use in the classroom.

The evaluation therefore does not stop with the selection of a textbook; rather, the reflective process of evaluation continues after the implementation period (Brown, 1995: 151). This entails assessment of whether the textbook remains the most appropriate one for the particular context and which additional materials and activities can enrich the learning experience. The inclusion of a portfolio element as part of the course assessment may, for instance, be one way of allowing students to engage with authentic language and cultural input beyond the textbook (see Chapter 13, this volume, for an example of using a portfolio to foster autonomous learning).

With blended learning approaches on the rise, modern textbooks face the challenge of continuous adaption and evolution in order to stay a relevant resource for today's language classroom. As the textbook evaluation in this chapter indicates, providing well-integrated online resources is not always a strength of current *ab initio* textbooks, but something that language practitioners will be increasingly expecting. Providing more integrated, innovative digital learning materials that can enhance virtual learning environments will therefore be key in offering materials that can be used flexibly in a variety of, increasingly blended or entirely online, learning and teaching settings.

References

Bernstein, N. and Guadalupe García Llampallas, C. (2015) 'Ein Verfahrensvorschlag zur Lehrwerkanalyse für DaF-Sprachenzentren'. *Deutsch als Fremdsprache* 52:2, 103–12.

Brown, J. (1995) *The Elements of Language Curriculum: A systematic approach to program development*. Boston, MA: Heinle.

Byram, M. (1997) *Teaching and Assessing Intercultural Communicative Competence*. Clevedon: Multilingual Matters.

Cunningsworth, A. (1995) *Choosing Your Coursebook*. Oxford: Heinemann.

Funk, H. (2004) 'Qualitätsmerkmale von Lehrwerken prüfen – ein Verfahrensvorschlag'. *Babylonia* 3, 41–7.

Hotho, S. (1996) 'Language teaching methodologies and coursebooks. Paradigms, changes and choices'. In *Ab initio Language Learning: A guide to good practice in universities and colleges: The example of German*, edited by G. Leder, N. Reimann and R. Walsh, 10–27. London: CILT.

Islam, C. (2003) 'Materials for beginners'. In *Developing Materials for Language Teaching*, edited by B. Tomlinson, 256–74. London: Continuum.

Kumaravadivelu, B. (2006) 'TESOL methods: Changing tracks, challenging trends'. *TESOL Quarterly* 40:1, 59–78.

McGrath, I. (2016) *Materials Evaluation and Design for Language Teaching*, second edition. Edinburgh: Edinburgh University Press.

Neuburg, U. and Ott C. (n.d.) *Analysedimensionen der Lehrwerksanalyse*. Online. www.daad.de/medien/6_workshop_ott_neuburg_lehrwerksanalyse_fragedimensionen.pdf (accessed 20 April 2021).

Neuner, G. (1989) 'Lehrwerke'. In *Handbuch Fremdsprachenunterricht*, edited by K. Bausch, H. Christ, W. Hüllen and H. Krumm, 240–3. Tübingen: A. Francke.

Niewalda, K., Schmidt, M. and Sakamoto, S. (2016) 'Ergänzungsvorschläge für Hörverstehensübungen in deutschen Lehrwerken im universitären Daf-Unterricht in Japan'. *Info DaF 6*, 623–46.

Richards, J. (2015) *Key Issues in Language Teaching*. Cambridge: Cambridge University Press.

Rösler, D. (1996) 'The context of ab initio language teaching. Factors influencing the development of ab initio courses'. In *Ab Initio Language Learning: A guide to good practice in universities and colleges: The example of German*, edited by G. Leder, N. Reimann and R. Walsh, 28–43. London: CILT.

Rösler, D. (2012) *Deutsch als Fremdsprache: Eine Einführung*. Stuttgart: Metzler.

Rösler, D. and Schart, M. (2016) 'Die Perspektivenvielfalt der Lehrwerksanalyse – und ihr weißer Fleck'. *Info DaF* 43:5, 483–93.

Tomlinson, B. (2003) 'Materials evaluation'. In *Developing Materials for Language Teaching*, edited by B. Tomlinson, 15–36. London: Continuum.

Ünsal, G. (2018) 'A study on the importance of learning styles in foreign language teaching'. *International Journal of Languages' Education and Teaching* 6:2, 184–91.

Textbooks

Aufderstraße, H., Bock, H., Eisfeld, K.-H., Gerdes, M., Holthaus, H. and Müller, J. (2003) *Themen aktuell 1. Kursbuch und Arbeitsbuch. Niveaustufe A1*. Munich: Hueber.

Aufderstraße, H., Müller, J. and Storz, T. (2003). *Delfin. Lehrwerk für Deutsch als Fremdsprache. Niveaustufe A1. Lehrbuch und Arbeitsbuch*. Munich: Hueber.

Braun, B., Doubek M., Fügert N., Kotas O., Marquardt Langermann M., Nied Curcio M., Sander I., Schäfer N., Schweiger K., Trebesius-Bensch U. and Walter M. (2016) *DaF kompakt neu A1-B1. Kursbuch*. Stuttgart: Ernst Klett Sprachen.

Braun, B., Doubek, M., Fügert, N., Kotas, O., Marquardt Langermann, M., Nied Curcio, M., Sander, I., Schäfer, N., Schweiger, K., Trebesius-Bensch, U., Vitale, R. and Walter, M. (2016) *DaF kompakt neu A1-B1. Übungsbuch*. Stuttgart: Ernst Klett Sprachen.

Buscha, A. and Szita, S. (2006) *Begegnungen. Sprachniveau A1+. Integriertes Kurs- und Arbeitsbuch für Deutsch als Fremdsprache*. Leipzig: Schubert Verlag.

Crocker, E. (2014) *Student Activities Manual. Neue Horizonte. Introductory German*, eighth edition. Boston, MA: Heinle, Cengage Learning.

Dollenmayer, D. and Hansen, T. (2014) *Neue Horizonte. Introductory German*, international edition. Boston, MA: Heinle, Cengage Learning.

Funk, H., Demme, S. and Kuhn, C. (2005) *Studio d. Deutsch als Fremdsprache, A1. Gesamtband: Kurs- und Übungsbuch*. Berlin: Cornelsen.

Glas-Peters, S., Pude, A. and Reimann, M. (2012) *Menschen. Deutsch als Fremdsprache, A1. Arbeitsbuch*. Munich: Hueber.

Krenn, W. and Puchta, H. (2014) *Motive. Kompaktkurs DaF, A1. Kursbuch. Deutsch als Fremdsprache*. Munich: Hueber.

Krenn, W. and Puchta, H. (2015) *Motive. Kompaktkurs DaF, A1. Arbeitsbuch. Deutsch als Fremdsprache*. Munich: Hueber.

Schenke, H. and Coggle, P. (2018) *Willkommen! German beginner's course: Activity book*, third edition. London: John Murray Learning.

Schenke, H. and Coggle, P. (2018) *Willkommen! German beginner's course: Coursebook*, third edition. London: John Murray Learning.

Sevin, D., Sevin, I. and Brockman, B. (2015) *Wie geht's? An introductory German course*, tenth edition. Boston, MA: Cengage Learning.

Specht, F., Evans, S. and Pude, A. (2020) *Menschen. Deutsch als Fremdsprache, A1. Kursbuch*. Munich: Hueber.

8
Intercultural awareness in the teaching and learning of German: the case of *ab initio*

Eva Gossner and Dagmar Paulus

Introduction

The concept of learning a foreign language often evokes first and foremost the notion of vocabulary lists and grammar rules, of conversation practice and writing drills. In other words, the focus tends to be on the linguistic aspects of the language that one wants to learn, and less on the culture associated with that language. In order to acquire both linguistic as well as intercultural competence, however, it is vital for learners as well as for teachers of a foreign language to take cultural aspects into account too.

In recent years, the spotlight has begun to shift away from an idealised native speaker as benchmark for foreign language competency (Wilkinson, 2012: 296). Instead, researchers underline that, in addition to acquiring linguistic skills, language learners have to be able to navigate an unfamiliar cultural context with all its complex implications and that the language classroom needs to equip them for this purpose (Noels, Yashima and Zhang, 2012: 58). Indeed, speakers of any language may find themselves in situations requiring intercultural skills even within their own culture. As Wilkinson points out, 'intercultural competence may be called for anywhere and at any moment' (Wilkinson, 2012: 301). For Mahon and Cushner, it is in fact the very nature of contemporary society that calls for language learners to acquire intercultural competence. They demand that 'educators must be able to prepare their students for a dynamic, changing, and global world' (Mahon and Cushner, 2012: 434). In such a setting, they argue, intercultural communication situations may arise at any time and place.

Other researchers agree, pointing out that 'regardless of the level of familiarity, a variety of sociopsychological and sociocultural processes operate within every intercultural interaction' (Noels, Yashima and Zhang, 2012: 52). Likewise, Risager notes that '[a]part from developing the students' communicative (dialogic) competence in the target language, language teaching ought also as far as possible to enable students to develop into multilingually and multiculturally aware world citizens' (Risager, 2007: 1). Language teaching, therefore, should go beyond the mere teaching of grammar and vocabulary. Successful intercultural communication requires participants to be equipped with at least a certain awareness of the unfamiliar culture that goes beyond linguistic proficiency. In their 2012 study, Noels and colleagues underline how

> [b]y definition, language learners lack the competence or the confidence to interpret host culture perspectives and/or the communication skills, including language skills, necessary to achieve effective communication outcomes … . These difficulties can contribute to poorer intercultural adjustment. To be an effective communicator, then, one must become more knowledgeable and skilled in the ways of the target culture. (Noels, Yashima and Zhang, 2012: 58)

In order to become a skilled intercultural communicator, it is not sufficient to acquire and use linguistic knowledge. Instead, one also needs to attain awareness of other cultures, other perspectives, other cultural contexts and signifiers (Wilkinson, 2012: 296). Byram supports this notion: 'Other perspectives such as sociocultural and social competence can be just as important' (Byram, 1997: 3). Foreign language teaching is concerned with communication,

> but this has to be understood as more than the exchange of information and sending of messages. … Even the exchange of information is dependent upon understanding on how what one says or writes will be perceived and interpreted in another cultural context; it depends on the ability to decentre and take up the perspective of the listener or reader. (Byram, 1997: 12)

Argyle also points out that non-verbal communication can vary between cultures and cause misunderstanding and confusion: 'When two people from two different cultures meet, there is infinite scope for misunderstanding and confusion' (Argyle, 1983: 189).

Intercultural communication settings are increasingly the norm in language classrooms. In a globalised world, we may find teachers and students from different cultural backgrounds who do not share the same first language. In such a scenario, Wilkinson notes,

> [t]eachers and pupils … require intercultural competence and skills of the intercultural speaker already at the point of departure – the foreign language classroom – as they are already crossing multiple boundaries here, long before they cross the nation-state border into the country of the foreign language they are learning. (Wilkinson, 2012: 298)

On the whole, it appears that research into the matter is quite unanimous about the fact that intercultural awareness is an important part of the language learning process and should therefore be part of the curriculum. However, while the need for culture as part of language curricula has been widely acknowledged in theory, it has not yet been implemented to the same degree in practice (Risager, 2007: 5). In German language classes in schools or language institutes, *Landeskunde* is part of the curriculum, a term usually translated as regional studies. *Landeskunde* covers general knowledge of the target culture, including geography, history, art, cuisine, customs and traditions. In many German textbooks, and *ab initio* textbooks in particular, *Landeskunde* also features, but cultural knowledge in the sense we defined above remains rare. As a rule, the focus here remains on the acquisition of linguistic skills, with the occasional bolt-on of a few short texts and exercises based on *Landeskunde*.

In the case of *ab initio* learners of German at UK universities, the need to familiarise students with the culture of German-speaking countries has additional relevance because a year abroad in direct contact with the target culture is an integral part of many degree programmes. How can we prepare *ab initio* students of German for this experience? They have not spent years at school learning about the German-speaking countries as their post-A-level peers have. What examples of cultural knowledge might these students be equipped with before they set out to encounter German culture for themselves? What are feasible ways of teaching German culture in a curriculum that, as a rule, is already packed with linguistic subject matter?

In order to address these questions, we will first discuss what the term 'culture' means for us in this context. Next, we will look at existing textbooks and outline to what degree they contain exercises or texts on cultural knowledge. Finally, we will present suggestions of how to intertwine cultural and linguistic aspects when teaching German to *ab initio* students in higher education.

Defining intercultural awareness and cultural codes

What does the term 'culture' mean? Claus Altmayer provides the following definition: 'Mit *Kultur* … beziehen wir uns … auf die Ebene der Bedeutungen, die wir der uns umgebenden Wirklichkeit, unseren Mitmenschen, uns selbst und unserem Handeln zuschreiben' (By the term culture we refer to the level of meaning that we attach to our reality, our fellow human beings, ourselves and our actions) (Altmayer, 2017: 11; our translation). Central here is the notion that culture resides not just in museums, schools or universities but that it permeates all aspects of an individual's existence in society. Culture, in this sense, has an everyday dimension that is highly relevant in the context of language learning, as linguistic exchange happens in everyday situations all the time. It is in the context of communicative situations involving speakers of a foreign language that intercultural awareness becomes relevant. Arasaratnam defines the term as follows:

> The phrase 'intercultural competence' typically describes one's effective and appropriate engagement with cultural differences. Intercultural competence has been studied as residing within a person (i.e., encompassing cognitive, affective, and behavioural capabilities of a person) and as a product of a context (i.e., co-created by the people and contextual factors involved in a particular situation). (Arasaratnam, 2016: n.p.)

In order to achieve this competence, it is necessary to combine the two aspects outlined by Arasaratnam: to develop awareness of elements that are the product of a context (that is, the target culture) and to make it part of each individual speaker's knowledge that they can then deploy in communication. Such elements can be customs and traditions, rules of social interaction as well as behavioural and communicative codes that native speakers often adhere to without being aware of them but which people from other cultural backgrounds need to learn and actively use in order to understand the other culture and, as a result, communicate successfully. For the purposes of this chapter, we call these elements cultural codes.

These codes differ from what many German textbooks call *Landeskunde*, that is, bite-size facts about a given country, such as its geography or history. While such factual knowledge of the target culture is certainly useful and important for a language learner to acquire, lack of this knowledge tends not to impede mutual understanding with a member of the foreign culture. If a speaker is not sufficiently aware of cultural codes, however, it can lead to misunderstandings, or even inadvertent rudeness.

A good example is the issue of when to use the formal way of addressing someone in German, 'Sie'. Learners whose native language is English may not be familiar with this concept, but they still have to use it on a daily basis nonetheless. The most straightforward explanation is that speakers use Sie in a formal context and du in more informal settings. But what counts as formal?

According to the current edition of Duden, the standard German dictionary, Sie is used for addressing adults who are neither relatives nor friends. Du, on the other hand, is for relatives, friends, children, animals and objects (Duden, n.d.). However, this is clearly not all there is to it, as the use of du has become much more widespread. In German advertising for example, the colloquial form has become increasingly common (Fronz, 2016). The use of du is now altogether much more widespread than it was in the past but there are still plenty of social situations where the use of Sie is required, even if the UK equivalent would be less formal. As a result, there is growing insecurity even among Germans when to use which pronoun (Schmedding, 2007).

When to address Germans by their first or by their surname mostly follows the same rules of Sie or du, perhaps with the exception that teachers will address students as Sie while using their first names. A slightly more complicated matter is the question of academic titles. Compared to the German-speaking countries, academic titles are less commonly used to address people in the UK. In Germany, this generally only extends to the titles Doctor and Professor, but in Austria, it is common practice to also address academics as Herr/Frau Magister (Mandl, 2005). Therefore, it would be beneficial for language textbooks to include not only the grammatical rules of application but also examples of when to use which form in different contexts, thereby taking into account the importance of intercultural competence in the language acquisition process. Teachers could add a short exercise, perhaps showing different social situations, and let students decide which pronoun or title would be appropriate in the given context.

Some may suggest that knowledge of such cultural codes can and should be taught primarily at higher levels in the language learning process, arguing that at the more basic level of ab initio, grammar and vocabulary acquisition is paramount. However, some cultural codes are embedded in the most basic features of language, such as the issue of how to address people. It would be quite unacceptable if a British person were to address an Austrian professor without using their academic title, let alone by their first name. These examples show that, in order for communication to be successful, it is vital for all participants to be aware of cultural codes. But unfortunately, none of the textbooks we studied includes specific guidelines explaining the matter of how to address people correctly.

German *ab initio* textbooks

Depending on the institution, *ab initio* courses usually cover levels A1 and A2 of the Common European Framework of Reference for Languages (CEFR) within one academic year, as shown in Chapter 1. So how do existing textbooks for *ab initio* students of German handle the issue of cultural codes? We looked at the following examples to evaluate the situation: *Berliner Platz* (Lemcke, 2010), *Begegnungen* (Buscha and Szita, 2007), *Motive* (Krenn and Puchta, 2016), *DaF kompakt neu*, chapters 1–18 (Braun et al., 2020) and *Themen aktuell* (Aufderstraße et al., 2009). All of these publications focus on *Landeskunde* throughout when addressing the topic of culture. Recurrent themes are German cities and their sights, especially Berlin and Munich, food culture, famous Germans such as artists or scientists and the educational system. *DaF kompakt* and *Berliner Platz* cover some aspects of everyday life in Germany, such as rules allocating chores to tenants in apartment blocks, waste sorting or the administrative process when going to the doctor. Apart from that, intercultural competence in the sense we outlined above hardly features at all. This is surprising, given that some of these aspects are closely linked to the process of language acquisition and use. For example, while the textbooks we analysed introduce the two forms of addressing, *Sie* and *du*, they do not explore the question of when each is appropriate in great detail. They just state that *Sie* is formal and *du* is not without giving concrete guidance.

Cultural and non-verbal communication: practical suggestions for teaching units at A1 and A2 level

As we have shown in the introductory section, there are several dimensions where problems may arise when people from different cultures communicate. The most obvious ones are linguistic differences. But there are also intercultural differences, verbal and non-verbal, which may pose a communicative challenge for language learners. This intercultural dimension includes for example kinesics (gestures, manners, postures, mannerisms), proxemics (personal space/distances), body adaptors (cosmetics, clothes) and also cultural memory (customs, festivals, texts, pictures, places, rites and so on) (Assmann, 2006: 368) – in short: this dimension is about the way of life in the other culture, including expected behaviour, values and living practices.

How can some of these dimensions and aspects form part of language lessons at A1 and A2 level? Byram points out that many aspects of non-verbal communication are often acquired unconsciously and may therefore be difficult to teach. He suggests that, rather than imitating a native speaker, it appears to be more important for the learner to compare their own and other cultures and look for similarities and differences, thus acquiring a better understanding of the other culture and ultimately achieving a higher degree of intercultural competence (Byram, 1997: 14). The next section explores and gives examples of how students can be encouraged to reflect on and deepen their intercultural competence, based on the topics of proxemics, cultural memory and gestures/facial expressions.

Proxemics

Interpersonal distancing can vary across cultures and people can feel threatened if their personal space is being invaded. Hall has identified four types of distances, namely public, social, personal and intimate (Hall, 1966: 116). 'In Germany, lots of physical distance and a moderate tone are appropriate in most situations. Hugging another person, patting them on the back or kissing their cheek is reserved for meetings with close friends and family members' (InterNations GO!, 2018). If a student is not aware of these unwritten rules that most people adhere to within the foreign country, then problems may arise. How can we introduce this aspect of non-verbal communication into the classroom?

The following classroom activity is based on a study titled 'Preferred interpersonal differences: a global comparison' (Haines, 2017).

In this study, researchers interviewed 8,943 people from 42 different countries to find out how close they could get to another person while still feeling comfortable. Participants in the study were given a graphic – which depicted two people standing two metres apart – and asked to indicate the point at which they would no longer feel comfortable in proximity to a close friend, a stranger, and a casual acquaintance. (Haines, 2017)

The activity covers four conventional linguistic topics while simultaneously making the student aware of non-verbal communication, in this instance, required personal space. It involves teaching and practising names of countries in German, numbers from one to 150, nationalities and comparisons based on proxemics.

1. Names of countries:
   a. Students receive a list of countries in German and are asked to match them up with their English equivalents.
   b. Numbers (1–150):
      – Students need to be familiar with basic numbers and the metric system (*Zentimeter/Meter*).
        Suggested activity:
        Two students stand in front of the class moving away from each other or closer to each other. Each time they move, the other students in the class need to estimate the distance between the two students in centimetres, write down their estimate and then call out their number. The actual distance can be measured with a measuring tape, or even better with a (typically German) *Meterstab* – a kind of foldable ruler. Points are awarded to the students who come closest.
      – Having established a feel for distance in centimetres, the students can then write down how far away they would need to be from a stranger not to feel uncomfortable. How would that compare with the distance they would normally keep with acquaintances?
   c. Nationalities:
      Using the given statistics in Figure 8.1, students answer country-specific questions: What is the average distance that Argentinians, Germans, Austrians, Swiss or British people keep from strangers?
   d. Comparisons:
      Again, using the statistics below, students make comparisons: In which country do people get closest to strangers without feeling uncomfortable? Where are people happier to stay closer to each other without feeling uncomfortable – Austria or Germany?
      More analytical questions for more advanced students:
      – How do Austria, Germany and Switzerland compare? Why do you think they differ?
      – Is your personal estimate in line with the statistics?
      – Which countries have the shortest social distances/the biggest social distances? What could the reasons be for these differences?
      – Analyse the second/third column.

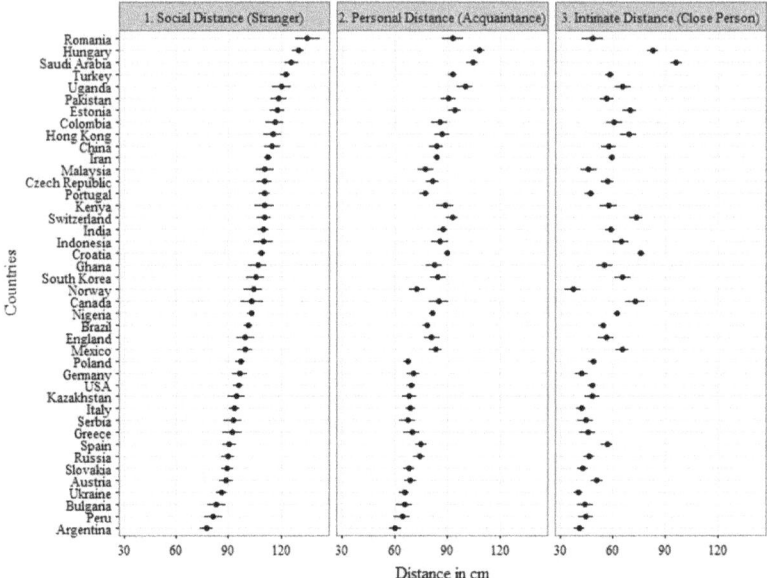

Figure 8.1 Mean values (cm) of social, personal and intimate distance across all nations. Source: Sorokowska et al. Reprinted by permission of SAGE Publications.

Cultural memory

In order to understand another culture and even become part of it, we need to understand and be aware of its cultural memory. Cultural memory includes not only customs and traditions but also texts, pictures, places, rites and so on (Assmann, 2006: 368). In the following section we offer some suggestions on ways to base language teaching on, for example, a specific custom and festival.

Cultural knowledge: 11 November

As an example, we have chosen 11 November, a day that means different things to different people. An unsuspecting French or British visitor to Germany might not only be taken by complete surprise about the role this day plays in the German calendar, but they may also be made to feel like an outsider. Equally, the same could happen to a German visitor to the UK.

This is because 11 November is a special day in many countries, but the cultural memories are very different. In the UK we remember all those who lost their lives in combat and at 11.00am many people observe a two-minute silence to mark the date of the end of the First World War in 1918.

By stark contrast, in some parts of Germany, the start of the 'fifth season', of Carnival, is celebrated on 11 November, starting exactly at 11.11am.

On that same day Germany also honours Sankt Martin (St Martin), a Roman soldier turned bishop, famous for his charity and good deeds and whose funeral took place on 11 November in the year 397. A St Martin's procession and, in many places, also a bonfire mark the day.

The following section gives suggestions on how to introduce learners of German to these 11 November celebrations at A1/A2 level.

Sankt Martin:

1. Fact-finding:

   Depending on their language level, learners could either do some research at home (that might include English sources for students at A1 level) or use the short video (see internet link 1b 'Die Geschichte von St. Martin') in order to be able to answer the following questions:

   a. Who was St Martin?

   b. Why is he celebrated?

   c. Why is goose a traditional dish on that day? Give two reasons. (One reason is explained in the short video, the other reason is based on the fact that a period of fasting starts on 12 November – 40 days before Christmas – and thus 11 November is the last chance to eat a substantial meal. Alternatively, it may be due to the fact that 11 November used to be the day when taxes had to be paid in crops or animals.)

   d. Students learn the song and sing along (link 1a) 'Ich geh mit meiner Laterne'.

   e. What are the connections between the St Martin's bonfire, the lanterns and Halloween?

2. Vocabulary exercise:

   a. The teacher shows a picture of St Martin on his horse, sharing his coat with a beggar:

   Students must describe the picture or come up with any word in connection with the picture. This could be 'rot, Pferd, Mantel, teilen, arm, Bettler, kalt'.

   b. Matching up vocabulary: students match up German and English words to do with St Martin's Day.

   c. Acting out the story of St Martin:

   Students could adopt some phrases and ideas from the video (link 1b), add their own ideas and create their own version of the story of St Martin.

   d. Watch authentic material (St Martin's procession: link 1d)

The official start of carnival:

The atmosphere in some German towns on 11 November – most notably Cologne, Düsseldorf and Mainz – stands in particular contrast to the UK; this is because 11 November marks the official beginning of carnival in Germany – the so-called 'fifth season' that ends on Ash Wednesday.

1. Fact-finding:
   a. Students do some research about carnival celebrations in their own countries and try to find answers as to when, how and why they celebrate carnival and present their findings in German.
   b. At the next stage, students research German carnival in order to answer questions like: Why is the official start on 11 November at 11.11am? What connotations does the number 11 have? What other words are used for *Karneval* and where? What does the word *Karneval* mean?
      What is the underlying idea of *Karneval*?
   c. Students discuss the differences (and the possible reasons) between German carnival and the carnival celebrations in their respective countries.

2. Vocabulary and grammar exercises:
   a. Students describe a typical photo of a carnival celebration.
   b. Students are asked to concentrate on colours: why are red, blue and white the dominating colours? (Cultural question: Why are some people dressed as Napoleonic soldiers?)
   c. The topic lends itself to practising/learning: ordinal numbers, seasons (five!), days of the week, the German names of important holidays, time expressions
      (von … bis, von … bis zum, am + day, um + time).
      – *Die Karnevalszeit geht vom 11. November bis (zum) Aschermittwoch. / Der Karneval beginnt am 11. November um 11 Uhr 11 und endet am Aschermittwoch.*
      – *Welches Datum (im jeweiligen Jahr) ist der Aschermittwoch/der Rosenmontag/der Altweiberdonnerstag etc. und was passiert an jenen Tagen?*
      – *Kulturelle Frage: Warum sind offizielle Partys ab Mitternacht am Aschermittwoch verboten?*

3. Watch authentic material: *Faschingsumzug in Köln* (link 2c)

German gestures and facial expressions:

InterNations GO!, a relocation company, points out '[our] gestures, facial expressions, and tone of voice say a lot more about us than the words we speak out loud. Not only that, these gestures and facial expressions also vary greatly from culture to culture' (Bruck, 2018: n.p.). Germans may not be known for their gestures or facial expressions, but there are some widely used German hand signals and facial expressions, and not knowing their meaning can lead to misinterpretation or confusion.

For the purpose of providing a teaching resource, we selected eight examples and present two ways of introducing them to the learner at beginners' level. Firstly, the teacher can act out the gestures and expressions, and students have to guess their meanings. Depending on the students' level of German, the language of the discussion could be German or English. Secondly, the teacher tells the students how to mimic these gestures and expressions by giving short commands, for example: 'Raise your right hand!'. Thus the teaching goal is twofold: discussions on the meanings of the gestures/expressions (and possibly how these meanings are expressed in different cultures) and learning how to form commands in German. The fact that German has three different types of imperative can easily be incorporated into the exercise.

The following section presents the selected examples of typical gestures and expressions, accompanied by suggestions (disguised as commands) of how to imitate them:

1. 'Are you mad?' (if vocalised at the same time, add: *Hast du einen Vogel?/Spinnst du?*)
    How to do it:
    • Raise your hand! / Tap your forehead with your index finger!
2. 'You have got to be kidding me' / 'That is madness' / '(S)he must be mad'
    How to do it:
    • Wave your hand in front of your face!
3. 'Good luck!' (if vocalised at the same time, add: *Ich drücke dir/euch/ Ihnen die Daumen*)
    How to do it:
    • Stretch out your arms! / Make a fist to enclose your thumb! (*ausstrecken* can be used as an example to teach separable verbs as commands)
4. Showing numbers to someone else with your hand: Germans start with and use the thumb for 'one', while British people start with and use the index finger for 'one'.
    How to do it:

- Number 3 = thumb + index finger + middle finger
  (Whereas in the anglophone world the number '3' is symbolised by the index finger, the middle finger and the ring finger.)
5. Saying/expressing 'Well done!' (in an academic context, for example at the end of a lecture)
   How to do it:
   - Lift your hand! / Knock against the surface of the table with your knuckles! / Do that quickly 5–7 times!
6. Showing that you are impressed (used in informal settings):
   How to do it:
   - Show surprise/astonishment with your eyes! / Pull back with your upper body! / Say *Boooooah* simultaneously!
7. Using/expressing sarcasm:
   How to do it:
   - Pull down one eyelid! / Keep talking!
8. Expressing 'Schadenfreude' (usually only used by children):
   How to do it:
   - Stick out your left index finger! / Rub over it gently with your right index finger! / Say *ätschebätsch* (or simply *ätsch*) at the same time!

Conclusion

Linguistic knowledge of a foreign language needs to be supplemented with cultural skills for the learner to feel comfortable and more at home in another culture. As mentioned in our introduction, Byram highlights the importance of the learner comparing their own and other cultures in order to achieve a higher degree of intercultural competence (Byram, 1997: 14). This goes beyond learning the details of the particular target culture. Ideally, language learners will become sensitised to such differences in general, and therefore be able to apply their intercultural skills in other contexts as well.

Most German coursebooks already include some specific comparative tasks on topics like the weather, the education system, celebrations and festivals, the political system and various geographical aspects, and we would advocate making best use of these tasks. However, this is only the first step towards becoming a good intercultural communicator. Successful communication is based not only on the acquired level of the language and an awareness of the differences of the cultures, but also on an awareness of non-language communication, behavioural and communicative codes, rules of social interaction and more in-depth knowledge of a country's customs, traditions and a country's history and geography.

Internet links (all accessed 27 May 2021)

1. St. Martin's Day:
   a. Song: 'Ich geh mit meiner Laterne'
      https://angelikasgerman.co.uk/ich-geh-mit-meiner-laterne/
   b. Video: Die Geschichte von St. Martin (4:11) (cartoon)
      www.youtube.com/watch?v=CdJPDlO3m6s&t=14s
   c. Der St. Martinstag: Hintergrund (in German)
      www.ndr.de/geschichte/Martinstag-Warum-feiern-wir-am-11-November-Sankt-Martin,martinstag106.html
   d. Martinsumzug und Martinsfeuer Konz 2016 (3:30)
      https://commons.wikimedia.org/w/index.php?title=File%3AMartinszug_und_Martinsfeuer_Konz_2016.webm

2. Carnival:
   a. Beginn am 11.11 um 11:11 (Text)
      www.t-online.de/leben/familie/id_52551444/karnevalsbeginn-am-11-11-start-in-die-fuenfte-jahreszeit.html
   b. Carnival photos and explanations in English:
      www.dw.com/en/carnival-starts-on-november-11-in-germany/g-18843065
   c. Kölner Karneval für Anfänger: DW (1:42)
      www.youtube.com/watch?v=HO893FeftYA
   d. Herkunft von Karneval, Fastnacht und Fasching erklärt (1:25)
      www.youtube.com/watch?v=6951Nj_kymo

3. Gestures and facial expressions:
   a. Body Language and Small Talk, InterNations GO!
      www.internations.org/go/moving-to-germany/living/body-language-and-small-talk
   b. 7 videos of German facial expressions that need explaining, Bruck, J., Deutsche Welle, 2018
      www.dw.com/en/7-videos-of-german-facial-expressions-that-need-explaining/a-19165041
   c. 9 uniquely German gestures and noises that need explaining:
      www.thelocal.de/20180621/8-uniquely-german-gestures-and-interjections-that-need-explaining/
   d. German hand gestures that throw off tourists:
      www.youtube.com/watch?v=h8Dul0MOvc8

Textbooks

Buscha, A. and Szita, S. (2007) *Begegnungen*. Leipzig: Schubert.
Lemcke, C. (2010) *Berliner Platz*. Berlin: Langenscheidt.
Braun, B., Doubek, M. and Schäfer, N. (2020) *DaF kompakt neu*. Stuttgart: Ernst Klett Sprachen.
Krenn, W. and Puchta, H. (2016) *Motive*. Munich: Hueber.
Aufderstraße, H. Bock, H., . Gerdes, M., Müller, J., Müller, H. (2009) *Themen aktuell*. Munich: Hueber.

References

Altmayer, C. (2017) 'Landeskunde im Globalisierungskontext: Wozu noch Kultur im DaF-Unterricht?'. In *Kulturelles Lernen im DaF/DaZ-Unterricht. Paradigmenwechsel in der Landeskunde*, edited by P. Hase and M. Höller, 3–22. Göttingen: Universitätsverlag.
Arasaratnam, L. (2016) 'Intercultural competence'. Online. https://oxfordre.com/communication/view/10.1093/acrefore/9780190228613.001.0001/acrefore-9780190228613-e-68 (accessed 1 June 2021).
Argyle, M. (1983) *The Psychology of Interpersonal Behaviour*, fourth edition. Harmondsworth: Penguin.
Assmann, J. (2005) 'Das kulturelle Gedächtnis und das Unbewusste'. In *Das Unbewusste in aktuellen Diskursen. Anschlüsse*, edited by M. Buchholz and G. Gödde, 368–92. Gießen: Psychosozial-Verlag.
Bruck, J. (2018) '7 Videos of German facial expressions that need explaining', Deutsche Welle. Online. www.dw.com/en/7-videos-of-german-facial-expressions-that-need-explaining/a-19165041 (accessed 24 June 2021).
Byram, M. (1997) *Teaching and Assessing Intercultural Communicative Competence*. Clevedon: Multilingual Matters.
Duden (n.d.) Entry 'du'. Online. www.duden.de/rechtschreibung/du (accessed 27 December 2020).
Fronz, H.-D. (2016) *Vom Ihrzen übers Siezen zum Duzen. Das Du ist auf dem Vormarsch - besonders in der Werbung*. Online. www.badische-zeitung.de/vom-ihrzen-uebers-siezen-zum-duzen-das-du-ist-auf-dem-vormarsch-besonders-in-der-werbung--127013396.html (accessed 27 November 2020).
Haines, G. (2017) 'Revealed: The nationalities most likely to invade your personal space'. Online. www.telegraph.co.uk/travel/news/the-nationalities-most-likely-to-invade-your-personal-space/ (accessed 30 April 2019).
Hall, E.T. (1966) *The Hidden Dimension*. New York: Doubleday.
InterNations GO! (2018) 'Body language and small talk'. Online. www.internations.org/go/moving-to-germany/living/body-language-and-small-talk (accessed 23 April 2021).
Mahon, J. and Cushner, K. (2012) 'The multicultural classroom'. In *The Routledge Handbook of Language and Intercultural Communication*, edited by J. Jackson, 434–48. London: Routledge.
Mandl, B. (2005) *Küss die Hand, Frau Magister! Titelverliebtes Österreich*. Online. www.spiegel.de/lebenundlernen/uni/titelverliebtes-oesterreich-kuess-die-hand-frau-magister-a-363231.html (accessed 27 December 2020).
Noels, K., Yashima, T. and Zhang, R (2012) 'Language, identity and intercultural communication'. In *The Routledge Handbook of Language and Intercultural Communication*, edited by J. Jackson, 52–66. London: Routledge.
Risager, K. (2007) *Language and Culture Pedagogy: From a national to a transnational paradigm*. Clevedon and Buffalo, NY: Multilingual Matters.
Schmedding, N. (2007) *Wann dürfen Sie Du sagen?* Online. www.ksta.de/wann-duerfen-sie-du-sagen--13516898?cb=1609061977469 (accessed 27 December 2020).
Sorokowska, A. et al. (2017) 'Preferred interpersonal distances: A global comparison'. *Journal of Cross-Cultural Psychology* 48:4, 577–92.
Wilkinson, J. (2012) 'The intercultural speaker and the acquisition of intercultural/global competence'. In *The Routledge Handbook of Language and Intercultural Communication*, edited by J. Jackson, 296–309. London: Routledge.

Part III
Innovative approaches

9
The 'flipped classroom' approach in the German beginner context
Mandy Poetzsch

'Flipped learning' (Bergmann and Sams, 2012) has gained popularity since the mid-2000s. It has been defined as a 'pedagogical approach in which direct instruction moves from the group learning spaces to the individual learning spaces' (Flipped Learning Network, 2014). The classroom is thereby transformed into a space in which more dynamic interactions can take place to facilitate higher-level learning.

In recent years, the flipped classroom has been widely adopted in higher education as a key pedagogy, and many UK institutions actively encourage their staff to implement this approach in their teaching practice. The flipped classroom is usually associated with online resources, particularly videos and other web-based applications. While this is undoubtedly the case, the concept behind the approach pre-dates new learning technologies and many key ideas of this approach have always been an essential part of language learning and teaching.

The aim of this chapter is to reduce the perceived barriers to 'flipping' the language classroom. The chapter will give a brief overview of flipped learning as a framework and provide examples of the application of the flipped learning approach in *ab initio* language teaching. This is followed by a critical evaluation of methods and materials for flipping the classroom, based on experience with *ab initio* learners of German.

The flipped learning approach

The flipped classroom, also known as the 'inverted classroom', is a learner-centred approach in which part of the traditional class content is provided outside of class time, traditionally in form of videos, to free up class time for practice and further exploration. In other words, the presentation phase of the traditional PPP (presentation, practice and production) lesson structure (Cotter, n.d.) is completed at home, so that class time can be devoted in its entirety to the practice and production phases. Due to the focus on technology, it can be considered a specialised form of blended learning.

Blended learning is very broadly defined as any form of educational setting where face-to-face and online instructions are combined (Graham, 2006: 4). In recent years, seven models of blended learning have emerged with the flipped classroom being one of them (Clayton Christensen Institute, 2021). Most of the blended learning models centre around rotation models. In these models, teachers retain their role as the providers of the direct instructions and students then complete tasks online to apply and deepen their knowledge and understanding. The aim of the flipped learning approach is to free up important classroom time by letting the students work through the theory at their own pace at home. The teacher's role is transformed into a guide and facilitator to enhance the practice and further exploration. The form, in which this theory is presented, is entirely up to the individual educator and the needs of the students. '[T]here is no single way to flip your classroom - there is no such thing as *the* flipped classroom' (Bergman and Sams, 2012: 11, emphasis in original).

Most of the literature emphasises the opportunities and learning gains in flipped learning compared to traditional lectures (for example Mason, Shuman and Cook, 2013; Baepler, Walker and Driessen, 2014) but lectures play at best a marginal role in language teaching. There is also a lack of comprehensive studies looking at the implementation of flipped learning in a language teaching context (Jiang et al., 2020). Many of the benefits, however, are still applicable in the language classroom: flipped learning allows students to work at their own pace, they have the chance to repeat sections of the online materials that they have not fully understood and can ask more precise questions in the face-to-face interactions (Roehl, Linga Reddy and Jett Shannon, 2013: 47).

With the direct instruction moved out of the classroom into the individual study time, there is more time in class to engage the students in active learning activities that allow them to use the target language (Roehl, Linga Reddy and Jett Shannon, 2013: 46). This is of great benefit in an *ab initio* course. Contact hours are often very few and students and teachers are required to cover a lot of content. Depending on the institution, these are usually levels A1 and A2 of the Common European Framework of Reference for Languages (CEFR) within a 24-week-long academic year as shown in Chapter 1. The flipped classroom enables teachers to dedicate more of that time to deepen and advance the language use in the communicative classroom. This approach can be used as the foundation for the entire course design with every lesson being flipped, or it can be used for individual lessons. Because of this, it offers great flexibility in content design.

Flipping a language classroom is in many ways easier to do than flipping a traditional university lecture as the language classroom does not follow the traditional pattern of long lecture phases with short application phases. Instead, homework is often not only consolidatory but also preparatory. Students are asked to learn vocabulary in advance, read a text at home in preparation for a classroom discussion or do independent research to be presented in class. The difference in the flipped classroom is the selection of topics and tasks that students are asked to work on at home. These are usually new topics, and the materials provide a first exposure for the students. The first phase of the face-to-face interaction needs to be dedicated to testing comprehension and answering questions to clear up any misunderstandings (Bergman and Sams, 2012: 14). The next phase can then move on to the application of the new information.

Integration of flipped learning in the *ab initio* classroom: benefits

The flipped classroom allows the students greater flexibility in their learning in so far as they can decide when and where they complete the preparatory materials for the face-to-face interactions. Nevertheless, it is still very much a teacher-centred and teacher-driven approach in that the teacher decides how to design the course (Wenner and Palmer, 2015: 356). It is up to the teacher to find the correct materials that will support the learning outcomes of each individual lesson and it is also the teacher's task to align these materials to the face-to-face sessions and ensure that learning takes place. This is especially important in an *ab initio* class. It means that despite the greater flexibility for the students, the teacher can still ensure that all necessary scaffolding is in place to support the learners.

Brame (2013) has summarised the key elements of the flipped classroom as (1) the first exposure (the presentation phase), (2) an incentive for students to learn, (3) a mechanism to assess students' understanding and (4) the in-class activities that focus on higher-level cognitive activities (practice and production phase). The higher-level cognitive activities need to be clearly linked to the materials studied at home, otherwise the incentive to engage with them is lost. After potential misconceptions have been addressed, a teacher needs to move on to creative and engaging activities. This is, again, an area in which language learning has long been leading. All classroom activities from the practice and production phase of the traditional face-to-face instructions can be used here. There is simply more time for them and more time for the teacher to focus on individual students and provide help where needed (Mehring, 2016).

Because the flipped classroom is designed to reduce the time spent on lecturing, certain topics are easier to flip. Grammar instructions are the most obvious choice. Instead of explaining a grammar rule in class, students can study the basic rules and examples at home. The materials can also include grammar drills as basic application exercises.[1] In class, the teacher can then focus on controlled and open-ended practice (Dörnyei, 2009: 39). Flipping the classroom in grammar instructions addresses the different learner abilities. The learning is self-paced, so students can decide how much time they spend on the tasks. They do not need to work at a comparable speed to their classmates but can be faster or slower, they can watch the explanations once or multiple times (Chilingaryan and Zvereva, 2017). It can be very helpful to provide further links. These can be in the target language or mother tongue of the students to enable further and deeper study or provide the content in a different format thereby addressing different learner needs.

Another area that lends itself well to flipping is vocabulary acquisition. The pre-learning of vocabulary items is not new, as previously stated. What is new is the richness of content in which the lexical items can be provided. 'Nicos Weg' (Deutsche Welle), for example, has short episodes that focus on different communicative situations. Students can watch these at home and recognise or identify key phrases. As the videos can be supported by captions and a script, students can identify and hear these and recognise them in writing. Further tasks at home can range from vocabulary drills with Quizlet (a flashcard-based learning tool) to some simple applications such as writing a short dialogue asynchronously with fellow students or recoding a short speaking sequence on Flipgrid (a web-based video recording tool) to which other students and the teacher can respond and provide feedback using the same software.

Mehring (2016) suggests flipping the classroom to prepare writing tasks by providing students with materials that focus on major specifications of the text type, such as the introduction and conclusion of a literary essay compared to a report or newspaper article, but the flipped classroom can also be used to address questions of style and register and introduce useful structuring phrases and idiomatic expressions.

Arguably, finding materials for the presentation phase is the easiest, but often also most time-consuming aspect of flipped learning. Thanks to YouTube, but also content providers such as Deutsche Welle or BBC Bitesize GCSE German, as well as additional digital offerings by textbook publishers, there are a plethora of materials available to support the *ab initio* classroom.[2] An alternative is to produce the required material, which has the benefit of a precise fit into the planned curriculum but requires familiarity with screencast and recording software. Sourcing materials should not be seen as an 'either/or' scenario. If a YouTube video on the perfect tense covers all aspects in the right detail, then there is no need to record a lecture on the same topic. Some YouTube channels, for example 'Learn German with Anja' or 'YourGermanTeacher', are very learner-friendly and designed for self-study. They can be highly engaging and, at the same time as providing first exposure, can serve as future resource for students' independent study. Additionally, they expose students to further examples of different German accents and dialects. The aforementioned 'Nicos Weg' on Deutsche Welle is a structured language course that fully integrates vocabulary, grammar and cultural knowledge about Germany. It can serve as excellent first exposure for vocabulary in context.

All chosen materials for the presentation phases should be relatively short (max. 15 minutes) and include several examples. Especially at *ab initio* level, they should not include too many new lexical items and come with the option of captions. If they focus on grammar items, they should also be supported by pictures or diagrams to aid comprehension. These visual aids can then be used again in the short comprehension check at the start of the face-to-face classes (Al-Naabi, 2020: 73). All videos and other materials should be supported by additional activities to guide and scaffold the learning (Straw et al., 2015: 7), especially at *ab initio* level where all language competencies in the target language are very basic.

All materials need to be in one place to minimise potential misunderstanding and confusion around when and which tasks should be completed. The Learning Management System (LMS) plays therefore an important role in a successfully flipped classroom. The LMS needs to allow educators to provide and structure the materials in a meaningful and easily accessible manner, otherwise they run the risk of students not having done the preparatory work. All modern LMS allow the integration of videos. LMS platforms such as Moodle go a step further with the flexible integration of a variety of sources and third-party content providers.

Challenges of the flipped classroom

The research report on flipped learning by the National Foundation for Education Research (Straw et al., 2015: 6) has highlighted four challenges for the implementation of the flipped classroom:

- Access to technology
- Identifying appropriate online resources
- Students not participating in preliminary homework
- Teachers' and/or students' preferences for face-to-face tuition as opposed to remote instruction

Wanner and Palmer (2015: 365) have further identified the high level of time commitment that is required to successfully implement flipped learning. A further obstacle, which is often not explicitly addressed, is the cost that is incurred by staff due to lack of support from their institution for required software and applications that can enhance and support students' learning. This is in addition to the cost of the required hardware and internet access that is an important concern for teachers and students.

A successful flipped classroom requires knowledge of modern technology. Hao and Lee (2016) demonstrated in their study regarding attitudes towards flipped learning that the technological aspect of flipped learning was a heightened concern for teachers with no or limited technological knowledge. A teacher does not only need to be aware of the subject matter but also be familiar enough with technology to decide which tool will help them best to support their students when they study autonomously at home in preparation for their classes. This step is essential. If a teacher spends a lot of time in the face-to-face interaction to go over the subject matter that was covered in the online study, it means the flipped classroom has failed. Al-Naabi (2020) addresses this in his small-scale study where students suggested that one way to improve the flipped classroom would be to watch the videos again at the beginning of the class. As he notes, this 'is not desirable and contradicts the flipped learning approach' (Al-Naabi, 2020: 73).

The biggest obstacle, however, is the buy-in from students. While most of the already listed studies report very positive results, there are always students who will not engage with the preparatory homework. This can be for various reasons. Fisher and colleagues (2017: 122) observed that good study habits are key to the success of the flipped classroom. The flipped classroom requires students to invest time in their studies. This has been reported as the feeling of having to spend more time on their preparatory work for the flipped class than their traditional classes. However, this might also be because students are not always aware of the amount of private study time recommended for each course (Fisher et al., 2017: 123).

The lack of preparedness in class can not only lead to a feeling of confusion and loss of motivation for the respective student but can also have a knock-on effect on the entire class if they are consistently stopped from exploring topics further in class. A simple example would be a role-play that cannot be practised by a group because one of their group has not done the homework and therefore lacks the required vocabulary. This is why the incentive to learn, one of the key elements mentioned earlier, is so important. Students need to know why they need to complete the preparatory homework. This is coupled with the need to explicitly prepare students for the flipped classroom. The preparation needs to go beyond explanations of the concept and expectations set by the teacher and needs to include demonstrations of important software. These demonstrations do not need to take place in class time, but user guides and instructive videos should be provided for students, so they can, whenever needed, consult them.

From the teaching point of view, flipped learning can seem less attractive because of the limitations in swiftly making changes to content once it has been released to the students (Roehl, Linga Reddy and Jett Shannon, 2013: 47). It might also lead to a reluctance to change the course content once the flipped classroom has been set up due to the work hours involved. While these are relatable objections, much of the basic content does not change that quickly in the *ab initio* classroom. Often the cultural information is modernised and updated, the underlying structures however are not. It is up to the individual teacher to decide which content should be flipped and in what way.

Finally, it is advisable to monitor the workload expectations across the degree programme. If every module went to fully flipped learning, there is a danger that workload for students could be too high (Straw et al., 2015: 8; Wanner and Palmer, 2015: 361). The listed challenges also give further strength to the argument that the flipped classroom should be considered as one among many approaches (Straw et al., 2015: 8; Chilingaryan and Zverva, 2017: 1504).

Applications to support flipped teaching

While some innate challenges of the flipped classroom are more difficult to solve, the technological component is one that has proven to be less of an obstacle than assumed. During the COVID-19 pandemic, many teachers were able to make the shift very quickly, though without much time for reflection on tools and strategies. To help identify useful digital tools, a framework of five aspects is suggested here. The following software and materials are used for illustrative purposes only and are based on the personal experience of the author. There is a plethora of software out there that offers very similar functionality. Alternatives might be a better fit depending on personal and institutional preferences. Given the speed at which new applications come to the market and others disappear, it is also possible that some of the software might no longer be available or will have already been overtaken by something new. The categories that have been used for the analysis, however, aim to provide a useful framework that will enable educators to decide quickly if a tool will fit with their intended learning outcomes. When assessing tools for their usefulness, the following aspects should be considered:

- **Functionality**: What can this application do? Does it offer a unique feature, or does it replicate the functionality of other software? There are, for example, many quiz apps to gamify the classroom and while they might all function slightly differently, it is advisable to have one preferred app with which students and staff can gain familiarity instead of having to adapt to ever new apps. Additionally, agreement between staff will result in a more consistent experience for students.
- **Cost**: Most software, especially in educational settings, offers free and premium accounts. Free accounts often have a limited functionality or have a trial period after which one must upgrade to a paid version. Additionally, free versions are often less secure and offer fewer or limited privacy setting. This is another argument for committing to fewer apps but using those consistently.
- **Ease of use for teachers and students**: The software needs to be user-friendly for both parties. Staff need to be able to set it up and ensure it works correctly while students need to be able to navigate it on their own without immediate help from the teacher. This means the interface has to be clear and intuitive. It is advisable to consult the developer support pages and the institutional support pages, link to these within the LMS and actively encourage students to consult these instead of contacting the teacher if they face any technical difficulties.

- **Analytics**: To ensure and monitor progress, a teacher needs to be able to access the students' work. Most educational apps provide rich analytics of the user data. Beyond accessing the results, teachers are often able to track the length of engagement, see where students spend the most time, what were the most common mistakes and other useful parameters. These can form the basis for the in-class activities.
- **Privacy**: Any software that students need to use as part of their course needs to comply with General Data Protection Regulations (GDPR). It should not require students to enter any private information and ideally, will not even require students to create an account.

Before selecting the software, it is always advisable to check with IT or see if comparable software is already licensed at the institution. Many institutions also offer ways to suggest or request software to be licensed for the specific needs of departments. While the process can take a while, it has the benefit of a thorough vetting process.

Many LMS offer functionalities that might already fulfil the requirements for the successful integration of the flipped classroom. As standard, they offer discussion boards, wikis and automated tests. If all can be achieved within one system, there is no need to go further. In reality, and based on exchanges with colleagues within higher education, the systems' functionality is often not satisfying and described as 'too clunky', 'not attractive' or even 'off-putting'. Hence, below are some suggestions that have worked well in my own and colleagues' flipped classrooms. They are grouped together under the phase in which they have been used and all fulfil the criteria above, though some of them only with a licensed version.

Support during the autonomous presentation phase at home

Once the materials for autonomous learning have been selected, the teacher needs to ensure that there is a structure in place for students to collect and retain key information and to ask any questions, if they occur. The simplest and most effective way forward is to treat the material like any other comprehension text and provide students with a list of questions that they should answer while working through the materials. This can be very low tech by providing them with a Word document to complete or can take the form of a Google/Microsoft Forms quiz where students can receive instant feedback after submission. These quizzes offer additional analytics that provide the teacher with insights into the number of students who have engaged with the task and their results.

Some video presentation software such as Kaltura or Mediasite also have a quiz function among their editing suite, so that comprehension questions in multiple-choice format are integrated into the video. Integrating the questions into the video can, however, be more time-consuming.

Whichever format is chosen, there always has to be space for students to record their questions while working with the materials. Moreover, students need to be explicitly encouraged to use the opportunity to submit their questions.

Students' questions need to be discussed during the comprehension check-up, but they can also be designed to encourage students to start a discussion among themselves before the face-to-face session. Encouraging this can be very difficult. Especially at the start of the year, *ab initio* students will not know each other yet, nor be clear about the teacher's expectations, but this can be cultivated in in-class discussions and over the term.

An extremely versatile platform that allows this is Padlet, a digital pinboard that offers many different design options depending on the learning outcomes. It is very easy to set up and use and works both asynchronously and synchronously. Compared to most discussion boards, all questions and responses are visible on one screen and can be scattered or grouped under specific headers. Using a platform like this means that students can easily post questions. These can then be opened on a screen in the classroom and answered. There is also a rating option in which students can rate questions up and down, making it easier for a teacher to see which points caused students the most confusion. Students can respond to each other and answer some of these questions, which can be steered by the task design. Finally, the board can be changed to 'read only' and integrated in the LMS as a permanent record.

Support during the comprehension check-up in the face-to-face class

In addition to the questions submitted by students, student response software, such as Kahoot, Quizizz and Mentimeter are a good way to check general comprehension.[3] All of these apps have the same basic principle; they gamify multiple choice tests that students can access via their phones and complete in real-time in direct competition with each other or as groups. They also serve as a quick assessment and provide the teacher with important feedback about students' progression (Mehring, 2016).

Kahoot is often used in schools, so students in the *ab initio* classroom would most likely be familiar with it, which can give it a slight advantage. Mentimeter allows open answers that are collected in a word cloud, which can serve well as a springboard for the next classroom activity and as a quick first check for the application of the new information. Quizizz allows multiple correct answers. All apps and other similar applications offer free versions with further and advanced features available with the licensed version.

The benefit of this type of gamified testing is that students really enjoy it and are often extremely engaged. The tests are very quick and timed, and the apps can be set to anonymous, so all students join in without the worry of making a mistake in front of the class. They all offer very good group and individual statistics, so that a teacher can track for example which question all students got wrong. These should form the basis for further discussion and clarification in class.

Because students spend more time in the digital world, it can also be very effective to retain this element in face-to-face classes depending on the learning outcomes and availability of devices in the classroom. For example, the outcome of small-group discussions can be posted onto a Padlet to compare the answers. At the same time, this would provide some organically integrated writing practice. Error analysis can be done in groups on a shared document, or students can create short presentations together via Google or Microsoft slides. Although all of this is possible without digital tools, they have the advantage of a document that can be easily accessed by the teacher and shared with the whole class, which creates a record that can be added to the LMS after class.

Conclusion

The COVID-19 pandemic forced the education sector to engage fully with online and blended learning. Teachers and lecturers had to switch to these new delivery modes in a very short time, often figuring out what worked in the new environment on a trial-and-error basis. Now is the time to reflect on these changes and analyse the long-term benefits and improvements to our teaching practice that these newly acquired skills can provide.

The flipped classroom can support *ab initio* learning in a highly structured way. Its flexibility means that a teacher can decide to flip the entire course or only certain aspects. While the impact on performance metrics in a flipped classroom might be less obvious, other factors such as better use of class time for active learning and student engagement and participation increase are clearly beneficial. The flipped classroom allows students to study essentials in their own time and at their own pace, so that they can participate with greater confidence in class. As more time in class can be spend on activities that require the students' active participation, teachers have more opportunities to monitor their students' progress and provide immediate and individual assistance where required.

Flipped learning can have a very positive impact on language learning but it is in the hands of the individual teacher to decide how to best use it.

Notes

1   For a detailed discussion on the teaching of grammar, see Chapter 6, this volume.
2   Chapter 7 provides more guidance on finding appropriate sources for ab initio students.
3   Winter discusses the use of software for feedback in more detail in Chapter 10, this volume.

References

Al-Naabi, I. (2020) 'Is it worth flipping? the impact of flipped classroom on EFL students' grammar'. *English Language Teaching* 13:6, 64–75. Online. https://eric.ed.gov/?id=EJ1255482 (accessed 20 May 2021).

Baepler, P., Walker, J.D. and Driessen, M. (2014) 'It's not about seat time: Blending, flipping, and the efficiency in active learning classrooms'. *Computers and Education* 78, 227–36.

Bergmann, J. and Sams, A. (2012) *Flip Your Classroom: Reach every student in every class every day*. Eugene, OR: International Society for Technology in Education.

Brame, C. (2013) 'Flipping the classroom'. Online. https://cft.vanderbilt.edu/guides-sub-pages/flipping-the-classroom/ (accessed 16 May 2019).

Clayton Christensen Institute (2021) 'Blended learning models'. *Blended Learning Universe*. Online. www.blendedlearning.org/models/ (accessed 15 July 2021).

Cotter, T. (n.d.) 'Planning a grammar lesson'. Online. www.teachingenglish.org.uk/article/planning-a-grammar-lesson (accessed 11 October 2020).

Chilingaryan, K. and Zvereva, E. (2017) 'Methodology of Flipped Classroom as a Learning Technology in Foreign Language Teaching'. *Procedia – Social and Behavioral Sciences* 237, 1500–4.

Dörnyei, Z. (2009). 'Communicative language teaching in the 21st century: The "principled communicative approach"'. *Perspectives. A Journal of TESOL Italy*, 36:2, 33–43.

Fisher, R., Ross, B., LaFerriere, R. and Maritz, A. (2017) 'Flipped learning, flipped satisfaction, getting the balance right'. *Teaching & Learning Inquiry* 5:2, 114–27. Online. https://doi.org/10.20343/teachlearninqu.5.2.9 (accessed 20 June 2021).

Flipped Learning Network (FLN) (2014) *The Four Pillars of F-L-I-P™*. Online. www.flippedlearning.org/definition (accessed 31 July 2019).

Graham, C.R. (2006) 'Blended learning systems. Definition, current trends, and future directions'. In *The Handbook of Blended Learning: Global perspectives, local designs*, edited by C.J. Bonk and C.R. Graham, San Francisco: Pfeiffer, 3–21.

Hao, Y. and Lee, K.S. (2016) 'Teaching in Flipped Classrooms: Exploring pre-service teachers' concerns', *Computers in Human Behavior* 57, 250–60.

Jiang, M., Jong, M., Lau, W., Chai, C., Liu, K. and Park, M. (2020) 'A scoping review on flipped classroom approach in language education: Challenges, implications and an interaction model'. *Computer Assisted Language Learning.* Online. www.tandfonline.com/doi/abs/10. 1080/09588221.2020.1789171 (accessed 18 January 2021).

Mason, G., Shuman, T. and Cook, K. (2013) 'Comparing the effectiveness of an inverted classroom to a traditional classroom in an upper-division engineering course'. *IEEE Transactions on Education* 56, 430–5.

Mehring, J. (2016) 'Present Research on the Flipped Classroom and Potential Tools for the EFL Classroom'. *Computers in the Schools*, 33:1. Online. www.tandfonline.com/doi/full/10.108 0/07380569.2016.1139912 (accessed 20 June 2021).

Roehl, A., Linga Reddy, S. and Jett Shannon, G. (2013) 'The flipped classroom: An opportunity to engage millennial students through active learning strategies;. *Journal of Family and Consumer Sciences* 105:2, 44–8.

Straw, S., Quinlan, O., Harland, J. and Walker, M. (2015) *Flipped Learning: Research report.* Slough: National Foundation for Education Research.

Wanner, T. and Palmer, E. (2015) 'Personalising learning: Exploring student and teacher perceptions about flexible learning and assessment in a flipped university course'. *Computers & Education* 88, 354–69.

10

New approaches to feedback in *ab initio* language classes: a case study

Ruth R. Winter

In higher education student surveys of recent years, the categories of 'assessment' and 'feedback' have often attracted relatively low scores, suggesting a general dissatisfaction with the amount and the type of feedback given (Boud and Molloy, 2013: 2; OfS, 2019). While most higher education lecturers would agree that feedback plays an important role in the learning process, William points out that we still 'know very little about feedback' (2018: 14).

This chapter aims to examine new approaches to giving effective feedback in *ab initio* language classes, focusing on the use of student response systems (SRS), an educational technology that until very recently has been primarily used for teaching in Science faculties (Herrada, Banos and Alcayde, 2020: 1). The chapter starts with an explanation of the term 'feedback' in the context of this study and a short introduction to SRSs in higher education in the UK and their strengths and challenges in terms of enhancing feedback.

Most German *ab initio* language classes offered as part of an undergraduate language degree are intensive courses, comprising several contact hours a week, and aim to equip students with the necessary knowledge and skills to become independent users of the target language within one or two years. This results in a steep learning trajectory, which in conjunction with an increase in the number of *ab initio* students (see Chapter 1, this volume) may pose new challenges for lecturers in terms of providing regular and inclusive feedback to students: a survey carried out by the author reveals that, about ten years ago, most higher education institutions in the UK had either no *ab initio* students or fewer than ten, whereas more than half of respondents stated that the number of students studying *ab initio* German in 2021 was more than ten and in some cases more than 20. Degree courses including *ab initio* German that were once reserved for the select few, comprising a handful of students at most, arguably offered language tutors more opportunities for closely following students' progress and for providing personalised feedback. With the increase in popularity of studying languages from scratch, *ab initio* class sizes have gone up in many institutions, prompting teachers to explore new ways of testing knowledge and comprehension, tracking progress and providing timely feedback to all participants while maintaining the same pace as before to ensure all students achieve a solid A2 level by the end of the first teaching year.

This study explores the uses of SRSs in *ab initio* language classes and the synergistic effects of providing feedback on formative tests making use of a technology that is aimed at enhancing student engagement and interaction with the lecturer. I will argue that this technology adds great value to language teaching and enhances students' experience of learning in multiple ways, irrespective of its use in in-class or live online lessons. The discussion includes a small-scale confirmatory study involving a Likert-type survey that examines the effectiveness of computer-mediated corrective teacher feedback and student feedback using the SRS Socrative.

Feedback

Hattie (cited in Busse, 2014: 157) identifies teacher feedback as one of the key factors underlying successful learning and teaching. However, this category still receives relatively low scores in student surveys compared to other aspects of the student experience (Boud and Molloy, 2013: 2). According to a 2019 press report by the Office for Students, 'universities should do more to improve feedback' (OfS, 2019: n.p.). Students want clear and fair marking and assessments, and value timely feedback on their work. They also want staff to listen to their feedback on their learning experience (OfS, 2019).

In an educational context, the term feedback has been broadly defined as 'procedures that are used to tell a learner if a response is right or wrong' (Kulhavy, 1977: 211). In recent years the shift to a more student-centred teaching style has led to formative feedback gaining significance. It refers to 'information communicated to the learner that is intended to modify his or her thinking or behaviour for the purpose of improving learning' (Shute, 2008: 154).

Formative feedback can be given either in written or in oral form, while a combination of both is also possible, for example when a written assignment is marked by the lecturer and followed up by a discussion in class. This chapter is concerned with tutor-led written and oral feedback on regular formative assessments testing receptive and productive grammar knowledge. It is based on the premise that students want to receive feedback on their performance from their lecturers and that immediate feedback that is explicit rather than implicit '[leads] to significant gains in accuracy' (Sheen and Ellis, 2011: 606). The focus of this discussion is how more traditional approaches to corrective feedback on writing tasks that are focused on grammar and vocabulary acquisition can be enhanced by the use of SRSs to provide a new and more immediate way of providing feedback to improve the learning experience of students.

As stated above, students are also keen to share their views on their learning with their lecturers. While in most university courses student feedback tends to be collected via end-of-term evaluation forms, providing more regular opportunities for informal student feedback throughout the semester or year is likely to enhance student satisfaction. This chapter will therefore also discuss the benefits of using SRSs to collect student feedback.

Short introduction to SRSs

One of the more recent inventions of e-learning are so-called SRSs that have been designed to enhance classroom interaction. SRSs allow lecturers to create digital materials in a simple way and to invite individual responses from all participants, thus enhancing engagement. While the earliest examples of this technology date back to the beginning of the century (Cerqueiro and Martín-Macho Harrison, 2019: 2), mobile versions allowing the use of personal devices as opposed to clickers handed out by the lecturer have been gaining popularity in many educational settings over the last few years.

Traditionally, SRSs have been used for large lectures in the science subjects and engineering, but there is strong evidence that suggests that this technology has similar benefits also for smaller groups in language education by providing insights into common errors and knowledge gaps and by stimulating 'attention and engagement' (Herrada, Banos and Alcayde, 2020: 7).

There is a significant number of web-based SRSs used in educational settings to 'improve the level of engagement, commitment, and learning of students' (Herrada, Banos and Alcayde, 2020: 2), with Kahoot, Mentimeter, Socrative and Poll Everywhere being among the most-used, freely available and reliable SRSs in higher education. They 'offer lecturers the opportunity to pose multiple-choice questions to their students, so that they respond individually using a handheld wireless transmitter, while these responses can be displayed immediately using charts' (Herrada, Banos and Alcayde, 2020: 2). While Mentimeter and Poll Everywhere are primarily designed to collect participants' views and to stimulate discussion, Kahoot and Socrative are quizzing tools with a gamified approach (Compton and Allen, 2018: 12–14). Kahoot appeals to many users due to its gamification elements and is more commonly used in schools; however, two of the main drawbacks are the emphasis on quick responses that 'may cause students to rush to answer questions … [generating] tension and anxiety' (Compton and Allen, 2018: 15) and the fact that it is not designed to provide written formative feedback to individual students. Moreover, the free version only offers two different question formats, that is, multiple choice questions (MCQs) and true/false questions.

On the other hand, Socrative allows lecturers to choose whether to opt for a gamified approach. Quiz questions, which include MCQs and fill-in-the-blank questions, can be displayed on students' own devices at different paces – either teacher-paced or student-paced. Moreover, as opposed to Kahoot, students' answers in Socrative are saved for reviewing by the lecturer and can be shared with individual students. Finally, Socrative allows lecturers to collect feedback easily from students on their learning.

Similar to other quizzing tools, creating questions in Socrative is relatively quick and easy, while adding feedback and explanations may be more time consuming, depending on how detailed they are. Once a quiz has been created, though, it can be reused and amended for other classes and shared with other lecturers. Questions prompting students to reflect on their learning are available through the so-called exit ticket function and can be deployed with little preparation. The first two questions are set in English by default and ask students to (1) evaluate how well they have understood the lesson topic(s) (from A = 'Totally got it' to D = 'Not at all') and (2) reflect on what they have learnt ('What did you learn today?'). There is also the option to add a third question as required by the teacher, which can be used either for further reflection or further testing of students' knowledge and ability to produce certain grammatical structures and/or vocabulary.

Using Socrative to enhance feedback in *ab initio* German classes

What new approaches can we develop to provide language students with more personalised feedback on their learning and progress in class? How can we achieve a greater effectiveness of feedback to enhance students' satisfaction? These were the questions that prompted an exploration of the use of the SRS Socrative for providing and gathering effective feedback in *ab initio* German classes. Over the course of two academic years, Socrative was used to deploy ten short formative assessment quizzes to two cohorts of *ab initio* German students to provide feedback on key grammar concepts and prompt students to reflect on their learning experience. The first cohort did the tests during in-person classes, whereas the second cohort completed the tests during live online lessons as the pandemic of 2020/1 required a move to online teaching. As the tests were all formative, the results did not count towards the unit mark. Students who missed a test were encouraged to take it in their own time before the next lesson.

The first seven quizzes comprised up to ten MCQs, whereas the last three consisted of fill-in-the-blank questions. Each quiz focused on one previously taught grammatical feature such as tenses, cases and adjectival declension, while at the same time testing students' vocabulary knowledge. All questions were in German and required students to complete a sentence with one word, with the aim to test not just their reading comprehension and ability to apply knowledge of grammatical rules but also their ability to retrieve the correct lexical item. Tests were shared via a virtual Socrative classroom that students accessed on their personal device via the Socrative student app. Questions were displayed one at a time and immediately after a response was given, students automatically received the correct answer as well as an explanation in English of why their answer was right or wrong. Once completed, students received the results of how they performed in the test.

In both *ab initio* groups, students were regularly prompted to reflect on their own learning and to feed this back to the lecturer by answering the two exit ticket questions described above. A third, open question, encouraging production of new grammatical forms and vocabulary, was added. Student responses thus provide immediate insights into the depth of learning, which help identify gaps of knowledge and inform future lesson planning.

A Likert-type, anonymous survey comprising ten statements in English on the use of the SRS Socrative was carried out in the two *ab initio* classes towards the end of the teaching year to explore the benefits of using this technology to enhance feedback and students' learning experience. Students were asked to rate each statement from 1 = strongly disagree to 5 = strongly agree. Overall, 20 students took part in the survey. Although the survey on its own should not be seen as main evidence to support the hypothesis stated above, it does confirm students' overwhelming acceptance of Socrative as a tool to facilitate and enhance learning and understanding in the language classroom (see Figures 10.1 to 10.4).

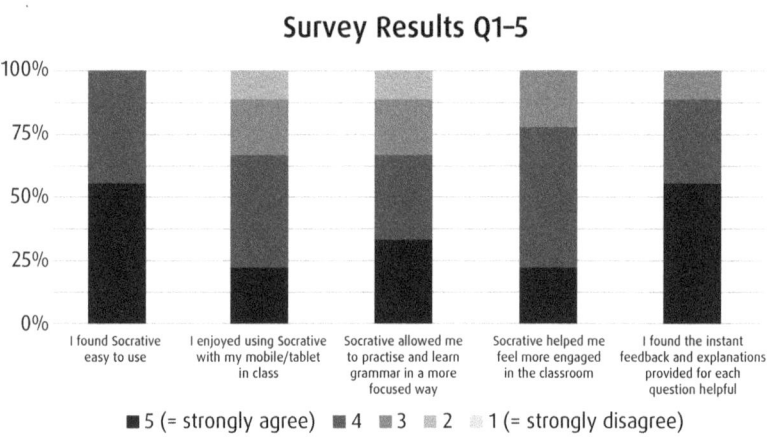

Figure 10.1 Student responses to Likert-type survey (2019) about Socrative use in-class (statements 1–5). Source: Author

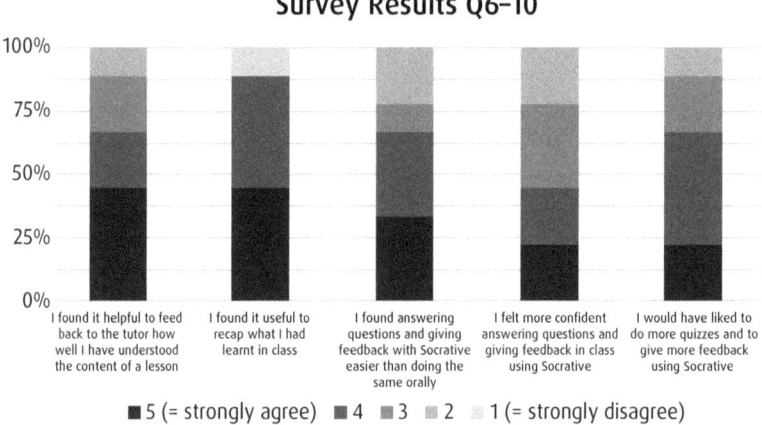

Figure 10.2 Student responses to Likert-type survey (2019) about Socrative use in-class (statements 6–10). Source: Author

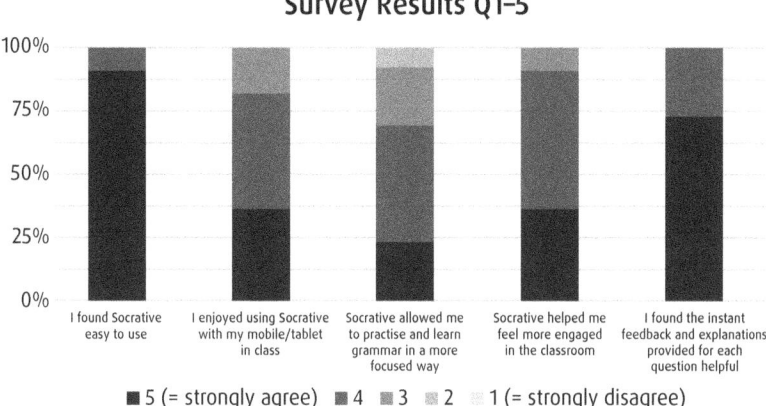

Figure 10.3 Student responses to Likert-type survey (2021) about Socrative use in online lessons (statements 1–5). Source: Author

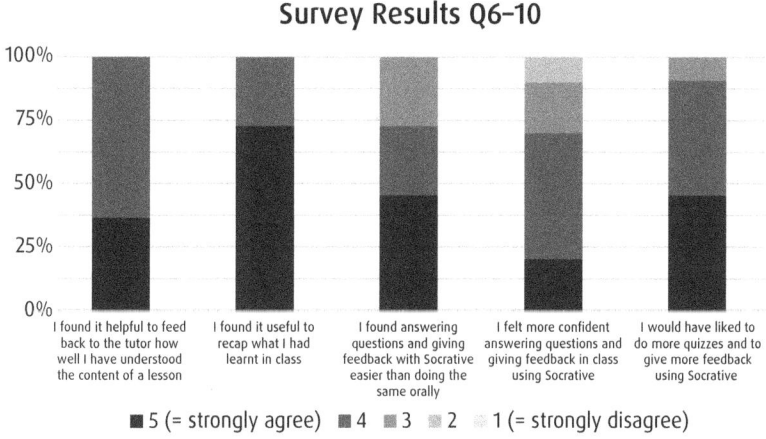

Figure 10.4 Student responses to Likert-type survey (2021) about Socrative use in online lessons (statements 6–10). Source: Author

As stated above, students need to receive regular corrective feedback to improve accuracy and to gauge how well they are performing in acquiring core language skills such as reading, writing, listening and speaking. SRSs can provide a useful tool to add to traditional ways of giving feedback because it allows for instant correction of errors and explanations to help '[understand] the nature of the error' (Sheen and Ellis, 2011: 596). For *ab initio* students who, by the time they graduate, must have achieved the same advanced productive skills as their peers who start their degree with an A-level in German, this kind of formative feedback is even more important. Students in the two *ab initio* groups clearly found the instant feedback and explanations helpful as confirmed by the survey results: all but one of them either agreed or strongly agreed with the statement 'I found the instant feedback and explanations provided for each question helpful' (see Fig. 10.1 and Fig. 10.3).

Using Socrative for regular quizzes on grammatical forms is therefore a very effective tool to improve students' acquisition of the target language (cf. Sheen and Ellis, 2011: 595). Effective language use is linked to the development of 'advanced productive skills of writing and speaking in the target language [that] both require a high level of knowledge of the grammatical, discursive and pragmatic conventions that govern language use' (QAA, 2019: 11). Formative assessments that include immediate explicit written feedback reinforce this knowledge. Sheen and Ellis's (2011: 606) cautious suggestion that focused written corrective feedback can lead to improvements of grammatical accuracy and acquisition can be backed up by Sánchez and colleagues' more recent study on the effect of quizzes on long-term learning (Sánchez, Diego and Fernández-Sánchez, 2017). This experimental research is the first one examining the effects of quizzes in foreign language learning on the acquisition of grammatical features. The authors conclude that the repeated retrieval of grammar aspects by using quizzes that include immediate feedback, 'produces better retention' and their use in foreign language lessons, whether in class or online, should be promoted 'because they are a quick and effective tool for long-term learning' (Sánchez, Diego and Fernández-Sánchez, 2017: 325).

An additional feature of Socrative that provides students with feedback on their performance is the report function. In the two *ab initio* groups, each of the formative tests was followed by sharing a summary of responses with the whole class that displays the number of correct answers as well as the wrong answers given for each question. This allows both lecturer and students to analyse the results and revisit those questions that appear to have been the most challenging. For lecturers the report function thus becomes a valuable tool for quickly identifying weaknesses or gaps in knowledge of the class. For students the oral repetition of correct answers and explanations provided during the tests enhances their cognitive and reasoning skills. Repeated and varied feedback reinforces the students' knowledge and understanding further, which most likely leads to even better retention.

As already mentioned, the exit ticket function in Socrative allows students to reflect on how well they have understood the lesson topic and what they have learnt. It is well-known that self-reflection supports learning by activating 'a range of cognitive skills', which leads to 'the development of an awareness of one's knowledge and practice that leads to responsible and autonomous action in order to transform one's way of knowing and doing' (Alderete Diaz, 2008: 2). Moreover, it is a means of providing regular, informal feedback to the lecturer about the learning experience, which students find useful. It is not surprising then to find that in the survey six out of nine students (67 per cent) taught in class and all respondents taught online either agreed or strongly agreed with the statement 'I found it helpful to feed back to the tutor how well I have understood the content of a lesson' (see Fig. 10.2 and Fig. 10.4).

Socrative is also effective in terms of inclusivity as it can provide students 'with a sense of active participation' (Cerqueiro and Martín-Macho Harrison, 2019: 3). Less confident students or those suffering from anxiety feel more able to take part in this kind of activity and interact with their peers and lecturer, safe in the knowledge that they do not need to speak out in front of the whole class. All students are able to see their individual results on their own device but can also compare their performance with the performance of their peers when anonymised results are shared by the lecturer, thus enhancing the learning experience of all students in the class. This can be backed up by the results of the survey: when asked to assess how Socrative might facilitate interaction in the classroom, six out of nine students (67 per cent) who were taught on campus and eight out of 11 students (73 per cent) who were taught online agreed or strongly agreed with the statement 'I found answering questions and giving feedback with Socrative easier than doing the same orally' (see Fig. 10.2 and Fig. 10.4). Four out of nine students (44 per cent) taught on campus and eight out of 11 students (73 per cent) taught online agreed or strongly agreed with the statement 'I felt more confident answering questions and giving feedback in class using Socrative' (see Fig. 10.2 and Fig. 10.4). The results suggest that the use of this SRS can boost participation levels, particularly in online teaching.

Using Socrative for grammar quizzes is particularly effective in terms of student engagement because it combines 'feedback ... with challenging goals [that] can enhance motivation and performance' (Busse, 2014: 160). In the two *ab initio* courses, the quizzes were student-paced and students were encouraged to take their time to read the correct answer and explanations carefully before moving on to the next question. At the same time, a table showing live results for the quiz for each participant (with names anonymised) and question (showing the number of correct answers in per cent) was shared with the whole class, thus allowing students to compare their own responses and performance with their peers in real time. By visualising results and achievements, students are able to see what they have learned and how their learning compares to their peers, which 'provides students with a sense of progress' and can help them feel more engaged (Busse, 2014: 159). Responses to statement four of the survey 'Socrative helped me feel more engaged in the classroom' overwhelmingly confirm that SRSs can enhance the learning experience both in-class and online: seven out of nine respondents (77 per cent) and ten out of 11 respondents (91 per cent) respectively either agreed or strongly agreed with this statement (see Fig. 10.1 and Fig. 10.3).

Regular opportunities for students to be assessed and receive formative feedback on their learning progress is important also in terms of motivation and engagement outside the classroom as confirmed by one Modern Languages student from Bristol University: 'Doing the course means regular assessments, through grammar quizzes, class debates, presentations and translations. This element of regular assessment encourages you to keep on top of learning the language rather than cramming work at the end of the year' (Thrale, 2017: para. 3). This suggest that there are benefits of using SRSs that go beyond the learning experience of students in the classroom.

Conclusion

The use of SRSs in *ab initio* language classes can enhance the learning experience of students in multiple ways. Using Socrative for deploying regular formative assessment quizzes has many benefits by providing students with feedback that is more immediate, focused and interactive than traditional approaches to teacher-led feedback. Apart from the more obvious advantages of increasing engagement and participation among students, Socrative also enhances two-way feedback between students and lecturers. It can help language learners improve both accuracy and acquisition while it is also a useful tool for students' self-reflection and for providing regular feedback to lecturers that empowers students and promotes learner autonomy and satisfaction. The results of the survey show that the effectiveness of using SRSs in language classes in terms of engagement and feedback is often even greater in live online classes than in in-class teaching; an interesting finding that requires further examination and research.

References

Alderete Diez, P. (2008) 'Reflection in language teaching/learning: Is the European portfolio the answer?' In *Estudios de Metodología de la Lengua Inglesa* (IV), edited by L. Pérez Ruiz, I. Pizarro Sánchez and E. González-Cascos Jiménez, 1–7. Valladolid: Ediciones Universidad de Valladolid.

Boud, D. and Molloy, E. (2013) *Feedback in Higher and Professional Education: Understanding it and doing it well*. London and New York: Routledge.

Busse, V. (2014) 'Visible learning and visible motivation: Exploring challenging goals and feedback in language education'. In *Motivation and Foreign Language Learning: From theory to practice*, edited by D. Lasagabaster, A. Doiz and J.M. Sierra, 157–74. Amsterdam: John Benjamins Publishing Company.

Cerqueiro, F.F. and Martín-Macho Harrison, A. (2019) 'Socrative in higher education: Game vs. other uses'. *Multimodal Technologies and Interaction* 3:3, 49.

Compton, M. and Allen, J. (2018) 'Student response systems: A rationale for their use and a comparison of some cloud-based tools'. *Compass: Journal of Learning and Teaching* 11:1. Online. https://journals.gre.ac.uk/index.php/compass/article/view/696/pdf (accessed 12 October 2018).

Herrada, R., Banos, R. and Alcayde, A. (2020) 'Student response systems: A multidisciplinary analysis using visual analytics'. *Education Sciences* 10:348, 1–23.

Kulhavy, R. (1977) 'Feedback in written instruction'. In *Review of Educational Research*, edited by the American Educational Research Association, 47:1, 211–32. Online. www.jstor.org/stable./1170128 (accessed 15 November 2019).

OfS (2019) 'Student satisfaction rises but universities should do more to improve feedback'. Online. www.officeforstudents.org.uk/news-blog-and-events/press-and-media/student-satisfaction-rises-but-universities-should-do-more-to-improve-feedback/ (accessed 2 February 2021).

QAA (2019) 'Subject benchmark statement, languages, cultures and societies'. Online. www.qaa.ac.uk/docs/qaa/subject-benchmark-statements/subject-benchmark-statement-languages-cultures-and-societies.pdf?sfvrsn=4ce2cb81_4 (accessed 12 May 2020).

Sánchez, M.J., Diego, C. and Fernández-Sánchez, A. (2017) 'Using quizzes to assess and enhance learning of English as a foreign language'. *Revista Española de Lingüística Aplicada /Spanish Journal of Applied Linguistics* 30:1, 325–41. Online. www.researchgate.net/publication/316712919_Using_quizzes_to_assess_and_enhance_learning_of_English_as_a_foreign_language (accessed 28 October 2020).

Sheen, Y. and Ellis, R. (2011) 'Corrective feedback in language teaching'. In *Handbook of Research in Second Language Teaching and Learning*, vol. II, edited by E. Hinkel, 593–610. New York and London: Routledge.

Shute, V.J. (2008) 'Focus on formative feedback'. In *Review of Education Research*, edited by the American Educational Research Association 78:1 (March), 153–89.

Socrative (2021) 'About us'. Online. www.socrative.com/about-us/ (accessed 24 April 2021).

Thrale, E. (2017) 'What it's like to study a modern languages degree'. Online. www.timeshighereducation.com/student/blogs/what-its-study-modern-languages-degree (accessed 5 January 2021).

William, D. (2018) 'Feedback'. In *The Cambridge Handbook of Instructional Feedback*, edited by A. Lipnevich and J.K. Smith, 3–28. Cambridge: Cambridge University Press Online. www.cambridge.org/core/books/cambridge-handbook-of-instructional-feedback/contents/DE8EB4DA51CCF3247BF562A3D8032E24/core-reader (accessed 14 July 2019).

11
Two for the price of one: using a cognitive theory of metaphors for vocabulary teaching and learning
Silke Mentchen

Introduction

An article by Novic (2021: n.p.) titled 'The harmful ableist language you unknowingly use' discusses conventional metaphors like 'to fall on deaf ears' or calling an idea 'lame'. Making students more aware of the effects of such language use is one of the aims of integrating insights from cognitive linguistics into language teaching methods, especially vocabulary learning. 'Even though vocabulary is considered to be one of the most important elements in language learning, it tends to be subordinated to the learning of grammar, and is largely left to take care of itself in language courses.' This quote, from Laufer and Nation's chapter 'Vocabulary' (2012: 167), summarises a problem learners face at all levels, but perhaps more acutely in *ab initio* language programmes, owing to the fast pace of these courses.

This chapter on vocabulary learning has been written with several teaching contexts in mind; first, the *ab initio* context in English speaking higher education institutions, including both the teaching for degree courses and at Institution-Wide Language Programmes (IWLPs); second, the teaching of German as a foreign language in schools. Of course, the number of contact hours will vary depending on institution and desired progression, and in turn will determine the shape of any approach in practice. My intention, however, is to show that using cognitive linguistics can help to encourage independent learning so that using the approach discussed in this chapter can have an impact on the learning process, even if the time available in the classroom is limited.

I will outline the theoretical background of my approach, survey literature on how to apply this theory to second language (L2) language teaching, provide examples for lessons and conclude by outlining the wider political relevance of this approach. I will look at the value of the cognitive linguistic approach for the understanding of L2 texts and the production of accurate and idiomatic German.

Learning new words

Experience shows that vocabulary acquisition is one of the areas causing *ab initio* students to lag behind their post-A-level peers in later years. Laufer and Nation (2012) describe the reasons for learners' difficulties when facing new words: if we assume that native speakers learn about 1,000 new word families per year until the age of 20, and that 98 per cent of a text's lexis can be understood if the reader can recall 8,000 word families, the sheer enormity of the task becomes clear (Laufer and Nation, 2012: 165 and 169, see also Schmitt, 2008). It is difficult to pin a number of vocabulary items to each Common European Framework of Reference (CEFR) level because opinions vary (see Milton and Alexiou, 2009). However, it is safe to assume that an *ab initio* learner has to acquire vocabulary in a relatively short time. L2 users also need to be able to understand a variety of features of the new word (inflection and derivation). In addition to this, input appropriate to a word's usefulness cannot be guaranteed. Tschirner has shown that compilations such as *Basic German* (Langenscheidt) do not necessarily list the most frequently used German words, his examples of such omissions include *verwenden*, *Bewegung* and *natürlich* (Tschirner, 2005: 11). The situation and environment of the learning process also play a significant role.

'Intentional learning' (Laufer and Nation, 2012: 171), defined as using lists, cards and computer-assisted methods, shows encouraging results.[1] In any case, 'attention, operationalized as involvement, is a key factor in learning' (Laufer and Nation, 2012: 171). A meaning-focused input used to stimulate learners' intellectual curiosity about their own cognitive processes can lead to a higher level of attention or involvement. Using conceptual metaphor theory (CMT) when introducing new words can lead to such stimulation and hence involvement.

The CMT approach can be linked to approaches in language teaching in which the focus is on the process of network building. Students learn the relationships (either paradigmatic: synonyms like 'drink' and 'beverage', antonyms like 'hot' and 'cold', or syntagmatic: collocational restrictions represented in idioms) between new and familiar words and establish a meaning network. This leads to depth of knowledge: L2 learners create connections between L2 words in their minds, rather than learning a list of L2 words and their equivalents in English (Haastrup and Henriksen, 2000: 221). In this sense, CMT is 'more a matter of system learning than of item learning' and leads to 'depth of knowledge' (Haastrup and Henriksen, 2000: 225). Haastrup and Henriksen describe the 'mental effort hypothesis' developed by Hulstijn (1992). They state that 'inferencing a word's meaning (rather than being given it) aids the retention of words. We believe that the process of network building can be seen as a parallel to inferencing, both requiring considerable mental effort' (Haastrup and Henriksen, 2000: 225). According to their findings, 'vocabulary acquisition is enhanced by directing learners' attention to lexical relations and to the analysis of words, thus supporting network building and depth of knowledge' (Haastrup and Henriksen, 2000: 238). Using a visual thesaurus like www.visualthesaurus.com, as suggested by Roche and Suñer (2017: 161), can help to reinforce this teaching method.

In Nation's extremely useful overview on the topic of learning L2 vocabulary, this mental effort is referred to as the 'learning burden' (Nation, 2001: 23), or as 'the amount of effort required to learn' the word. Once learners have understood that meanings of words can be accessed because they are conceptually motivated, learning can become 'explicit' (Nation 2001: 34) and the burden or effort may become intellectually enjoyable. EL-Bouz (2016: 89) calls this a *'spannender Entdeckungsprozess'*, an exciting process of discovery. Nation's observation that 'defining a word by looking for the concept that runs through all its uses reduces the number of words to learn' describes this process well (Nation, 2001: 51). He goes on to explain how using this teaching and learning method opens up 'educational values' as the learner comes to see the world from different perspectives. The example Nation uses is 'fork'. In English, the word is used to describe a shape rather than a function and thus it can refer to a piece of cutlery as well as to a road system or lightning. In languages where the meaning of 'fork' only activates its function, it cannot be used to describe a junction in the road, for example. Nation's description of the 'generative processing' of new words (the example given is that of 'cement' as in 'We cemented the path' and its metaphorical extension 'We cemented our relationship with a drink') (Nation, 2001: 52) highlights this intellectually challenging process. He states that it 'can lead to a form of mental elaboration that deepens or enriches the level of processing of a word and thus enhances learning' (Nation, 2001: 69). I believe that this approach will be appealing to a university student embarking on a course at beginners' level. Rather than learning lists of words, learners are encouraged to engage intellectually with learning as a process.

What is CMT?

A good overview of CMT can be found in Kövecses (2017). He states that many conceptual metaphors, like for instance 'knowing is seeing', 'can be found in a large number of genetically unrelated languages' (Kövecses, 2017: 19). Such examples for English are: 'I see', 'this is a bright idea', 'she is in the dark', and for German: *etwas erklären, ein heller Kopf, einen Kontext erhellen* and *im Dunkeln tappen*. Kövecses concedes that 'not *all* conceptual metaphors [...] will be the same from one language/culture to another language/culture'. Metaphors can 'derive from the body, cultural specificities and also the more general context' (Kövecses, 2017: 19, emphasis in the original). I am using Kövecses' definition, 'a conceptual metaphor is understanding one domain of experience (that is typically abstract) in terms of another (that is typically concrete)' (Kövecses, 2017: 13).[2]

Although the concepts of metaphors are discussed in linguistics and literary criticism research, they are largely absent in literature about second language teaching (MacArthur, 2017: 413). This is surprising, especially since CMT, described by Fludernik as having had a 'tremendous impact, displacing almost all other theoretical approaches to metaphor' has resulted 'in what could well be described as a paradigm shift' (Fludernik, 2011: 5).

It is important to realise that CMT describes the way we think and not only the way we speak: 'Conceptual metaphors can be said to represent ways of thinking, in which people typically construe abstract concepts such as time, emotions, and feelings in terms of more easily understood and perceived concrete entities, such as places, substances and containers' (Littlemore and Low, 2006: 5).

The connection between two domains is established from concrete to abstract. For example, we can describe relationships in terms of temperature ('They gave me a warm welcome') but we would not describe temperature in terms of relationships (*The temperature in this room got very passionate'). The link between the two domains is asymmetrical and one-directional, presumably because we monitor the concrete experience (temperature) more consistently than we monitor the abstract topic (relationships). While many conceptual metaphors seem to be similar in many European languages, variation, sometimes even within the same language, is also found (Kövecses, 2017: 19) and can depend on a number of factors. These can be culturally or environmentally determined.

It will have become clear that metaphor in this context is not the rhetorical feature reserved for poems, polemical speeches and literature. It is not 'an anomaly, an unusual or deviant way of using language' representing 'a minority interest or something you do in a literature class', but an 'indispensable basis of language and thought' (Goatly, 1997: 1). Metaphors are not only relevant in 'advanced use by a minority of speakers' and therefore of little use in L2 teaching. Metaphor is not a niche feature but ubiquitous (Littlemore and Low: 2006). Other terminology about metaphors goes back to Richards, as referred to by Ricœur (1975: 26), where the 'vehicle' is what in CMT is referred to as 'source domain' and 'tenor' as 'target domain'.[3] The German word for vocabulary itself, *Wortschatz*, can serve as a good example of this principle as its literal translation is 'treasure of words'. Aitchison's influential book *Words in the Mind* (1987) on the 'Mental Lexicon' uses metaphors such as 'The human word-store' (Aitchinson, 1987: 3) 'Attempts to pin down the meaning of words' (Aitchinson, 1987: 53), 'Word-webs: Semantic networks' (Aitchinson, 1987: 99) or 'The internal architecture of words' (Aitchinson, 1987: 145) to make her descriptions more accessible to a wide range of readers by tapping into underlying conceptual metaphors.

As Koch (2010: 36) observes, a metaphor's career which may at one point have started as an innovative addition can lead to the metaphor's integration into the standard lexicon. It is no longer perceived as a metaphor by native speakers but has entered the lexicon and is only noticed again as an innovation when L2 learners are amused by words like *Handschuh* (the German word for glove which translates literally as 'shoe for the hand') or *Glühbirne* (the German word for light bulb which translates as 'glowing pear'). Since lexicalised metaphors (sometimes referred to as 'dead metaphors') are fundamental, it seems appropriate to make learners aware of this process, and thereby allow access to understanding them, as early as possible. What seems part of the conventional vocabulary can be experienced as innovative by learners. Weininger (2013: 27) recommends the inclusion of the teaching of conceptual metaphors at a low language level for that reason.

Similarities and differences of concepts and therefore of use of metaphors between L1 and L2 must be of interest to any language teacher, starting at *ab initio* level. But as Littlemore (2017) points out, teachers of *any* subject in a context with international students should be made aware of the potential problems in understanding academic discourse caused by the teacher's (often unconscious) use of metaphors. For an excellent overview, including short videos and recommendations for lecturers, see Littlemore and colleagues (2016).

This problem is further complicated by the fact that many second language users are unaware of their own gaps and misunderstandings. Identifying overlaps between L1 and L2, and just as importantly their differences, will be crucial. Koch points out another benefit. She sees the discussion of metaphors in language teaching, including at *ab initio* level, as preparation and addition to the teaching of literature. This will minimise the 'shock' experienced by many students when moving from textbooks to authentic literature:

> Eine Thematisierung von Metaphern im Sprachunterricht – und zwar von Anfang an (!) – ist ihrerseits als Vorbereitung auf bzw. Ergänzung zum Literaturunterricht sinnvoll, da sich Autoren auf alltägliche Metaphern berufen [...] und der „Literaturschock" (Weinrich 1983:201), der beim Übergang von didaktisierten Lehrwerktexten zu authentischer Literatur entsteht und die Motivation der Lernenden sinken lässt, abgemildert werden kann. (Koch, 2010: 44)[4]

Engelbrecht (2014) demonstrates convincingly how 'metaphor-awareness' can be raised in the beginners' classroom. She outlines two lesson plans based on chapters 8 and 9 of the textbook *Menschen* (Hueber), in which the topics *Zeit* (time) and *Essen* (food) are introduced. She explains in some detail how the learners' previous cultural knowledge about the concept of time can be activated and used to understand new vocabulary and how the grammatical phenomenon of compound nouns (examples in this context include *Meeresfrucht, Spiegelei, Tortendiagramm*) can be explained by referring to metaphors.[5]

If the way in which human beings understand the world around them is mostly metaphorical, and if words are manifestations of these concepts, then the acquisition of new words in L2, and therefore concepts, can lead to a different way of comprehending the world. CMT almost automatically leads to intercultural and transcultural teaching (see, for example, Weininger, 2013: 28). It is important to keep in mind that this theory of metaphor tries to explain our understanding of words as well as our thinking. 'Metaphor resides not only in language but also in thought' (Kövecses, 2017: 16).[6]

Experiments by Kövecses and Szabo suggest that learners who were given motivated explanations involving metaphors rather than simply translations when learning new phrasal verbs including 'up' and 'down' were better at understanding previously unencountered phrasal verbs that also used 'up' and 'down' in a similar way (Kövecses and Szabo, 1996: 345–51;

MacArthur, 2017: 415). An example of how this may work for German is given by Hoffmann who looks at *Funktionsverbgefüge* in German, using an approach from cognitive linguistics. She discusses highly idiomatic expressions like *in Gang bringen* (to set into motion), *in Betracht ziehen* (to take into account) or *zur Verfügung stellen* (to put at someone's disposal), for example, illustrating that they are all based on the concept of space (Hoffmann, 2018: 77). Exercises involving these could be used towards the end of an *ab initio* course, depending on the level learners are supposed to achieve. For limitations and potential counterproductive effects caused by too much meta-language used in the classroom, see Low (2008: 217ff).

Based on an approach informed by cognitive linguistics, a team at LMU Munich are developing teaching materials that employ visualisation (https://granima.de/). This is used to animate or illustrate examples for A1 to B2 including prepositions, the passive, prefixes, modal verbs, and syntax. Their material is designed for learners from heterogenous backgrounds while I am focusing on learners who use English as their common language.

Using metaphors in language teaching

Learning about metaphors will equip students with additional tools needed in order to access authentic texts in the target language. This competence can be fostered from A1 level onwards and can also lead to more idiomatic text production. In this section I will sketch lesson plans. Roche and Suñer (2017: 62–8) discuss the existing research on strategies that learners develop when confronted with new metaphors and find that these include relying on analogies, using figurative thinking, relying on context and on knowledge about metaphors in L1. In their overview of L2 vocabulary learning in general they include the teaching of meta-cognitive strategies (Roche and Suñer, 2017: 150–64). Liebscher reminds us to recognise 'the benefits of the learner's first language as a cognitive and meta-cognitive tool, as a strategic organizer, and as a scaffold for language development' (2013: 127) and Wei points out in an article about the concept of translanguaging that practices in which teachers make use of the learners' other language can help to 'maximize the learner's, and the teacher's, linguistic resources in the process of problem-solving and knowledge construction' (Wei, 2018: 15). He calls this '*a process of knowledge construction* that goes beyond language(s)' (Wei, 2018: 15, emphasis in the original).[7] What follows are ideas for lessons.

Step 1. Discussion in English to raise awareness of conceptual metaphors. Here, examples from Computer Science work well. Students can discuss the use and meaning of expressions like: the net, the web, to surf, to go to a website, the server, a page, a folder, to leak information, to upload, to download, threads, breadcrumbs, cookies, spam, bug, virus, mouse. At this stage, the teacher can decide whether to introduce metalanguage or not. Goatly refers to 'filling the lexical gap' (1997: 154) to describe the use of metaphors in contexts as the one above.

Step 2. The teacher then introduces a conceptual metaphor like 'time is money' and asks students to map expressions relating to 'Geld' onto expressions relating to 'Zeit':

sparen, ausgeben, investieren, verdienen, bezahlen, gewinnen, schenken, verlieren, rauben, stehlen, nicht/genug haben, verschwenden, verbrauchen, kostbar, wertvoll.

Of the list above, *ausgeben, verdienen* and *bezahlen* are not used idiomatically in the *Zeit* context. It is interesting to discuss possible reasons for the connection between the two domains. Depending on the language level, vocabulary relating to *Geld* could first be discussed to make sure that meanings are understood. Once students are confident using the expressions relating to *Geld* they can apply them to the new context of *Zeit* thereby making use of this 'Dual Coding' (MacArthur, 2017: 417). Understanding the motivation behind figurative meanings makes the meaning of new vocabulary more memorable. Koch refers to this as 'Synergieeffekt' (2010: 51). Students acquire two new words for the price of learning one. It will be just as important though to identify those expressions that do not work.

Another example could be to introduce the conceptual metaphors GOOD is UP and BAD is DOWN by presenting a list of expressions, asking the students to sort them into *gut* und *schlecht*. Depending on the students' previous knowledge, this list can be trimmed or expressions involved could be introduced first. A revision of adverbs and verbs involved would be useful.

1. *die Stimmung war auf Null*
2. *ich bin ganz unten*
3. *es geht bergauf*
4. *es herrscht Hochstimmung*
5. *die Stimmung war im Keller*
6. *die Hoffnung sinkt*
7. *das heitert mich auf*

8.   *der Aufschwung*
9.   *mit der Wirtschaft geht es aufwärts*
10. *die Chancen steigen*
11. *das zieht mich runter*
12. *ich bin hochvergnügt*

In my experience, this exercise invariably leads to discussions about why 'up' is associated with positive things, and 'down' with negative experiences. Whether or not the discussions resonate with everyone, students will remember this lesson and the metaphors involved.

Step 3. Students study authentic German texts chosen for their use of metaphors. Texts about the economy, politics or sports work well. Depending on the level of proficiency, the teacher may have to adapt the text or add a glossary. The task involves identifying metaphors used in the text. For examples from a wide variety of texts see Semino (2008). Even though her examples are all for English texts, they can still serve as prompts for where to look. Useful texts can be found in the politics, economics, science or sports sections of newspapers. An example taken from a text used in a textbook's lesson one can illustrate this further: '**Herz**lich Willkommen in Tübingen! Die Universität Tübingen wurde 1477 gegründet und ist eine der deutschen **Spitzen**universitäten. Traditions**reich**tum **trifft** hier auf Innovation und Kreativität. [...]' (Braun et al., 2016: 20, emphasis added). Students are asked to discuss, in English, the use of the words *Herz*, *Spitze*, *reich* and *treffen* regarding their metaphorical content. This kind of task can reinforce some of the metaphors discussed in Step 2 and also introduce new ones.

Step 4. Students are asked to write a short text using some of the metaphors they have studied. This step could also be a gap-filling exercise. The tasks described above can also involve aural and oral exercises.

Step 5. As a further step, students can be encouraged to watch out for conceptual metaphors, to notice them in idiomatic expressions and to add them to their lists. Flashcards (or other methods of adding new vocabulary like Quizlet) can be produced and shared. One group could hunt for German expressions using metaphors from the source domain of buildings (*aufbauen, zementieren, der Grundstein, gegen die Wand, die Schwelle, Türen öffnen, ruinieren* ...), for example, while others could focus on different domains: journey, eating, body, machine....

I would argue that this method will add a dimension to the learners' vocabulary. It will not replace all other ways of learning new words, rather, it will make learners aware of the process itself and can lead to reflection on word acquisition. Hopefully, it will also identify those expressions which are not productive as metaphors in German. The fact that 'way', for example, is productive in English ('there is no way I can do this', 'they did this in a different way', 'in which way shall I do this?', 'which way to turn' and so on), but not in German, can be observed.

In the ideas for teaching material above I have mostly included nouns and verbs. The same approach can also be used to introduce prepositions. For an example of how this can work see the online interactive grammar programme 'Just-in-Time-Grammar' (Künzl-Snodgrass and Mentchen, 2013): The unit on prepositions is organised by case but also by the context (space or time) that the preposition is used for:

> There are quite a few prepositions used for both, space and time. In a way, measuring time is articulated by borrowing ideas from measuring space. We speak of a 'short' or 'long' time, and we say things like: 'I am glad that's behind me' or 'this still lies ahead'. You can have a 'house between other houses', but you can also do something 'between 4pm and 6pm'. Consider: *Er lief vom Start bis zum Ziel in 30 Sekunden.* [He ran from start to finish in 30 seconds.] *Ich habe von 15.00 Uhr bis 16.00 Uhr auf dich gewartet!* [I waited for you from 3pm to 4pm!]. (Künzl-Snodgrass and Mentchen, 2013: n.p.)

The fact that individual prepositions like *ab* (from a certain place/time onwards), *aus* (from a certain place/time), *in* (inside a building/time period), or *durch* (through/out a place/time period) double up to locate events in space and time can be made transparent making students intellectually curious and engaged. The online programme uses visualisations and animations to support the learning process. It is also important to include the idea of 'objects moving in space' to explain the idea that time passes, as expressed in *im Laufe der Zeit* or in *die Ferien sind schnell vorbei gegangen*, for example.

Depending on the learners' interests, the idea that we can only describe time by recycling concepts from space can lead to interesting discussions. Fauconnier and Johnson (2008: 54) state: 'the fact that time is measurable and stable – inferences for which we do not have independent evidence – comes from the domain of space.' It can make for a very memorable lesson on prepositions if students learn that the linear and horizontal concept of time in which events that happened in the past are 'behind' us and events in the future are 'in front of us' is a construct. Many Asian languages use a vertical axis, for example, and in some languages the future is conceptualised as behind the speaker as it is unknown and can therefore not be seen.[8]

Apart from benefits relating to the process of learning and remembering new words, the theory of conceptual metaphors, and the understanding of 'frames' can make students more aware of reader manipulation in texts.[9]

The 'ability *not* to be swayed by another person's use of figurative language' is listed by Littlemore and Low (2006: 277, emphasis in the original) as one of the communicative language abilities established through metaphorical competence. They continue: 'In order to avoid being positioned by the writer, readers need to identify the conceptual metaphors and metonymies underlying the arguments' (Littlemore and Low, 2006: 277). They give a good example: 'The welfare state can be described as an umbrella or a safety net, depending on one's political vantage point' (Littlemore and Low, 2006: 279). Musloff (2017) discusses the 'parasite' metaphor used in different genres in the context of debates about immigration in the UK, and Goatly's discussion of the metaphorical concept 'immigrants are disease' in his article 'Conventional metaphor and the latent ideology of racism' (Goatly, 2011: 272) is another good case in point.

My recommendations for further work in this field includes the production of a textbook dedicated to vocabulary learning using CMT based on word lists compiled by frequency grammars (for example, Tschirner, 2020). This could be similar to books produced for ESOL, like Lazar's *Meanings and Metaphors* (2003). More effective though would be the introduction of CMT-based learning strategies for regular L2 textbooks, including at *ab initio* level.

Notes

1   For a more detailed discussion on the effectiveness of using vocabulary learning apps see Chapter 12.
2   For a much broader discussion of the theory, and its first formulations, see the works by Lakoff and Johnson. In Lakoff (2008: 24–5) one can find an excellent summary of the theory.
3   For a good overview of the study and use of metaphor in general see Kohl's (2007) book, *Metapher*.
4   'Discussing metaphors in language teaching – and from the very beginning (!) – is for its part useful as a preparation for or support of the teaching of literature, since authors use everyday metaphors [...] and the "literary shock" (Weinrich, 1983: 201), which arises during the transition from didacticised texts to authentic literature and causes the learners' motivation to decline can be mitigated' [my translation]. For more reflections and advice on teaching literature to beginners, see Chapter 4, this volume.

5 Practitioners interested in reading more about applications in the classroom are referred to MacArthur (2017), Roche and Suñer (2017) and Blomberg and Jessen (2018).
6 Recent thinking about neuroscience and its implications for language learning ought to be considered as well, for an initial overview see Grein (2013). It seems to be the case that neurons storing particular memories or meanings can be activated simultaneously when associations or connections between the two memories or meanings are established. For example, if a certain event is associated with feeling sick, then this pair will be activated frequently at the same time, resulting in an organic link (or an 'action potential', also referred to as 'spike') between the two nerve cells. What makes this possible is synaptic plasticity. These 'circuits' (Lakoff, 2008) link the source and target domains in one step. The two areas are activated simultaneously. For a discussion of intercultural awareness in the *ab initio* classroom see Chapter 8, this volume.
7 See Chapter 14, this volume, for more details about engaging with learners' strengths.
8 For further discussions see Roche and Suñer (2017: 69–80) and Nuñez and Sweetser (2006). Roche and EL-Bouz (2020) discuss how understanding metaphors can help to visualise and animate exercises. For more information on studies about the 'metaphoricity' of prepositions ('some prepositions are more metaphorical than others'), see Nacey (2014). Schröder (2014) has an excellent overview of the discussion of 'space' as a topic within linguistic research.
9 For good examples see recent tweets by Lakoff about Donald Trump on https://georgelakoff.com/framingforactivists/.

References

Aitchison, E. (1987) *Words in the Mind*. Oxford: Blackwell.
Blomberg, J. and Jessen, M. (2018) 'Theoretische Säulen der Kognitiven Linguistik'. In *Kognitive Linguistik*, edited by M. Jessen, J. Blomberg and J. Roche, 42–52. Tübingen: Narr.
Braun, B., Doubek M., Fügert N., Kotas O., Marquardt Langermann, M., Nied Curcio, M., Sander, I., Schäfer, N., Schweiger, K., Trebesius-Bensch, U. and Walter, M. (2016) *DaF kompakt neu A1-B1. Übungsbuch*. Stuttgart: Ernst Klett Sprachen.
EL-Bouz, K. (2016) 'Grammatik neu gedacht: Innovatives didaktisches Konzept für die deutschen Modalverben'. *Zeitschrift für Interkulturellen Fremdsprachenunterricht* 21:2, 85–98.
Engelbrecht, N. (2014) 'Zur Rolle von Metaphern im Unterricht Deutsch als Fremdsprache auf A1 Niveau'. Stellenbosch University. Online. http://scholar.sun.ac.za. (accessed 24 April 2021).
Fauconnier, G. and Turner, M. (2008) 'Rethinking metaphor'. In *The Cambridge Handbook of Metaphor and Thought*, edited by R. Gibbs, 53–66. Cambridge: Cambridge University Press.
Fludernik, M. (2011) *Beyond Cognitive Metaphor Theory*. New York: Routledge.
Goatly, A. (1997) *The Language of Metaphors*. New York: Routledge.
Goatly, A. (2011) 'Conventional metaphor and the latent ideology of racism'. In *Beyond Cognitive Metaphor Theory*, edited by M. Fludernik, 258–80. New York: Routledge.
Grein, M. (2013) *Neurodidaktik. Grundlagen für Sprachlehrende*. Ismaning: Hueber.
Haastrup, K. and Henriksen, B. (2000) 'Vocabulary acquisition: Acquiring depth of knowledge through network building'. *International Journal of Applied Linguistics* 10:2, 221–40.
Hoffmann, I. (2018) 'Räumlich konzeptualisierte Funktionsverbgefüge – eine Erwerbsstudie'. *Zeitschrift für Interkulturellen Fremdsprachenunterricht* 23:2, 74–85.
Hulstijn, J.H. (1992) 'Retention of inferred and given word meanings: Experiments in incidental learning'. In *Vocabulary and Applied Linguistics*, edited by P.J.L. Arnaud and H. Bejoint, 113–25. New York: Macmillan.
Koch, C. (2010) 'Lexikalisierte Metaphern als Herausforderung für den Fremdsprachenunterricht'. https://www.metaphorik.de/sites/www.metaphorik.de/files/journal-pdf/18_2010_koch.pdf (accessed 16 June 2022).
Kohl, K. (2007) *Metapher*. Stuttgart: J.B. Metzler.
Kövecses, Z. (2017) 'Conceptual metaphor theory'. In *The Routledge Handbook of Metaphor and Language*, edited by E. Semino and Z. Demjén, 13–27. New York: Routledge.
Kövecses, Z. and Szabo, P. (1996) 'Idioms: A view from cognitive semantics'. *Applied Linguistics* 17:3, 326–55.

Künzl-Snodgrass, A. and Mentchen, S. (2013). Just-in-time grammar. Online. www.langcen. cam.ac.uk/opencourseware/german/german.html (accessed 26 September 2021).

Lakoff, G. (2008) 'The neural theory of metaphor'. In *The Cambridge Handbook of Metaphor and Thought*, edited by R. Gibbs, 17–38. Cambridge: Cambridge University Press.

Lakoff, G. and Johnson, M. (1980) *Metaphors We Live By*. Chicago and London: University of Chicago Press.

Laufer, B. and Nation, I.S.P. (2012) 'Vocabulary'. In *The Routledge Handbook of Second Language Acquisition*, edited by S.M. Grass and A. Mackey, 163–176. New York: Routledge.

Lazar, G. (2003) *Meanings and Metaphors*. Cambridge: Cambridge University Press.

Liebscher, G. (2013) 'Multilinguals in the language classroom and curricular consequences'. In *Traditions and Transitions. Curricula for German Studies*, edited by J.L. Plews and B. Schmenck, 125–41. Waterloo, ON: Wilfrid Laurier University Press.

Littlemore, J. (2017) 'Metaphor use in educational contexts: Functions and variations'. In *The Routledge Handbook of Metaphor and Language*, edited by E. Semino and Z. Demjén, 283–95. New York: Routledge.

Littlemore, J. and Low, G. (2006) 'Metaphoric competence and communicative language ability'. *Applied Linguistics* 27:2, 268–94.

Littlemore, J., MacArthur, F., Cienki, A. and Holloway, J. (2016). 'How to make yourself understood by international students: The role of metaphor in academic tutorials'. British Council. Online. www.teachingenglish.org.uk/sites/teacheng/files/B458%20ELTRP%20 Report%20-%20Littlemore_final.pdf (accessed 24 April 2021).

Low, G. (2008) 'Metaphor and education'. In *The Cambridge Handbook of Metaphor and Thought*, edited by R. Gibbs, 212–31. Cambridge: Cambridge University Press.

MacArthur, F. (2017) 'Using metaphor in the teaching of second/foreign languages'. In *The Routledge Handbook of Metaphor and Language*, edited by E. Semino and Z. Demjén, 413–25. New York: Routledge.

Milton, J. and Alexiou, T. (2009) 'Vocabulary size and the Common European Framework of Reference for Languages'. In *Vocabulary Studies in First and Second Language Acquisition*, edited by B. Richards, M.H. Daller, D.D. Malvern, P. Meara, J. Milton and J. Treffers-Daller, 194–211. London: Palgrave Macmillan.

Musloff, A. (2017) 'Metaphor and persuasion in politics'. In *The Routledge Handbook of Metaphor and Language*, edited by E. Semino and Z. Demjén, 309–22. New York: Routledge.

Nacey, S. (2014) 'Metaphorical prepositions in L2 English'. AELCO/SCOLA. Online. https:// susannacey.hihm.no/wp-content/uploads/2017/09/Presentation-AELCO-SCOLA2014.pdf (accessed 24 April 2021).

Nation, I.S.P. (2001) *Learning Vocabulary in Another Language*. Cambridge: Cambridge University Press.

Novic, S. (2021) 'The harmful ableist language you unknowingly use'. Online. www.bbc.com/ worklife/article/20210330-the-harmful-ableist-language-you-unknowingly-use (accessed 24 April 2021).

Nuñez, R. and Sweetser, E. (2006) 'With the future behind them: Convergent evidence from Aymara language and gesture in the crosslinguistic comparison of spatial construals of time'. *Cognitive Science* 30, 401–50.

Ricœur, P. (1975) *The Rule of Metaphor*. New York: Routledge.

Roche, J. and EL-Bouz, K. (2020) 'Zur Räumlichkeit temporaler Präpositionen – Ein kognitionsdidaktischer Ansatz'. *Zeitschrift für Interkulturellen Fremdsprachenunterricht* 25:1, 1395–405.

Roche, J. and Suñer, F. (2017) *Sprachenlernen und Kognition, Kompendium DaF/DaZ 1*. Tübingen: Narr.

Schmitt, N. (2008) 'Instructed second language vocabulary learning'. *Language Teaching Research* 12:3, 329–63.

Schröder, U. (2014) 'Die metaphorische Bedeutungsvielfalt von Präpositionen im DaF-Unterricht an brasilianischen Hochschulen'. *Zeitschrift für Interkulturellen Fremdsprachenunterricht* 19:2, 146–70.

Semino, E. (2008) *Metaphor in Discourse*. Cambridge: Cambridge University Press.

Tschirner, E. (2005) 'Korpora, Häufigkeitslisten, Wortschatzerwerb'. In *Deutsch als Fremdsprache – Konturen und Perspektiven eines Fachs*, edited by A. Heine, M. Hennig and E. Tschirner, 133–49. Munich: Iudicum.

Tschirner, E. and Möhring, J. (2020) *A Frequency Dictionary of German Core Vocabulary for Learners*. New York: Routledge.

Wei, L. (2018) 'Translanguaging as a Practical Theory of Language'. *Applied Linguistics*, 39:1, 9–30.

Weininger, A. (2013) 'Grundlagen, Funktionen und kognitive Potentiale alltagssprachlicher Metaphern im Fremdsprachenunterricht'. *Zeitschrift für Interkulturellen Fremdsprachenunterricht* 18:1, 21–3.

12
Effective vocabulary learning apps: what should they look like?
An evaluation with a particular view to German language acquisition

Annemarie Künzl-Snodgrass, Theresa Lentfort and Maren de Vincent-Humphreys

Introduction

It is possible to communicate in a foreign language, after a fashion, just by using words. Adjectival endings don't matter if, for example, what you want is an ambulance, and quickly. So you need the words for ambulance and accident in the foreign language. Words come first, grammar follows (Wilkins, 1972: 111–12). In practice, of course, only grammatical context enables the learner to extract more than merely basic meaning from words. But without words, there is no grammar. It follows that effective strategies for vocabulary learning must be central to any attempt to learn a foreign language. Particularly in the context of *ab initio* language learning, acquiring a basic vocabulary is one of the most pressing challenges that students face (Dräxler and Kühn, 1998: 307).

One method of learning vocabulary is from lists in a behaviourist way, whether isolated from context, or embedded in a context (for example, in a coursebook). This still seems to have a place (Kühn, 2013: 158; Kurtz, 2016: 446), not only in textbooks, but also, surprisingly and despite the digital turn, in commercially produced mobile language learning apps (Heil et al., 2015: 32).

The comparatively recent development of computer-assisted language learning (CALL) has brought into sharp focus its potential for uses in second language teaching and learning; more recently, the development of mobile-assisted language learning (MALL) technologies has opened possibilities of independent and flexible technological support for language learners (Li, 2017: 103; Kukulsa-Hume, 2018), demonstrating its potential for learners to mediate their second language learning (Ma, 2017: 197).

Benefits of CALL include, for example, quick access to authentic linguistic materials, individualised instruction and feedback for students (Li, 2016: 463). The question here is how CALL can most efficiently support successful vocabulary acquisition, especially for *ab initio* learners.

How can CALL support vocabulary acquisition?

In the following, we will present criteria that we have identified as crucial for the development of a successful vocabulary learning app, namely: knowing which words to select for the transition from *ab initio* learning to an advanced stage; which aspects constitute 'knowing a word' (Nation, 2013); how to practise retrieval; how to use timing and sequencing; how multimedia presentation supports the learning process and how feedback can be incorporated.

Selection of lexical items

Especially for *ab initio* learning, a pressing question is what vocabulary needs to be learned in order to reach basic communicative skills as quickly as possible. Word frequency is 'one of the most important features of words to be acquired at various levels of language learning' (Tschirner and Möhring, 2020: 1) and is therefore a highly relevant criterion for selecting lexical items. Identifying high-frequency words and collocations should be a priority, before moving on to less frequent items (Gardner, 2007: 242; Nation, 2013: 486). This is now embedded in the Common European Framework of Reference for Languages (CEFR): for basic use at A2 level, learners are expected to understand 'frequently used expressions related to areas of most immediate relevance' (Council of Europe, 2021).

Tschirner (2019: 100) identifies a threshold of about 2,000 words that are necessary for covering 90 per cent of conversation vocabulary in German, and about 3,000 words for an adequate understanding of best-selling literature. Vocabulary learning apps for *ab initio* should focus on reaching these thresholds as quickly as possible. In order to save the learners' time, many vocabulary learning apps are equipped with import features that allow the downloading of external content, for example, pre-prepared vocabulary lists from coursebooks. However, it is important to stress that vocabulary lists should ideally be based on frequency information. To date, this is not always the case (Tschirner, 2019: 101; Schmitt and Schmitt, 2020: 84). One advantage of CALL is that digital corpora like the DWDS (*Digitales Wörterbuch der Deutschen Sprache*) already facilitate access to frequency information. Large corpora can provide a reliable overview and a selection of examples from authentic and frequently updated sources.

While the required range of receptive vocabulary is expected to be more or less the same for all beginners, the mid- or even low-frequency vocabulary needed for the productive skills of speaking and writing may vary, depending on the learner's individual biography (Tschirner, 2019: 106). An ideal vocabulary learning app should therefore allow students to create their own content that is relevant for talking about their own lives and everyday routines, in addition to high-frequency words: for *ab initio* learners in the UK, a word like *Pfund* (pound) will surely have a higher priority than for learners in a different cultural setting. Such learner-generated content can be added either individually or collaboratively (for example in a classroom or in online communities).

Knowing a word

'Knowing a word' (Nation, 2013: 49) is the result of successful vocabulary learning. This does not refer merely to the learner's familiarity with the semantic aspects of a single lexical item and its parts, but also with its pronunciation, its grammatical integration and its potential to form 'meaningful units' with other words (Takač, 2008: 16). Fundamental objectives are the understanding and acquisition of form (spoken, written, word parts), meaning (form and meaning, concepts and referents, associations) and use (grammatical functions, collocations, constraints of use) (Nation, 2013: 49). For German *ab initio* learning through CALL, we find the following aspects particularly important.

Knowing a word means knowing how to spell it, but also what it sounds like and how to pronounce it correctly on a phonological level: word stress, for example, should be considered here. There are various ways in which this can be achieved, for example by including appropriate audio materials and providing listening and pronunciation exercises, but also by facilitating learner-to-native-speaker contact through purpose-designed digital resources, for example, the apps *tandem* or *italki*, or by the repurposing of existing resources such as WhatsApp (Clancy and Murray, 2016: 507).

Nation emphasises that a learner's understanding of a word can also be deepened significantly by gaining insight into the morphological level, that is, by understanding the parts that make up the word (Nation, 2013: 72–3). For example, learners can easily understand the word *trinkbar* (drinkable), if they are already familiar with the meaning of the suffix *-bar*. Words consisting of different parts make up a large part of the German thesaurus (Barz and Fleischer, 2012: 18), so learners should be made aware of the principles of word formation from a very early learning stage, for example, of compound nouns, in German a highly productive variety of word formation. German being an inflected language, acquisition of inflected forms, for example plural forms or verbs that change vowels in conjugation, is strongly driven by the amount of input in teaching materials (Wegener, 2016: 212).

Furthermore, analysis of written and spoken German language clearly reveals the vital role of 'multi-word units' (Nation, 2013: 479). The use of specific words is subject to various semantic restrictions, which can only be acquired by learning a word as part of a sequence. For example, the sentence *Ich musste diese Entscheidung machen* (literally: I had to make this decision) is grammatically correct and can be understood, but it is not idiomatic. For an L2 learner, especially at *ab initio* stage, it is therefore important to know that *Entscheidung* frequently co-occurs with the verb *treffen*.

It follows that memorising words in context, rather than isolated units, should be encouraged (Neveling, 2016: 112; Li, 2017: 118; for an overview, see Schmitt and Schmitt, 2020: 32–74). Nation suggests that 'at least three quarters of the learning opportunities should come from meeting and using items in communicative contexts' (Nation, 2013: 482). This does not imply that learning individual words is obsolete; quite the opposite, knowing the meaning of the individual words that make up the multi-word unit facilitates its acquisition and vice versa (Nation, 2013: 481).

It has also been pointed out that multi-word units help to generate frequently occurring sentence structures. Pawley and Syder (1983) have demonstrated that L1 speakers to a very high degree rely on what they call 'institutionalized/lexicalized sentence stems' (chunks), enabling them to produce and predict frequently occurring sentence structures at a very impressive speed. For foreign language acquisition, it is therefore highly desirable to have a useful repertoire of chunks at hand, which learners can then use as set pieces to increase fluency in language production.

For *ab initio* learning, this means that learners should be given the chance to expand their understanding of a word by being exposed to input that contains an already familiar lexical item in novel contexts. For example, a learner of German, who encounters the verb *schließen* for the first time, will come across this word in its literal sense first, as in *die Tür schließen* (to close the door), before moving on to the metaphorical use of the word, for example, *ein Abkommen schließen* (to make an agreement) *or jemanden ins Herz schließen* (to take someone to one's heart). Repeated presentation of words in different specific contexts and visual enhancement of multi-word units, for example, through highlighting (Nation, 2013: 497), will help learners to remember their usage. One of the most prominent aspects in the use of language which needs to be improved in future CALL applications is that of 'generative use', by 'showing the target word, used in different senses, collocations, inflections, or grammatical functions every time the word is practised' (Nakata, 2011: 33).

A good example for this is the e-reading tool LingQ, where texts can be imported and annotated by the learner. In the reading process, learners can click on unknown words, look up their meaning in an online dictionary and then save their individualised L2 translations for each word. Notably, not only can single words, also in their inflected form, be annotated, but also multi-word units. Based on this information, the app will optically enhance all annotated words or multi-word units whenever they are encountered in a new context.

Based on the words already annotated by the learner, the import tool will help them to estimate the difficulty level of new texts, by indicating in a preview the percentage of unknown words and the number of annotated words. Annotated words can also be reviewed with a flashcard feature, showing the sentence in which the word was first presented, with the learner having to retrieve the missing word.

Retrieval practice

Based on Nation's concept of what is necessary for learners to 'know a word' – in terms of form, meaning and use – three different strategies or learning skills to access vocabulary knowledge can be distinguished: noticing, retrieving and creative use (Nation, 2013: 331–2). The first step, noticing (Schmitt, 1990: 139), implies that a learner consciously perceives a lexical item as useful when it is first presented to them; the second, retrieval, means that these items are encountered again; this can happen receptively (by seeing the written or spoken form of a word and retrieving its meaning) or productively (for example, by having the meaning or use of a word as a cue and retrieving the word form). Trying to retrieve a word actively by trying to remember it without looking it up again is superior to simply noticing (Nation, 2013: 331). Apps should therefore strongly encourage retrieval practice: rather than simply presenting a word and its translation, learners should be required to retrieve meanings and word forms by way of exercises that encourage remembering without re-study; a simple example would be multiple-choice exercises.

Learners are more likely to retrieve a word successfully if retrieval practice follows increasing levels of difficulty (Pyc and Rawson, 2009). Nakata (2011: 21–2) suggests the stimulation of an increasing retrieval effort: apps should be designed in a way that they first ask learners to choose the meaning of a target word (receptive recognition) or to choose the correct word form from different options (productive recognition). Subsequently, learners should try to retrieve the meaning of a target word themselves (receptive recall) or to produce the word form (productive recall). Although receptive retrieval is easier than productive retrieval (Laufer, 2004: 208), it is important to train both skills; a good vocabulary learning app should therefore implement a variety of exercises to strengthen both aspects.

With Quizlet, for example, retrieval practice is possible in the 'learn mode': for instance, in form of multiple choice exercises or a prompt for learners to write a sample sentence with a gap for the word to be learned (Barr, 2016: 39). The aim is to encourage the learner to retrieve the word without re-study. In the 'test mode', there are four different types of retrieval practice exercises to support both receptive and productive recall.

Lastly, creative use involves connecting a word with new levels of knowledge: this can happen through semantic mapping, creating contexts or mnemonic strategies such as the keyword technique. Miyatsu and McDaniel suggest that a keyword mnemonic supports retrieval of vocabulary by 'creating an interactive image between the key-word and the English translation of the foreign word' (Miyatsu and McDaniel, 2019: 1329).

Two such mnemonic encoding techniques were employed by the winning team of researchers from Radboud University in Nijmegen in the Memprize competition in 2017. The aim was to find the most effective vocabulary learning technique. This was achieved by combining mnemonic learning strategies (in this case, visualisation) with retrieval practice, which was found to be a particularly powerful combination: the researchers developed a strategy which combined the 'method of loci', an ancient technique already mentioned by Greek and Roman orators with the keyword mnemonic method (Worthen and Reed Hunt, 2011: 55–9, 62–5). Learners had to imagine words in certain rooms. Visualising these rooms and re-entering them later helped learners to recall the words through association with each room. Another innovative mnemonic approach, the use of a cognitive theory of metaphors to enhance vocabulary teaching and learning, is presented in Chapter 11 of this volume.

Timing and sequencing

In current research, there is still a discussion about how often, in the context of intentional vocabulary learning, a word must be repeated in order to be remembered. Figures vary between three and 20 times, depending on the word itself, the learning environment and the learner's level of proficiency (Schuetze, 2014: 12). There are also different views on how many lexical items should be studied in a single learning session, that is, what the 'block size' should be. In terms of vocabulary acquisition through flashcard-based software, Nakata suggests flexibility (2011: 23). Some current research focuses on whether words should be learned in a graduated way, with an increased interval over time and an increasing number of distractor items in between, or in a uniform way, with an equal interval between each practice and the same number of distractors in between. In their long-term retention research based on an online vocabulary learning programme, Schuetze and Weimar-Stuckmann (2011: 466) perceive a slight advantage for the uniform method. Furthermore, Schuetze points out that function words are more likely to be forgotten than content words and therefore should be repeated more often in language learning materials. A flashcard system should take both word type and interval type into account (Schuetze, 2014: 13).

A further advantage of CALL applications is that, through adaptive sequencing, computers can keep track of a learner's performance, so that hard-to-learn items can be studied more frequently (Nakata, 2011: 23). For example, the vocabulary learning apps Anki and phase6 identify the words that the learners find most difficult to retrieve and encourage them through sequencing to repeat retrieval practice of those words more often than others.

Multimedia presentation

In terms of vocabulary acquisition, one striking advantage of CALL is that in addition to text (L1 or L2 glossing, that is, providing an explanation for a word or phrase), additional input through audio, images, animation and videos can be provided and individualised very easily, enabling multimedia-supported learning, which includes 'building mental representations from words and pictures' (Mayer, 2014: 2). Generally, studies on the efficacy of multimedia presentation in vocabulary learning applications suggest that, as an 'interactive, context-based and learner-oriented strategy' (Ramezanali and Faez, 2019: 106), it has several positive effects: among others, facilitating and improving L2 vocabulary learning and retention (Li, 2017: 119–20).

However, this should not be taken to imply that these positive effects on vocabulary acquisition can be achieved automatically through multimedia presentation alone. It is also important that the material is presented in a way that supports long-term retention and, most importantly, that it follows a pedagogical concept (Krauß, 2015: 34). Even extensive use of multimedia presentation (for example, by adding more glosses) does not necessarily improve vocabulary acquisition, as it is 'influenced by a range of variables, for example, learner proficiency and learning goals' (Ramezanali, Uchihara and Faez, 2021: 105, 127–8). Learners' individual learning styles and preferences are also a key factor when evaluating the efficacy of multimedia glossing (Proctor, Dalton and Grisham, 2007: 73; Ramezanali and Faez, 2019: 107–8). The human brain has a limited capacity for processing and retaining information (Mayer, 2014: 49), so information overload should be avoided and materials should be presented in a structured way that allows the learner to integrate new vocabulary according to pre-existing knowledge.

Aural and oral learning

As has already been pointed out, it is important for learners to familiarise themselves with the pronunciation of new vocabulary, which is crucial at *ab initio* stage. Most online dictionaries have a facility that enables learners to listen to the spoken word. Video and audio clips, including podcasts, in the target language provide an opportunity for learners to listen to authentic spoken language, which in turn supports the development of general listening comprehension skills.

Listening to a spoken word is, however, inextricably linked to learning how to speak this word (Clancy and Murray, 2016: 494). Among language learning tools which allow learners to practice oral skills in various ways are *tandem*, *langblog* and *videochat*. Some apps foster productive skills through independent and autonomous interaction, which lets students comment on online material that they have produced (Stollhans, 2015). Such interaction can also be achieved through asynchronous discussion, for example, with the apps Flipgrid or Padlet. Learning vocabulary with music and mobile devices also has a positive effect on retention (Dorairaju and Jambulingam, 2017: 43). Singing a song or watching a video clip, ideally with subtitles, further improves vocabulary knowledge (Chen, 2020: 387). Students using the Lyrics Training App watch a music video and then have to either choose the right word from a range of four, or type missing words into the lyrics while listening to the song – which fits in with the principles of retrieval practice.

Visual learning

Some studies found that combining verbal information with visual information has a highly positive effect on L2 vocabulary learning, as new words can be acquired more successfully if text is presented with additional imagery (Chun and Plass, 1996: 193). Others concluded that video glossing is more effective than audio or even imagery glossing for the acquisition of certain words (Lin and Tseng, 2012: 349; Ramezanali and Faez, 2019: 116).

Some specific areas of German grammar have proven to be especially suited to presentation via computer-animated visualisations, which enable highly effective learning and retention (Scheller, 2008: 4). Good examples for this are noun-verb collocations (*Funktionsverbgefüge*) related to spatial concepts (Hoffmann, 2018: 74; Roche and EL-Bouz, 2018), for example, *in Gang bringen* (to get something off the ground), or two-way prepositions governing the accusative or the dative (*Wechselpräpositionen*).

Whether and how subtitling aids like the Google add-on Learning Languages with Netflix (Türkmen, 2020: 469) and the 'rich context' of digital games (Rasti-Behbahani, 2021: 115–16) facilitate vocabulary learning has to be further investigated.

Virtual and augmented reality

As fairly new technologies, virtual reality (VR) and augmented reality (AR) offer promising perspectives for language learning. As computer-generated 3D environments, virtual reality scenarios allow learners to immerse themselves in quasi-authentic situations. While VR learning scenarios are already common in vocational training, for example, to practise action patterns in dangerous situations (for example in flight simulators), their potential for foreign language acquisition has yet to be explored in more detail.

Augmented reality learning scenarios take this concept of 'localized, contextual learning' (Godwin-Jones, 2016: 9) one step further: through AR technology, learners can engage interactively with their own 'real' world environment through their mobile devices. Real-world objects in the learners' immediate surroundings can be glossed on the screens of their mobile devices with additional information, such as audio glossing, imagery or animations to improve vocabulary retention (Santos et al., 2016: 20). In addition, AR technology allows learners to move beyond the traditional classroom setting, for example, by using a walking and vocabulary app (Hautasaari et al., 2019).

Corrective feedback

One of the most striking advantages of CALL is the possibility of immediate feedback. Overall, three different types of feedback can be identified. The first is feedback provided by the computer programme itself; the second is feedback given in social media environments and the third is feedback provided by the language instructor as tutor.

As for computer-generated feedback, the first and simplest stage merely involves presenting the correct answer. This type of feedback is the most common type. The students are given no indication as to why or how their input doesn't match the right answers, which is why most of them 'learn no more from grammar on the computers than they do from grammar in the workbooks' (Garrett, 1987: 174). This kind of behaviouristic feedback is still common in computer programmes today (Roche, 2019: 111) and is seen in some authoring tools, such as H5P, often implemented on Moodle. These allow the creation of online materials by instructors, such as quizzes, and support vocabulary acquisition, particularly if they are paired with retrieval practice. Computer-generated feedback, in its most sophisticated form, is built on the natural language processing (NLP) approach. Based on this, the computer can react to learners' individual performances and store information about their cognitive characteristics (Hemard, 1997: 15), also in the context of phonetics. A good example is the English language learning app ELSA, which not only corrects the pronunciation output of the learner, but also assesses it and gives suggestions for improvement, so that the learner can imitate native speaker output. This illustrates the notion that feedback should be 'timely, accurate and individualised' (Li, 2017: 158). Especially for *ab initio* learners, such a tool can be invaluable.

The second type of feedback that has emerged in recent years is based on peer and self-evaluation. Through blogging, vlogging or writing on platforms or language learning sites, users can provide, receive and edit their peers' feedback (Caws and Heift, 2016: 132). With the development of gaming and serious games, these possibilities have become even more relevant.

The third type of feedback involves a language instructor using technology-enhanced feedback (such as the track changes function in Word). Overall, it remains the task of the language instructor to 'guide the learner, set up appropriate tasks and evaluate the quality of interaction', especially in a blended learning environment (Caws and Heift, 2016: 133).

Conclusion

To sum up, effective foreign vocabulary learning apps should:

1. Offer vocabulary import, based on frequency, allowing learners to add self-generated mid- to low-frequency vocabulary.
2. Encourage learning a word by taking into account all three aspects of form, meaning and use. This includes information about pronunciation, word parts, inflected forms and collocations.
3. Present activities based on the principles of retrieval practice, if possible in conjunction with mnemonic strategies.
4. Enable the learner to progress through the learning of lexical items in spaced repetition and keep track of their performance through adaptive sequencing.
5. Use multimedia glossing to generate mental representations of vocabulary.
6. Be built on the NLP approach, giving immediate and explanatory corrective feedback with advice on how to improve.

Even though using apps for vocabulary learning offers considerable potential to boost learning outcomes, we must not forget the individual circumstances of the learner, which can also influence the acceptance of this technology. Ma (2017: 197) draws our attention to the important role of L2 learners' agency and beliefs in order to define how they are using the technologies for language learning, but also the role of the teacher for enhancing language learning through technologies. Only if this can be positively achieved can apps make a difference, including in *ab initio* vocabulary learning.

References

Barr, B. (2016) 'Checking the effectiveness of Quizlet as a tool for vocabulary learning'. *The Center of EFL Journal* 1:2, 36–48.

Barz, I. and Fleischer, W. (2012) *Wortbildung der deutschen Gegenwartssprache*, fourth edition. Berlin and Boston, MA: de Gruyter.

Caws, C. and Heift, T. (2016) 'Evaluation in CALL: Tools, interactions, outcomes'. In *The Routledge Handbook of Language Learning and Technology*, edited by F. Farr and L. Murray, 127–40. London and New York: Routledge.

Chen, I. (2020) 'Music as a mnemonic device for foreign vocabulary learning'. *English Teaching & Learning* 44, 377–95.

Chun, D.M. and Plass, J.L. (1996) 'Effects of multimedia annotations on vocabulary acquisition'. *The Modern Language Journal* 80:2, 183–98.

Clancy, U. and Murray, L. (2016) 'CALL tools for listening and speaking'. In *The Routledge Handbook of Language Learning and Technology*, edited by F. Farr and L. Murray, 491–508. London and New York: Routledge.

Council of Europe (2021) Common European Framework of Reference for Languages. Online. www.coe.int/en/web/common-european-framework-reference-languages/table-1-cefr-3.3-common-reference-levels-global-scale (accessed 22 April 2021).

Dorairaju, R. and Jambulingam, M. (2017) 'The role of music and m-learning in English: Vocabulary gain among tertiary students'. *Journal of Language and Education* 3:2, 39–44.

Dräxler, H. and Kühn, B. (1998) *Methodik des Fortgeschrittenenunterrichts*. Munich: Goethe-Institut.

Gardner, D. (2007) 'Validating the construct of word in applied corpus-based vocabulary research: A critical survey'. *Applied Linguistics* 28:2, 241–65.

Garrett, N. (1987) 'A Psycholinguistic perspective on grammar and CALL'. In *Modern Media in Foreign Language Education: Theory and Implementation*, edited by W. Smith, 169–96, Lincolnwood, IL: National Textbook Company.

Godwin-Jones, R. (2016) 'Augmented reality and language learning: From annotated vocabulary to place-based mobile games'. *Language Learning & Technology* 20:3, 9–19.

Hautasaari, A., Hamada, T. Ishiyama, K. and Fukushima, S. (2019) 'VocaBura: A method for supporting second language vocabulary learning while walking'. *Proceedings of the ACM on Interactive, Mobile, Wearable and Ubiquitous Technologies* 3:4, 1–23.

Heil, C., Wu, J., Lee, J. and Schmidt, T. (2016) 'A review of mobile language learning applications: Trends, challenges, and opportunities'. *The EuroCALL Review* 24:2, 32–50.

Hemard, D.P. (1997) 'Design principles and guidelines for authoring hypermedia language learning education'. *System* 25:1, 9–27.

Hoffmann, I. (2018) 'Räumlich konzeptualisierte Funktionsverbgefüge – eine Erwerbsstudie'. *Zeitschrift für Interkulturellen Fremdsprachenunterricht* 23:2, 74–85.

Krauß, S. (2015) 'Apps for learning German vocabulary – what does the digital landscape look like?'. *German as a Foreign Language* 2, 32–57.

Kühn, P. (2013) 'Wortschatz und Wortschatzdidaktik: Tradition und Neuansätze'. In *Deutsch als Fremdsprache*, edited by I. Oomen-Welke and B. Ahrenholz, 153–64. Baltmannsweiler: Schneider.

Kukulska-Hulme, A. (2018) 'Mobile-assisted language learning' [revised and updated version]. In *The Concise Encyclopedia of Applied Linguistics*, edited by C.A. Chapelle, 1–9. Hoboken, NJ: Wiley.

Kurtz, J. (2016) 'Lehr-/Lernmaterialien und Medien zum Wortschatzlernen'. In *Handbuch Fremdsprachenunterricht*, sixth edition, edited by E. Burwitz-Melzer, G. Mehlhorn, C. Riemer, K.-R. Bausch and H.-J. Krumm, 445–8. Tübingen: Francke.

Laufer, B. (2004) 'Size and strength: Do we need both to measure vocabulary knowledge?'. *Language Testing* 21:2, 202–26.

Li, L. (2016) 'CALL tools for lexico-grammatical acquisition'. In *The Routledge Handbook of Language Learning and Technology*, edited by F. Farr and L. Murray, 461–77. London and New York: Routledge.

Li, L. (2017) *New Technologies and Language Learning*. London: Palgrave.

Lin, C. and Tseng, Y. (2012) 'Videos and animations for vocabulary learning: A study on difficult words'. *The Turkish Online Journal of Educational Technology* 11:4, 346–55.

Ma, Q. (2017) 'A multi-case study of university students' language-learning experience mediated by mobile technologies: A socio-cultural perspective'. *Computer Assisted Language Learning* 30:3–4, 183–203.

Mayer, R.E. (2014) (ed.), *The Cambridge Handbook of Multimedia Learning*, second edition. Cambridge: Cambridge University Press.

Miyatsu, T. and McDaniel, M. (2019) 'Adding the keyword mnemonic to retrieval practice: A potent combination for foreign language vocabulary learning?' *Memory & Cognition* 47, 1328–43.

Nakata, T. (2011) 'Computer-assisted second language vocabulary learning in a paired-associate paradigm: A critical investigation of flashcard software'. *Computer Assisted Language Learning* 24:1, 17–38.

Nation, I.S.P. (2013) *Learning Vocabulary in Another Language*, second edition. Cambridge: Cambridge University Press.

Neveling, C. (2016) 'Verfügen über sprachliche Mittel: Wortschatz'. In *Handbuch Fremdsprachenunterricht*, sixth edition, edited by E. Burwitz-Melzer, G. Mehlhorn, C. Riemer, K.-R. Bausch and H.-J. Krumm, 116–21. Tübingen: Francke.

Pawley, A. and Syder, F.H. (1983) 'Two puzzles for linguistic theory: Native-like selection and native-like fluency'. In *Language and Communication*, edited by J.C. Richards and R.W. Schmidt, 191–225. London and New York: Longman.

Plass, J. and Jones, L.C. (2005) 'Multimedia learning in second language acquisition'. In *Cambridge Handbook of Multimedia Learning*, edited by R.E. Mayer, 467–88, Cambridge: Cambridge University Press.

Proctor, P., Dalton, B. and Grisham, D. (2007) 'Scaffolding English language learners and struggling readers in a universal literacy environment with embedded strategy instruction and vocabulary support'. *Journal of Literacy Research* 39:1, 71–93.

Pyc, M.A. and Rawson, K.A. (2009) 'Testing the retrieval effort hypothesis: Does greater difficulty correctly recalling information lead to higher levels of memory?' *Journal of Memory and Language* 60, 437–47.

Ramezanali, N. and Faez, F. (2019) 'Vocabulary learning and retention through multimedia glossing'. *Language Learning & Technology* 23:2, 105–24.

Ramezanali, N., Uchihara, T. and Faez, F. (2021) 'Efficacy of multimodal glossing on second language vocabulary learning: A meta-analysis'. *TESOL Quarterly* 55:1, 105–33.

Rasti-Behbahani, A. (2021) 'Why digital games can be advantageous in vocabulary learning'. *Theory and Practice in Language Studies* 11:2, 111–18.

Roche, J. (2019) *Medienwissenschaft und Mediendidaktik*. Tübingen: Narr Francke Attempto.

Roche, J. and EL-Bouz, K. (2018) Das aktuelle Grammatikstudio. Online. www.granima.de (accessed 23 April 2021).

Santos, M.E., in Wolde Lübke, A., Taketomi, T., Yamamoto, G., Rodrigo, M.M.T., Sandor, C. and Kato, H. (2016) 'Augmented reality as multimedia: The case for situated vocabulary learning'. *Research and Practice in Technology Enhanced Learning* 11:4, 1–23.

Scheller, J. (2008) 'Grammatik, Kognition und Imagination'. *Zeitschrift für Interkulturellen Fremdsprachenunterricht* 13:2, 1–8.

Schmitt, D. and Schmitt, N. (2020) *Vocabulary in Language Teaching*, second edition. Cambridge: Cambridge University Press.

Schmitt, R. (1990) 'The role of consciousness in in second language learning'. *Applied Linguistics* 11, 129–58.

Schuetze, U. (2014) 'Spacing techniques in second language vocabulary acquisition: Short-term gains vs. long-term memory'. *Language, Teaching, Research* 19:1, 28–42.

Schuetze, U. and Weimer-Stuckmann, G. (2011) 'Retention in SLA processing'. *CALICO Journal* 28:2, 460–72.

Stockwell, G. (2016) 'Mobile language learning'. In *The Routledge Handbook of Language Learning and Technology*, edited by F. Farr and L. Murray, 296–307. London and New York: Routledge.

Stollhans, S. (2015) 'The e-learning tool Voxopop and its benefits on oral skills: Activities for final year students of German'. In *10 Years of the LLAS elearning Symposium: Case studies in good practice*, edited by K. Borthwick, E. Corradini and A. Dickens, 185–92. Dublin: research-publishing.net.

Takač, V.P. (2008) *Vocabulary Learning Strategies and Foreign Language Acquisition*. Bristol: Multilingual Matters.

Tschirner, E. (2019) 'Der rezeptive Wortschatzbedarf im Deutschen als Fremdsprache'. In *IDT 2017: Band 1: Hauptvorträge*, edited by E. Peyer, T. Studer and I. Thonhauser, 98–111. Berlin: Erich Schmidt.

Tschirner, E. and Möhring, J. (2020) *A Frequency Dictionary of German: Core vocabulary for learners*, second edition. London: Routledge.

Türkmen, B. (2020) 'Utilising digital media as a second language (L2) support: A case study on Netflix with translation applications'. *Interdisciplinary Description of Complex Systems* 18:4, 459–70.

Wegener, H. (2016) 'Regeln versus Muster'. In *Formen und Funktionen*, edited by A. Bittner and C. Spieß, 193–214. Berlin and Boston, MA: de Gruyter.

Wilkins, D. (1972) *Linguistics in Language Teaching*. London: Edward Arnold.

Worthen, J.B. and Reed Hunt, R. (2011) *Mnemonology: Mnemonics for the 21st century*. New York and London: Taylor & Francis.

Part IV
Learner focus

13
Developing learner autonomy in German *ab initio* programmes
Thomas Jochum-Critchley

Introduction

Ab initio programmes as part of Modern Languages degree programmes are designed to enable beginner learners to make rapid progress in their language proficiency and to reach C1 level according to the Common European Framework of Reference (CEFR) after four years of study (QAA, 2019: 18–19). Given the constraints of accelerated language learning, considerations of learner autonomy have not been front and centre of *ab initio* language learning pedagogy. As with the notion of autonomy in a more general sense and derived from its philosophical and broader educational background (Schmenk, 2010: 19–21), autonomy is generally associated with adults or more advanced learners. And yet, autonomy is mentioned in the quoted QAA document above as an essential learning outcome of language degree programmes (QAA, 2019: 14), and thus merits a more detailed discussion.

Since about the 1990s, the concept of learner autonomy in the field of language learning and teaching has gained considerable attention across all institutional settings, including higher education. Benson's seminal work can be regarded as the first attempt to give a systematic overview of research, scholarship and practices of autonomy in the field of language education (Benson, 2001). At the same time, autonomy has acquired the status of a 'buzzword' (Little, 1991; Irie and Stewart, 2012) or 'slogan' (Schmenk, 2008), not least because the notion of autonomy seems to align smoothly with current developments in higher education emphasising neo-liberal values, such as individualisation, choice and commodification (Evans, 2020: 574).

Drawing on the experience of encouraging learner autonomy in the German *ab initio* programme at the University of York, this chapter argues that learner autonomy can be fostered through a portfolio approach that provides a structured approach to students' engagement with authentic language use. Greater autonomy thus enables students to develop essential learning skills and strategies for merging successfully with the post-A-level cohort.

Learner autonomy in language learning – a productive concept?

Learner autonomy in the context of language learning was initially defined by Henri Holec as 'the ability to take charge of one's own learning' (Holec, 1979: 3). He originally developed the concept of learner autonomy in language learning in the context of adult education. The main aim was to support learners to make informed decisions about how, when, where and to what extent they engage in the learning process making use of the growing body of materials available outside the classroom, for example through self-access centres (Holec, 1979: 3). The responsibility for learning is thus shifted from the teacher to the learner. However, as Dam has pointed out, this does not mean that learners are left to their own devices (Dam, 2002: 137). On the contrary, in the context of formal educational settings, such as secondary schools, she promotes the idea that the teacher has a responsibility to plan and organise learning in a way that the learner can participate in the decisions about the content and the organisation of the learning.

Benson concludes that autonomy is a 'capacity to exert control over one's language learning' (Benson, 2001: 47). Observing autonomy is observing what learners can do in terms of selecting materials and using specific learning strategies, as well as communicating successfully about their choices in structured reflections. Introducing autonomy in an *ab initio* programme means setting the conditions that these types of behaviour can develop over time and designing tasks that give language learners a space to allow for discovering how they learn through making choices, which will become better informed over time.

David Little's understanding of autonomy is grounded in developmental psychology: 'Autonomy in language learning depends on the development and exercise of a capacity for detachment, critical reflection, decision-making and independent action' (Little, 1991: 4). 'Independent action' refers here to the ability to use language spontaneously in authentic communicative situations in the real world. Little therefore adds the principle of 'appropriate target language use' to the general educational principles of 'learner reflection' and 'learner involvement' (Little, 2020: 5).

Beginning autonomy? Challenges for *ab initio* learners

As Little (1991) and others (Vieira, 2009: 7, 162; Irie and Stewart, 2012) have pointed out, fostering autonomy in institutionalised settings, such as higher education, is not a frictionless process. The challenges lie equally on the personal level in that learning habits, attitudes and conditioned behaviours are put into question and have troublesome effects on the learners (cf. Holec, 1985: 183). It can be considered a 'threshold concept' (Cousins, 2006: 4) that places the learner in a 'liminal space' that requires a reset of points of reference for the learner. Autonomy has also the potential to unsettle the institution as the conditions of learning themselves come into the focus of the learner through reflection, and thus can lead to more critical or even subversive action (Evans, 2019: 581).

It seems clear that *ab initio* language learning and autonomy do not necessarily make for natural or easy partners. The elements necessary to promote autonomy, such as informed selection, evaluation of resources, engagement in authentic communication and evaluation of the learning experience, seem difficult to tackle, with only limited prior exposure to the German language, as well as little or no experience with specific learning materials and resources.

On the other hand, the lack of prior language learning can also be an advantage, particularly when the transition from secondary to university education is taken into consideration. Learners are confronted with new approaches, less tightly structured sequences and many more open-ended tasks that are often less clearly aligned with specific elements of the assessment. If developing learner autonomy responds to these more general challenges of studying in higher education, the question remains how *ab initio* learners can engage meaningfully and authentically with the language, society and cultures of the countries where the language of study is spoken.

Another challenge of developing autonomy in the *ab initio* programme is that these programmes are intended to prepare students for merging with the post-A-level cohort at some point in the programme, in most cases after the first or second year. The learning outcomes of the *ab initio* programme have their real-life reality check when the two cohorts merge either in the second or in the final year. The prospect of following the same curriculum and thus interacting with peers whose perceived level of proficiency is higher might leave little room for *ab initio* learners to engage in activities that do not promise instant advancement of language proficiency, such as learning about autonomy, reflecting upon one's own strengths, weaknesses and needs, as well as evaluating one's own learning. In other words: does the focus on autonomy detract from the first and foremost goal of developing language proficiency at an accelerated pace?

Finally, second language acquisition (SLA) research such as processability theory argues that the development of language proficiency follows developmental stages or patterns (Pienemann, 2015). Learning certain grammar structures that are typically part of the German *ab initio* syllabus, such as word order in main and subordinate clauses, verb morphology and case assignment, is constrained by the learners' state of development, and therefore learner choice is limited.

Although this point is by no means undisputed, my experience with language learning materials such as textbooks for beginners do indeed follow similar patterns of progression, particularly with regards to grammar and vocabulary. This more linear learning curve at *ab initio* level is mirrored in learner perceptions of learning gains.

Introducing autonomy in the *ab initio* programme requires a structured approach that supports the learners in their individual journeys to become more autonomous language learners and users. It also requires a slight shift of emphasis in the conception of the use of the language of study as the primary indicator for autonomy (Little, 1991: 27). All available language resources for successful communication, whether this is language of study, or English as the first language of most students of German at British universities, are considered as having a role to play in the development of autonomy. Rather than in opposition, they complement each other, working together towards the goal of greater autonomy.

Encouraging learner autonomy: German *ab initio* at the University of York

The undergraduate (UG) German programmes at the University of York have been offering an *ab initio* pathway alongside the traditional post-A-level route since 2012. A formal separation of the two cohorts takes place only in the first year, where students are required to take 60 credits of dedicated *ab initio* modules in German. The current module configuration divides these 60 credits into three year-long modules, each of which provides two weekly contact hours. All UG language programmes at York follow a content and language integrated learning (CLIL) approach, which means that language skills are not only developed in the dedicated module (*Ab initio* German Language Skills), but also a grammar module (*Ab initio* German Grammar) and a module focusing on an introduction to social, political and cultural issues in contemporary Germany (*Ab initio* German Language and Society).

The development of learner autonomy takes place in the context of the module *Ab Initio* German Language Skills. This module aims at developing communication skills in German addressing all four language skills and the learners achieve approximately B1 level at the end of the year. The module also aims to develop students' ability to acquire language independently and their ability to reflect upon their learning. The textbook *DaF kompakt A1–B1* provides a framework for developing communicative skills as well as lexical, grammatical and cultural knowledge.

In addition to student work in the seminars, seminar preparation and homework tasks, students must complete an assessed language learning portfolio, which constitutes 40 per cent of the module mark. An end-of-year written exam covering reading skills, vocabulary knowledge and writing skills (worth 60 per cent) completes the module assessment. It is through a specific design of the portfolio that learner autonomy is developed.

Designing autonomy: a portfolio approach

The portfolio approach and learner autonomy share several crucial characteristics, not least a conceptual and practical multiformity. This makes them almost natural partners in education. 'There is no such thing as the one portfolio' states Sandra Ballweg (2009: 469; my translation from the German). She identifies three fundamental characteristics of portfolios shared by most uses: portfolios are (1) a collection of work from students, (2) this collection of work is a result of selection and (3) they include a form of reflection (Ballweg, 2009: 470). Portfolios understood in that way serve a double function: they document student learning, and they are a way of enabling reflection, and thus address both the outcome and the process of learning, which makes them an effective approach to support learner autonomy.

The language learning portfolio designed for *ab initio* German learners at York is inspired by a portfolio approach developed and implemented by Antonio Martínez-Arboleda (2011) at the University of

Leeds. It was originally designed for second year post-A-level students in Spanish and adapted for German in 2010 (Jochum-Critchley, 2012).

The portfolio approach for *ab initio* students at the University of York follows the same basic framework. It comprises a set of structured authentic language-learning activities (see list below), each of which have a specific points value attached to them. To complete the portfolio, students have to collect activities worth a set number of points. The allocation of points is derived from an estimation of workload as well as level of difficulty. A reflective task in English prompts students to describe and evaluate their learning. Thus, all three principles for autonomy set out by Little (2007) are present.

The portfolio is assessed using three criteria: the evaluation of the presented portfolio activities follows conventional criteria subsumed under 'content' and 'language' (together 80 per cent of the mark), and a specific criterion of 'reflection and autonomy' (20 per cent). The weightings of the assessment criteria make clear that the main focus is on the evaluation of the language learning progress and the ability to use language effectively, while also reminding of the relevance of reflection and its role in the development of autonomy.

The portfolio is, however, not meant to be primarily about 'testing autonomy' in the sense that Benson (2010: 91) conceptualises the construct. The criteria of reflection and autonomy take into account some of the choices documented in the portfolio work, such as the selection of activities, choice of language forms and vocabulary, and the rationale for the selection given, but the main focus is on the quality of the reflective writing based on Moon's approach to teaching and assessing learner reflection (Moon, 2005).

Learners complete the portfolio in two parts: the first part is submitted at the end of the autumn term, and the second part at the end of the spring term. Students complete a reflective task for each of the submitted parts. This structure requires students to plan and organise their learning over a longer time period and they receive feedback for each submission. Thus, the first submission has a formative aspect as it marks a formal point of dialogue between student and teacher and thus provides an additional opportunity to inform students' learning. The following list gives an overview of the portfolio activities that engage students as language learners and language users.

- *Ein Kinderbuch lesen* (30 points)
  A list with seven titles of illustrated children's books in German is shared with students. The list includes books such as *Die Geggis*

(Mira Lobe), *Columbus Bär entdeckt das Meer* (Katja Reider), *Winzig der Elefant* (Erwin Moser). The selection of the books is based on three criteria: it is a narrative text, the story has a minimum of approximately 1,000 words, and no published translation into English is readily available.

- *Einen Kurzfilm sehen* (20 points)
  A list of suggested German-speaking short films is shared with students. The list includes films from well-known directors such as Hans Weingartner (*Gefährder*, 2008), Fatih Akin (*getürkt*, 1996) or Dani Levy (*Joshua*, 2008), or actors such as Julia Jentsch (*Sprachlos*, 2011). The selection of the short films is based on three criteria: a length of approximately ten minutes, no release in English or version with English subtitles available and at a minimum amount of spoken dialogue of approximately three minutes. Students may also choose their own short film based on the three criteria.

- *Fernsehnachrichten sehen/ Radionachrichten hören* (15 points)
  Students select four news items from television or radio over a period of time. They answer wh-questions, summarise one item and compare one item with another on the same topic. They also write a short news story about an on-campus event.

- *Zeitungsnachrichten lesen* (15 points)
  Students select four written news items over a period of time and/ or from different sources. They answer wh-questions, summarise one item and compare one item with another on the same topic. They also write a short news story about an on-campus event.

- *Musik hören* (10 Points)
  Students listen to a German-language song of their choice. They answer questions on the content of the song, create a grammar task with the transcript. One possible production task is to record a short podcast with a song review.

- *Einen Tandem-Austausch durchführen* (15 points)
  Students engage in a tandem exchange with a German native speaker. This is usually another student on campus. They document a minimum of four meetings and include a recording of an interview with the tandem partner.

- *Eine Reise in ein deutschsprachiges Land machen* (15 points)
  Students document a trip to a German-speaking country that lasts at least four days. The documentation includes an interview with a German speaker they meet on the journey.

Each of these activities is accompanied by a generic task sheet that has a three-part structure to cover different aspects of the language learning process, namely communicative competence as in receptive and productive task elements, as well as knowledge of grammar and vocabulary.

The first part of the task sheet focuses on the documentation of the engagement with the chosen source material and/or chosen type of interaction and/or exposure to German. This can be either answering questions on the content of the selected material where the task is about engaging with textual or audio-visual material, or documenting activities related to tasks that involve an engagement with speakers of German.

The second part prompts students to work on specific aspects of the language encountered. It consists of at least one question that encourages students to adopt a 'focus on form' (Long, 1991), that is to identify and analyse specific grammatical features of the language, and at least one question to work on vocabulary. The third and final part of the task sheets focuses on language production and offers a choice of open-ended oral and written tasks where students can reuse and practise the language encountered in the chosen activity in a creative way, for example, producing an audio book, writing a news story, creating a fictitious interview or interviewing a fluent or native German speaker. Each of these activities focuses on at least two different skills, one receptive skill (listening and/or reading) and one productive skill (writing and/or speaking).

Overall, the portfolio offers a structured way for *ab initio* learners to engage in authentic language use that also encourages them to develop increased awareness of the learning process, their learning preferences and styles and, last but not least, learning strategies that work for them.

Discussion and reflection of outcomes and experiences

After seven years of using the portfolio, some interesting findings have been emerging. Overall, the module feedback has been positive with consistent scores of above 4.4 (out of 5) or higher for satisfaction with the module.

In total, 39 students who have completed the module have submitted 243 tasks and 107 learner reflections. All types of possible activities have been chosen so far, but there is a clear preference for the more structured activities. The most popular activity was reading a children's book, which was selected 80 times, with watching a short film coming second (51) and reading news articles and listening to music as close third and fourth options (48 and 44 respectively). The two most popular activities were those which had a list of suggested titles. Students preferred the activities that provided guidance in selecting materials.

The least popular activity was the travel activity. Given the resource implications and specific conditions, only two students in total used a trip to a German-speaking country for their portfolio work.

With regards to specific reasons for choosing activities as cited by students in their learning reflections, a number of aspects of learner autonomy are clearly visible. Particularly at the start of the year and for the submission of the first part of the portfolio, the reading and writing tasks were more popular than the activities involving listening and speaking. Accessibility of the language and the fact that learners can exert more control over the processing and production of written language were mentioned as a rationale. Reading a children's book was seen as 'a lot easier than the TV/radio task'. When students chose activities that focused on listening, they often reported these in the reflections as particularly challenging in the beginning. This can be interpreted as a positive aspect of increased awareness of different types of source material and language use. A second group of motivations for selecting specific tasks were areas of language learning that needed particular attention. Reasons given for the task selection included points such as the chosen tasks covering areas in which 'I need to improve' or being an area 'I generally have trouble with'.

A third group of motivations for the choice of activities is related to personal interest and enjoyment. Students mentioned this particularly in relation to choosing to listen to German music, but also when explaining the choice of narrative materials, such as books or short films. 'I like stories' or 'I like listening to German music' were repeatedly mentioned. Some reflections went a step further and showed more explicitly an awareness of the positive impact of enjoyment to progress in learning.

A final point to note here is the specific reflection on learning strategies and approaches to tackling more complex and challenging materials. Many students reported that they had changed their approach to reading or watching a longer narrative authentic text, such as a children's book or a short film. They documented that a word-for-word approach or sentence-to-sentence (line-to-line) approach to reading a longer text did not prove effective and they thus changed to a more holistic and meaning-oriented approach.

Overall, the reflections show that students have gained a better awareness of their learning and that the learners' behaviour has changed as a result of engagement with the portfolio activities. Some limitations in the active involvement of their learning remain as only a minority of students opted for the more creative and open-ended activities and tasks. Individual differences and preferences as to how to approach language learning might play a role here, but it could also indicate that there is a need for more scaffolding of how to select appropriate tasks. Additional qualitative data needs to be gathered to answer this question.

Whether the students' reported feedback is truly a genuine reflection of their thoughts and experiences or whether they are a manifestation of 'masked autonomy' (Benson, 2010: 84) cannot be determined at this stage.

Autonomy and the digital – towards a brighter future?

The relative sudden, yet almost complete move of language learning online in the context of the COVID-19 pandemic has accelerated the expansion of the use of and engagement with digital technologies in language learning and teaching. New digital language-learning environments and associated technologies and tools bring about affordances and limitations for the development of autonomy (Reinders and White, 2011: 2). Becoming aware of these resources and fully understanding their potential benefits as well as drawbacks is becoming increasingly important.

I only want to focus on three types of digital technologies as these have potential to be successfully integrated into the portfolio:

1. The internet has developed from a repository of information and knowledge to a ubiquitous platform for communication, interaction, and collaboration (Stanley, 2013: 2). The portfolio format described above can easily accommodate a structured engagement with new and hitherto less practised forms of authentic online language use, such as synchronous chatting or asynchronous participation in social media platforms. The suggestion is here to create new task sheets that focus on activities such as online gaming or participating in specialist online forums or social media in German. A list with suggestions for online games and platforms can help to provide a starting point for exploring this type of resource. Learner motivation and engagement are expected to increase as a result of the inclusion of such activities and will give students a foundation for pursuing their language learning journey beyond the formal educational context.

2. Language learning apps and platforms have become widely available through mobile technologies, and many have freely accessible resources that cater in particular for *ab initio* learners. Mobile assisted language learning (MALL) for tutorial apps (Morgana, 2019: 2), such as Duolingo or Memrise, are just two examples of digital tools that allow *ab initio* learners to engage in structured language learning activities in a flexible yet structured and directed way. In order to contribute to the development of autonomy, the suggestion is to encourage learners to compare their experience with different apps to better understand the affordances and limitations of these platforms.

3. More recent developments in language processing, speech recognition and AI-based machine learning are also becoming increasingly available for language learners. These resources employ large-scale computing capabilities that represent a qualitative shift, as they operate at a level of language processing that connects learners with levels of language use that have been beyond their language proficiency. The use of online machine translation, speech-to-text software and automatic captioning help *ab initio* learners to gain at least a general understanding of a wide range of complex authentic resources and to assist them to produce language of a complexity that is far beyond their natural level of language proficiency. Language awareness as well as noticing are thus excluded or at least neglected, with compromising effects for the learners' acquisition of more complex forms or the storage of lexical items in their long-term memory. In addition, asynchronous language use, especially in writing, loses its documentation function as a reliable link for monitoring and self-evaluation of language learning. In other words, language use becomes disconnected from language learning in a way that is barely understood. To a certain extent, these resources can be seen as limiting the autonomy of language use as *ab initio* learners become over-reliant on these resources and will not develop the ability to communicate in German in situations where these resources are not available.

Conclusion

Introducing learner autonomy at *ab initio* level has helped the students at York to successfully manage the integration with post-A-level students after just one year and to complete the German programme. The portfolio approach chosen provides a structured and standardised, yet open-ended and flexible framework that brings together the principles of engagement, reflection and authentic use of German. It also allows for the integration of digital technologies and tools for language learning into the formal curriculum and thus constitutes an effective framework for the promotion of learner autonomy. The latter also benefits from the increased integration of formal and informal language learning opportunities, which have gained increased attention and presence through the online and remote learning situation.

At the same time, the role and potential of learner autonomy has to be further investigated. In light of emerging digital resources that operate at the level of language processing, teachers and learners have yet to establish how best to integrate these resources without compromising the language acquisition process. This may well mean revisiting certainties and established approaches not only to autonomy itself (Holec, 2008: 4) but also to *ab initio* language learning in general.

References

Ballweg, S. (2009) "'… und dann bringen Sie in der letzten Sitzung Ihr Portfolio mit." Portfolioarbeit im Unterrichtsalltag'. *IDV Magazin* 81, 468–78.

Benson, P. (2001) *Teaching and Researching Learner Autonomy in Language Learning*. Harlow: Pearson Education/Longman.

Benson, P. (2006) 'Autonomy in language teaching and learning: State-of-the-art article'. *Language Teaching* 40, 21–40.

Benson, P. (2008) 'Teachers and learners' perspectives on autonomy'. In *Learner and Teacher Autonomy: Concepts, realities, and response*, edited by T. Lamb and H. Reinders, 15–32. Amsterdam: Benjamins.

Dam, L. (2002) 'Developing learner autonomy: The teachers' responsibility'. In *Learner Autonomy in the Foreign Language Classroom*, edited by D. Little, J. Ridley and E. Ushioda, 135–46. Dublin: Authentik.

Evans, M. (2020) 'Navigating the neoliberal university: Reflecting on teaching practice as a teacher-researcher-trade unionist'. *British Journal of Sociology of Education* 41:4, 574–90.

Cousins, G. 'An introduction to threshold concepts'. *Planet* 17:1, 4–5.

Holec, H. (1979) *Autonomy and Foreign Language Learning*. Strasbourg: Council for Cultural Co-operation of the Council of Europe.

Holec, H. (1985) 'On autonomy: Some elementary concepts'. In *Discourse and Learning*, edited by P. Riley, 173–90. London: Longman.

Holec, H. (2008) 'Foreword'. In *Learner and Teacher Autonomy: Concepts, realities, and response*, edited by T. Lamb and H. Reinders, 3–4. Amsterdam: Benjamins.

Irie, K. and Stewart, A. (2012) 'Realizing autonomy: Contradictions in practice and context'. In *Realizing Autonomy: Practice and Reflection in Language Education Contexts*, edited by K. Irie and A. Stewart, 1–17. Basingstoke: Palgrave Macmillan.

Jochum-Critchley, T. (2012) 'Back to the future. Autonomous language learning reloaded'. Paper presented at Language Futures. Languages in Higher Education Conference, Edinburgh, 5–6 July 2012. Online. https://www.llas.ac.uk//sites/default/files/nodes/6672/TJC%20 Presentation%20Autonomy%20Edinburgh.ppt (accessed 14 July 2021).

Lai, C. (2018) *Autonomous Language Learning with Technology: Beyond the classroom*. London: Bloomsbury.

Little, D. (1991) *Learner Autonomy 1: Definitions, issues and problems*. Dublin: Authentik.

Little, D. (2007) 'Language learner autonomy: Some fundamental considerations revisited'. *Innovation in Language Learning and Teaching* 1:1, 14–29.

Little, D. (2020) 'Language learner autonomy: Rethinking language teaching'. *Language Teaching* 55:1, 64–73.

Long, M. (1991) 'Focus on form. A design feature in language teaching methodology'. In *Foreign Language Research in Cross-Cultural Perspective*, edited by K. de Bot, R. Ginsberg and C. Kramsch, 39–52. Amsterdam: John Benjamins.

Martinez-Arboleda, A. (2010) 'Autonomous learning portfolio in Spanish: Personalised learning and motivation in a regulated learning environment'. Paper presented at Supporting students' learning outside the classroom: Promoting independence and autonomy in LLAS disciplines, Leeds, 13 June 2012. Online. http://humbox.ac.uk/2882/ (accessed 4 July 2021).

Moon, J. (2005) *Guide for Busy Academics No. 4. Learning through reflection*. Online. https://nursing-midwifery.tcd.ie/assets/director-staff-edu-dev/pdf/Guide-for-Busy-Academics-No1-4-HEA.pdf (accessed 21 July 2021).

Morgana, V. (2019) 'A review of MALL: From categories to implementation. The case of Apple's iPad.' *The EUROCALL Review* 27:2, 1–12.

QAA (2019) Subject Benchmark Statement. Languages, Cultures and Societies. Online. https://www.qaa.ac.uk/docs/qaa/subject-benchmark-statements/subject-benchmark-statement-languages-cultures-and-societies.pdf (accessed: 22 July 2021).

Pienemann, M. (2015) 'An outline of processability theory and its relationship to other approaches to SLA'. *Language Learning* 65:1, 123–51.

Reinders, H. and White, C. (2011) 'Learner autonomy and new learning environments'. *Language Learning and Technology* 15:3, 1–3.

Schmenk, B. (2008) *Lernerautonomie. Karriere und Sloganisierung des Autonomiebegriffs*. Tübingen: Gunter Narr Verlag.

Schmenk, B. (2010) 'Bildungsphilosophischer Idealismus, erfahrungsgesättigte Praxisorientierung, didaktischer Hiphop? Eine kleine Geschichte der Lernerautonomie'. *Profil* 2, 11–26.

Stanley, G. (2013). *Language Learning with Technology – Ideas for integrating technology in the classroom*. Cambridge: Cambridge University Press.

14
Individual differences in *ab initio* language learning: working with learners' strengths

Ulrike Bavendiek

Introduction

Not all learners benefit equally from the teaching environment that teachers, departments and institutions provide for them. Individual learners progress differently, depending on a variety of factors that influence their experiences and achievements as language learners. Individual variation includes psychological factors, such as cognitive and affective abilities and styles, which are traditionally classified as individual differences (IDs). In addition, learners also differ regarding the knowledge and previous learning experiences that they bring to the process. Languages they have previously acquired or learned in particular affect their *ab initio* language learning. Although the exact effects are still unclear, these cross-linguistic influences have been shown to play a role in the acquisition of other languages. Finally, each learner is embedded in different learning conditions outside the classroom. Factors including exposure to the target language outside the institutional learning context also affect their learning of a new language. Such environmental factors, although not discussed here, should be explored and considered by the language teacher if possible.

This chapter explores learner variables and their significance in the beginners' language classroom. It aims to bridge the gap between new research in second language acquisition (SLA) and applied linguistics on the one hand, and classroom practice on the other, to enable teachers and institutions to create learning environments that are sufficiently rich, flexible and multifaceted to meet the needs of all *ab initio* learners. The focus lies on the didactic implications of this dynamic interaction between individual learner variables and the *ab initio* teaching context. There is no attempt to provide a comprehensive overview of all learner variation.

Language and learner characteristics as complex adaptive systems

IDs are not static components but interact with each other as well as with situational and environmental factors in systems that are still largely uncharted. Language learning itself is not a straightforward, linear process, in which individual learner variables can be neatly dissected and their effects calculated. Instead, language is now seen as a complex adaptive system (Larsen-Freeman, 1997). Its constituent parts, including the phonologic, morphologic, lexic, syntactic, semantic and pragmatic rule systems, interact and constantly shape and reshape the emerging learner language. The learner dependent variables, including psychological factors, knowledge, experience, and the environment of the learners, further influence this system, resulting in multifaceted, dynamic, constantly changing constellations of factors which are difficult to unravel. Yet I would argue that awareness of isolated variables and their potential influences is still important for teachers, advisors and policy makers, so that they can aim to cater for all learners and understand differences in language growth. The goal is to encourage teachers and institutional providers to adjust their programmes and practices with a view to empowering both teachers and learners.

I will start the discussion with the internal, psychological learner variables that impact on the language-learning process, captured under the term ID, before I move on to the diverse linguistic skills that our students bring to the classroom. Finally, I will suggest approaches to a differentiated classroom to account for less researched or more complex variables.

Individual differences

Language learners are unique in many ways, yet not every attribute is relevant in the language-learning context. In addition, many constructs, such as personality traits and language learning aptitude variables, need further research before any conclusions for pedagogic practice can be drawn. For example, language learning aptitude is 'one of the most reliable indicators of L2 learning success' (Dörnyei and Ryan, 2015: 68), but the complex of interacting factors makes it difficult to isolate and test discrete components and, so far, the links between individual aptitude clusters and pedagogical interventions are not sufficiently clear (Dörnyei and Ryan, 2015: 68). Similarly, apart from conscientiousness, researchers have not yet established a consistent relationship between personality factors and achievement, nor is it feasible or advisable for practicing teachers to identify personality factors in the classroom. As a result, knowledge and awareness of such factors and their didactic implications are not yet applicable in the pedagogic context. This discussion of IDs in the context of the beginners' classroom therefore focuses on some well-researched motivational factors that are selected for their malleability and applicability in the *ab initio* context.

Motivation

Motivation involves the 'attitudes and affective states that influence the degree of effort that learners make to learn an L2' (Ellis, 1997: 75). Although practitioners intuitively understand its relevance for the learning process, motivation is difficult to conceptualise for the researcher. As a complex, dynamic psychological notion with temporal variation (Dörnyei and Ryan, 2015: 93) it is in constant interaction with the wider (learning) context. In practical terms this means that external factors, such as teacher behaviour and the learning experiences that they create, can influence the motivation of their students. An awareness of significant motivational factors enables teachers to cultivate motivational learning experiences or at least avoid demotivating influences. More importantly, it allows them as well as language advisors and other support staff to pinpoint and address individual student problems and therefore help them with their subjective challenges.

The dynamic nature of motivation also means that, once the students arrive in the beginners' classroom, teachers will strive to sustain the initial motivation to learn German. However, faced with the pressures of intensive language learning and the competing demands and attractions of university life, this motivation can wane quickly or not translate into effort. To help teachers keep their students motivated in the foreign language class, I will discuss selected motivational components which are most likely to be influenced by institutional provision or teacher behaviour. The list is therefore not exhaustive but based on the potential application of research findings in the beginners' classroom.

The socio-psychological component

The first researcher exploring motivation from the perspective of the language learner was Robert Gardner (1985). Although he developed a complex concept of motivation with multiple variables that still informs current discussions, the two dimensions, 'integrative' and 'instrumental' motivation resonated most strongly with the teaching community. Gardner emphasised the fact that language learning, as opposed to most other learning, contains a social and cultural dimension. In this view, the learners' attitudes towards the target language community have consequences for their learning. Learners who are predominantly driven by the desire to interact and communicate with speakers of the target language show an integrative attitude, whereas learners who learn the language for other purposes, such as better career prospects, are instrumentally motivated. Since both dimensions are not exclusive but cumulative, a positive attitude towards the community of speakers is an important motivational factor in addition to the instrumental motivation that the students bring to their degree studies. In the case of German in the UK, integrative motivation is often lower than it is for languages with a more positive image in the national and institutional discourses.

The concept of integrative motivation is more complicated in today's globalised world than it seemed in the 1980s. Due to migration, trade, tourism and the internet, German-speaking communities are dynamic, shifting and not as nationally or culturally bound as in the late twentieth century. According to the UN world migration report 2020, Germany has the largest foreign-born population in Europe, while Austria and Switzerland together with Sweden have the highest percentage of migrants in their population (International Organization for Migration, 2019: 87–8). A vibrant scene of German-speaking authors, filmmakers, performers, bloggers and so on with migrant and multilingual backgrounds reflects this changing demographic. For language learners, such open and fluid communities can offer an entry point to develop a sense of belonging. As Ryan (2006) argues in the context of English, becoming part of an imagined global community can be a strong driving force for the language learner. Encouraging learners from the beginning of their journey to participate, actively or passively, in such multicultural online discourses can help them develop that integrative motivation. Up-to-date materials that resonate with the learners are easy to find online, however, the nature of the *ab initio* language class demands a carefully scaffolded approach to the use of authentic texts. Exploratory tasks, for example identifying the key points of a passage, the general attitude of its author or finding a detailed piece of information, can be used as incentives for students to engage with difficult texts without overwhelming the teacher with preparatory work. At the same time, such texts, signs, conversations and music have the potential to index and symbolise a community of speakers that the students may be able to identify with more easily. This approach is notably different from the traditional 'othering' and 'exoticising' that can be seen in many textbooks, with their rigid depiction of the L2-speaking countries and their focus on differences rather than commonalities.

The notion of self

An important component in many motivational theories is the concept of self. How learners interpret past experiences and events, how they perceive themselves in relation to the wider learning context as well as the task in front of them and the future visions of themselves, are important drivers or inhibitors of learning behaviour. They also differ from one student to the next. This motivational self-system, complex and interwoven as it is, is nevertheless an important access point to a student's motivational disposition. Education providers, but first and foremost the teachers, can help to actively co-construct positive learner identities through their communication with the students. The following discussion will focus on three related motivational theories, which are sufficiently researched to venture conclusions for pedagogic practice: attribution theory, self-efficacy and the ideal self.

Attribution theory builds on the view that individuals tend to 'search for understanding, seeking to discover why an event has occurred' (Weiner, 1984: 18). Learners are inclined to find explanations for past events of perceived success or failure, such as a high mark in a grammar test or a failed conversation. Weiner (1980) calls these interpretations attributional causes and suggests a taxonomy, classifying causes as stable or unstable and as internal or external. In the event of perceived failure, an attribution to a stable, internal cause such as ability has particularly negative consequences. In other words, it is extremely difficult for a student to persist in the face of perceived failure, for example after a conversational breakdown, when they attribute the failure to their general lack of German-language abilities as a stable and internal cause. Attributing the lack of success to an external, stable cause, such as task difficulty, is not helpful either, but at least it leaves the self-concept of the learner intact. The key here is the feeling of control that the learners have over the learning process, since this influences their motivation. Teachers, advisers and other social agents can help students develop that feeling of control by carefully framing the discourse around performance and achievement and emphasising internal, unstable causes such as effort over external or stable causes, which the students have no control over. If effort is seen as having a qualitative as well as a quantitative dimension, this opens the room for learning conversations around strategies and learning behaviours.

However subjective they are, interpretations contribute to the learner's self-concept, or the 'knowledge and perceptions about one's competencies and attributes, along with resultant emotional reactions' (Ahn and Bong, 2019: 64). Teachers should not shy away from actively engaging with the feelings and assumptions resulting from the sense of success and failure of their students. An ongoing learning conversation, even in passing, is especially important in intensive beginners' classes, where the pace of the programme almost inevitably leads to a seeming loss of control at some stage. Simply explaining this fact can turn the focus from the perceived lack of ability of the learner to the strategies to cope with the demands of the task.

Ultimately, such conversations aim to preserve the self-efficacy of the learner, which Bandura defines as the 'beliefs in one's capabilities to organize and execute the courses of action required to produce given attainments' (1997: 3). Self-efficacy is a subjective, future-oriented, cognitively defined construct that is likely to vary between individual learners at any given time. Different from self-esteem and self-confidence, self-efficacy relates directly to the task ahead. For the teacher it is important to remember that repeated perceived failure can become a vicious circle with a lack of self-efficacy beliefs regarding the task ahead, a lack of motivation and the potential consequence of further disappointments. Studies have repeatedly shown that 'students with low self-efficacy often choose less challenging academic tasks, apply minimal effort and strategy use, and show higher signs of anxiety in the face of obstacles' (Mills, 2014: 9). SLA research further established 'a relationship between self-efficacy and FL [foreign language] achievement, FL reading and listening proficiency, language learning strategy use, FL anxiety, and self-efficacy for self-regulation' (Mills, 2014: 12).

Particularly challenging to self-efficacy in the *ab initio* context is the mix of beginners and false beginners in many intensive degree courses. The structure of the degree usually offers only two entry points, as a complete beginner or as a student with an A-level in the language. In practice, this results in complete beginners sharing a class with students with GCSE or even higher competencies in the language. Existing linguistic knowledge and language learning experiences and other ID variables also result in different progression routes. For complete beginners or inexperienced language learners, who would otherwise have to cope with a sense of relative failure, it is important to address these different starting points openly and to demonstrate or explore strategies to work around them. Furthermore, classroom practices that provide opportunities for students 'to collaborate on sequential tasks and integrate language and content in the collective development of a final project' (Mills, 2014: 14) can enhance the self-efficacy beliefs of students, by enabling them to demonstrate a variety of skills, receive regular feedback and experience success. Mills (2014: 8) further asserts that 'teachers, in particular, can enhance students' self-efficacy with credible feedback and guidance that encourages and motivates students'. Evaluating students' performances with a strong element of constructive feedforward guidance focuses weaker learners on achievable future tasks. Tasks and projects with distinct personalised goals and clear end points structure the learning process and provide regular opportunities for feedback.[1] Finally, authentic texts and language tasks can look daunting to beginners. Managing expectations carefully through detailed instructions and learning goals can give students a sense of achievement despite their relatively low proficiency.

The most future-facing cognitively defined construct is that of the possible self, which Dörnyei and Ryan define as 'specific representations of one's self in future states, involving thought, images, and senses', which are 'in many ways the manifestations, or personalized carriers, of one's goals and aspirations (and fears, of course)' (2015: 87). According to this theory, learners strive to close the gap between their vision of the ideal possible self and their current self, if the conditions are right and the vision remains plausible. In many ways, language classrooms are ideal places to construct and substantiate vivid, colourful narratives around such ideal future selves (Dörnyei and Kubanyiova, 2014). Traditional writing and conversation tasks that invite students to imagine themselves in the future, foster elaborate, vivid motivational visions and narratives. Literary texts, films and other cultural artifacts with multilingual and multicultural characters can also stimulate the creation of such positive future self-images.

Finally, sustaining or boosting the students' motivation is a valid goal, and the discussed strategies will help teachers create a motivating atmosphere and avoid demotivational practices. However, it has to be noted that much of the motivational disposition of the students is based on internal traits and the external environment. Students may discontinue their studies for a variety of reasons, on which the teacher has little influence.

Cross-linguistic influences

The languages of bi- and multilingual speakers are not isolated but interact and affect the acquisition and learning of new languages (Odlin, 1989; Gabryś-Barker, 2012; Gutiérrez Mangado, Martinez Adrián and Gallardo-del-Puerto, 2019). Existing knowledge of other languages, including the L1(s) acquired in infancy, as well as languages learned or acquired later in life, the L2(s), affects the learning of another target language, also referred to as L3 (Hammarberg, 2009: 5). The L3 is therefore the language the learner is focused on learning, in the context of this article, the *ab initio* language.

For teachers in the *ab initio* classroom, it is important to gauge the diverse linguistic knowledge and language-learning histories of their students. Cross-linguistic influences are especially frequent at the beginning of the learning process at lower proficiency levels (Lindqvist, 2009; Sanz, Park and Lado, 2015: 2), when the access that students have to other linguistic systems can almost entirely determine their interlanguage, that is, what they are able to produce or comprehend in the new language. Since learners ultimately need to be able to distinguish facilitating transfers from less beneficial interferences, teachers should explicitly activate such existing linguistic knowledge and draw attention to similarities and differences between languages. This can, at the same time, raise the students' confidence as proficient and reflective adult language speakers, which is especially important for learners starting out in a new language.

Learning a second language, with only access to an L1, differs from the learning of a third language, where the learner is already an experienced language learner and brings their competences as a bi- or multilingual speaker to the learning process (Jessner, 1999; Cenoz, Hufeisen and Jessner, 2001). The Cumulative Enhancement Model suggests that 'language acquisition is accumulative, i.e. the prior language can be neutral or enhance subsequent language acquisition' (Flynn, Foley and Vinnitskaya, 2004: 14; Berkes and Flynn, 2012), thus making the process easier with every language learned. The most obvious effect of previous language learning experiences is on strategy use. In addition, L3 learners have extensive linguistic knowledge in multiple interconnected language systems to draw on, whereas others have to rely almost entirely on their first language. Awareness of the linguistic histories of the learners in the classroom helps teachers understand achievement patterns and direct their support where needed. Being highly visual, language portrait silhouettes (LPS) (Dressler, 2014; Kusters and De Meulder, 2019) can be used even with complete beginners in the *ab initio* classroom, to gauge their linguistic repetoires. LPS invite learners to colour and draw their languages and language varieties using empty silhouettes of the human body. They thematise linguistic identities and therefore make a perfect introductory activity for students and teachers in a higher education language class.

Influences between individual language systems are not one-directional but bi- or multidirectional (Slabakova, 2017: 653), making multilingualism a dynamic process (de Bot and Jaensch, 2015: 140), in which newly acquired languages influence previously acquired linguistic systems. This has pedagogical implications especially for language degree courses, where many learners study several languages simultaneously, for example in joint or triple languages programmes. Explicit metalinguistic reflections on the full language repertoire present in the classroom develops linguistic knowledge and sensitivity, enriching all the learners' languages and turning them into more effective, profound communicators.

Bardel (2019) identifies several conditioning factors that govern the selection of the transfer language when learners have more than one language available. These include the L2 status, suggesting that languages acquired through a comparable process of formal language learning are more influential than languages acquired in infancy, because explicit metalinguistic knowledge, obtained by formal learning, transfers more easily to languages learned through similar cognitive processes (Falk, Lindqvist and Bardel, 2015). However, in contradiction to this theory, evidence suggests that the most powerful factor is the perceived typological similarity between the two languages, or else linguistic relatedness, two distinct but linked concepts. Bardel (2019) shows that cross-linguistic influences from typologically similar languages are indeed more frequent than those from other languages. The fact that all learners in a UK higher education German class are proficient users of English, a closely related language with plenty of opportunities for positive transfer, makes this a welcome unifying aspect in the context of *ab initio* German in the UK. Students are likely to use English for interlanguage transfers, regardless of it being a first or a second language. Encouraging them to notice similarities and differences is therefore a legitimate practice, since it does not disadvantage students for whom English is, or is not, their first language. It also authorises the use of all linguistic knowledge for the learning of the new language, a practice that may contradict some deep-seated beliefs about language learning.

Multilingual learners and teachers have long recognised the opportunities that familiarity with other languages brings to the classroom, often despite prevailing teaching and learning theories. Garciá and Wei observe that, in the foreign language classroom 'code-switching between the so-called mother tongue, "L1" or "native" language and the "foreign" or "L2" language is often seen as a sign of linguistic and cognitive deficiency', because '"foreign language" study was centered on a nation-state ideology that perceived "other" languages as alien, external and spoken only overseas' (2014: 53). More recently, projects like the award-winning MELT Multilingual Readers' Theatre, a multilingual reading programme which gives students and teachers a voice in any of the languages and variations they are competent in, can be used to inspire a more linguistically inclusive classroom (Massler et al., 2016).

Translanguaging practices, which allow and encourage learners to deploy all available meaning-making systems, including previously acquired languages, are making a comeback in the SLA literature. Garciá and Wei describe the potential of a translanguaging pedagogy 'to develop more sophisticated discourse, deeper comprehension of texts, production of more complex texts, authentic and meaningful evaluation of what students know, as well as to question linguistic inequalities and to include the voices of learners who have been minoritized' (Garciá and Wei, 2014: 125). Contrary to the target-language-only practices still dominating many language classrooms today, translanguaging pedagogies encourage the use of another shared language for mediation or translation exercises, or for contrastive analyses to clarify complex grammar points. Especially for beginners of German with English in their repertoire, drawing on common structures and shared lexical items while highlighting distinct features can save time on lengthy explanations and allow access to challenging texts. Facilitating transfers of phonological, lexical, morphological, syntactic or pragmatic structures should therefore be used as an empowering pedagogic practice that can give learners a much-needed sense of success, especially beginners. In addition, the teacher should celebrate multilingualism in the classroom and honour all languages and varieties by showing curiosity about the full linguistic repertoires of the students and using multilingual teaching practices such as back translations.

Learner variability and differentiation

Historically, teachers and learners have long been aware of real or perceived factors that influence the pace and trajectory of the learning process, and often adapted their practices accordingly (McLelland, Coffey and Fisher, 2021). However, with the new understanding of language and learning as complex adaptive systems, researchers are now more hesitant to predict direct effects of such variables or even propose straightforward didactic solutions. Age, gender, social class, culture, identity, personality, willingness to communicate, aptitude, beliefs, affects, anxiety, motivation, learning and cognitive styles, strategies and many other ID constructs are not static or fixed binary sets, but multi-componential and dynamic. Previous language-learning experiences and linguistic knowledge, the institutional settings and the wider environment of the learner further add to the complexity. To respond to the uniqueness of each student, teachers are therefore best advised to retain an acute awareness of different learner needs and to differentiate the content, delivery and intended outcome of their sessions accordingly. As Tomlinson explains, 'in differentiated classrooms, teachers ensure that students compete against themselves as they grow and develop more than they compete against one another, always moving toward – and often beyond – designated content goals' (2014: 4). A learner-centred approach turns the focus to the students' learning away from the teaching methods, providing alternative materials, tasks, activities and explanations in response to the students' needs. Flexibility and a wide repertoire of instructional strategies that draws on a variety of methods and methodologies to reach the identified learning aims and outcomes are key elements of a responsive language class. A mix of activities, switching regularly between the focus on meaning and the focus on form, from plenary to group-, pair- and individual work, from written to oral or from closed to open tasks creates space for all learners to progress.

Learner autonomy, as well as active engagement with the task, are integral parts of a differentiated language pedagogy.[2] Coffey argues that 'differentiation … allows pupils to understand their own preferred learning styles and to negotiate their own targets' (2011: 198). For adult learners in higher education, with their capacity for reflection, an ongoing learning conversation enables them to identify their strengths, weaknesses and preferences, leading to greater control of their learning. Learning conversations can be conducted almost in passing, for example explaining in a few sentences why an activity is supposed to develop certain skills or asking about the strategies students have used to arrive at an answer. Such conversations focus the attention on the learning processes and activities, encouraging students to review and evaluate them critically and thus expand their repertoire of strategies to become more autonomous learners. Weaker students often benefit from a more individual learning dialogue, such as a learning log with regular feedback from the teacher or language adviser. The resulting consciousness of the learning process 'allows for increasing self-regulation, for deeper processing, for more efficient learning actions, and for feelings of knowing, unknowing, and appropriate levels of confidence in one's own abilities' (van Lier, 1996: 71). Such '*organizing*, *controlling*, and *evaluating* of experience' (van Lier, 1996: 73, emphases in the original) is especially beneficial in higher education, where the relative focus on independent learning provides ample opportunities to differentiate tasks and outcomes.

Conclusion

The context of *ab initio* language teaching in higher education institutions has changed considerably over recent years. *Ab initio* German in traditional, single-honours degree programmes requires fast-track progression for students to reach C1 level in the Common European Framework of Reference (CEFR) in their final year. Such language programmes are often embedded in a wider programme focusing on German culture and history. At the other end of the spectrum are standalone, co- or extra-curricular German language modules for students of other subjects or members of the public, often offered by language centres. With this increasingly broad range of teaching contexts comes a growing diversity of learners. The profile of the traditional *ab initio* student, a competent language learner with an A-level in at least one other language and motivated to study the *ab initio* language to access its culture and history, has given way to students with a multitude of aptitudes, motivations, linguistic knowledge and previous learning experiences. Teachers therefore benefit from an awareness of those components in their learners' profiles that impact on the direction and pace of their progress. The ability to build on the learners' strengths while mitigating their limitations can be a decisive factor especially in the intensive language courses of traditional degree programmes. Co-constructing positive self-images, developing a feeling of belonging to the speaker community, fostering learner autonomy and drawing on already-existing linguistic knowledge are all strategies for teachers to empower their *ab initio* learners. Ultimately, a learner-centred, creative, responsive and differentiated language pedagogy will help all students reach their potential and, hopefully, enjoy the experience.

Notes

1 For more reflections on feedback see Chapter 10, this volume.
2 Learner autonomy is discussed in detail by Jochum-Critchley in Chapter 13, this volume.

References

Ahn, H.S. and Bong, M. (2019) 'Self-efficacy in learning'. In *The Cambridge Handbook of Motivation and Learning*, edited by K.A. Renninger and S.E. Hidi, 63–86. Cambridge: Cambridge University Press

Bandura, A. (1997) *Self-Efficacy: The exercise of control*. New York: W.H. Freeman.

Bardel, C. (2019) 'Syntactic transfer in L3 learning. What do models and results tell us about learning and teaching a third language?'. In *Cross-Linguistic Influence: From empirical evidence to classroom practice*, edited by M.J. Gutiérrez Mangado, M. Martinez Adrián and F. Gallardo-del-Puerto, 101–20. Cham: Springer.

Berkes, E. and Flynn, S. (2012) 'Enhanced L3...LN acquisition and its implications for language teaching'. In *Cross-Linguistic Influences in Multilingual Language Acquisition*, edited by D. Gabryś-Barker, 1–22. Berlin: Springer.

Cenoz, J., Hufeisen, B. and Jessner, U. (eds) (2001) *Cross-Linguistic Influence in Third Language Acquisition: Psycholinguistic perspectives*. Clevedon: Multilingual Matters/Channel View Publications.

Coffey, S. (2011) 'Differentiation in theory and practice'. In *Becoming a Teacher: Issues in secondary teaching*, edited by J. Dillon and M. Maguire, 197–209. Maidenhead: McGraw-Hill Education.

de Bot, K. and Jaensch, C. (2015) 'What is special about L3 processing?'. *Bilingualism: Language and Cognition* 18:2, 130–44.

Dörnyei, Z. and Kubanyiova, M. (2014) *Motivating Learners, Motivating Teachers: Building vision in the language classroom*. Cambridge: Cambridge University Press.

Dörnyei, Z. and Ryan, S. (2015) *The Psychology of the Language Learner Revisited*. New York: Routledge.

Dressler, R. (2014) 'Exploring linguistic identity in young multilingual learners'. *TESL Canada Journal* 32:1, 42–52.

Ellis, R. (1997) *Second Language Acquisition*. Oxford: Oxford University Press.

Falk, Y., Lindqvist, C. and Bardel, C. (2015) 'The role of L1 explicit metalinguistic knowledge in L3 oral production at the initial stage'. *Bilingualism: Language and Cognition* 18: 227–35.

Flynn, S., Foley, C. and Vinnitskaya, I. (2004) 'The cumulative enhancement model for language acquisition: comparing adults' and children's patterns of development in first, second and third language acquisition of relative clauses. *International Journal of Multilingualism* 1, 3–16.

Gabryś-Barker, D. (ed.) (2012) *Cross-Linguistic Influences in Multilingual Language Acquisition*. Berlin: Springer.

García, O. and Wei, L. (2014) *Translanguaging: Language, bilingualism and education*. London: Palgrave Pivot.

Gardner, R.C. (1985) *Social Psychology and Second Language Learning: The role of attitudes and motivation*. London: Edward Arnold.

Gutiérrez Mangado, M.J., Martinez Adrián, M. and Gallardo-del-Puerto, F. (eds) (2019) *Cross-Linguistic Influence: From empirical evidence to classroom practice*. Cham: Springer.

Hammarberg, B. (ed.) (2009) *Processes in Third Language Acquisition*. Edinburgh: Edinburgh University Press.

International Organization for Migration (2019) IOM UN Migration: World Migration Report 2020. Online. www.un.org/sites/un2.un.org/files/wmr_2020.pdf (accessed 25 April 2021).

Jessner, U. (1999) 'Metalinguistic awareness in multilinguals: cognitive aspects of third language learning'. *Language Awareness* 8:3–4, 201–9.

Kusters, A. and De Meulder, M. (2019) 'Language portraits: Investigating embodied multilingual and multimodal repertoires'. *Forum Qualitative Sozialforschung / Forum: Qualitative Social Research* 20:3, art. 10.

Larsen-Freeman, D. (1997) 'Chaos/complexity science and second language acquisition'. *Applied Linguistics* 18:2, 141–65.

Lindqvist, C. (2009) 'The use of the L1 and the L2 in French L3: Examining cross-linguistic lexemes in multilingual learners' oral production'. *International Journal of Multilingualism* 6:3, 281–91.

McLelland, N., Coffey, S. and Fisher, L. (2021) *Language Teaching: Learning from the past. 1. Differentiation and Diversity*. Online. www.nottingham.ac.uk/clas/documents/research/

language-teaching-learning-from-the-past/differentiation-instructor-handbook.pdf (accessed 9 May 2021).

Massler, U., Antony, A.-M., Götz, K, Hendel, R., Ilg, A., Kutzelmacher, S., Ludescher, F., Peter, K., Seraina, P., Theinert, K. and Unterthiner, D. (2016) MELT Multilingual Readers' Theatre. Online. https://melt-multilingual-readers-theatre.eu/en/ (accessed 15 July 2021).

Mills, N. (2014) 'Self-efficacy in second language acquisition'. In *Multiple Perspectives on the Self in SLA*, edited by S. Mercer and M. Williams, 6–22. Bristol: Channel View Publications.

Odlin, T. (1989) *Cross-Linguistic Influence in Language Learning*. Cambridge: Cambridge University Press.

Ryan, S. (2006) 'Language learning motivation within the context of globalisation: An L2 self within an imagined global community'. *Critical Inquiry in Language Studies* 3:1, 23–45.

Sanz, C., Park, H.I. and Lado, B. (2015) 'A functional approach to cross-linguistic influence in *ab initio* L3 acquisition'. *Bilingualism: Language and Cognition – L3 Acquisition: A Focus on Cognitive Approaches* 18:2, 236–51.

Slabakova, R. (2017) 'The scalpel model of third language acquisition'. *International Journal of Bilingualism* 21, 651–65.

Tomlinson, C.A. (2014) *The Differentiated Classroom: Responding to the needs of all learners*. Alexandra, VA: ASCD.

van Lier, L. (1996) *Interaction in the Language Curriculum: Awareness, autonomy and authenticity*. London: Longman.

Weiner, B. (1980) *Human Motivation*. New York: Rinehart & Winston.

Weiner, B. (1984) 'A theory of motivation'. In *Research on Motivation in Education*, edited by R. Ames and C. Ames, 15–38. London: Academic Press.

Index

Ingram Content Group UK Ltd.
Milton Keynes UK
UKHW051630240423
420504UK00010B/19